A PRIMER IN
POWER POLITICS

A PRIMER IN POWER POLITICS

STANLEY MICHALAK

A Scholarly Resources Inc. Imprint
Wilmington, Delaware

Scholarly Resources Inc.
104 Greenhill Avenue
Wilmington, DE 19805-1897
www.scholarly.com

Michalak, Stanley J.
   A primer in power politics / Stanley Michalak.
   Includes index. p. cm.
   ISBN 0-8420-2950-8 (alk. paper) — ISBN 0-8420-2951-6 (pbk. : alk. paper)
   1. International relations—Political aspects. 2. Balance of power. I. Title.

JZ1310.M53 2001
327.1'01—dc21

00-066105

∞ The paper used in this publication meets the minimum requirements of the American National Standard for permanence of paper for printed library materials, Z39.48, 1984.

This book is dedicated to superb teachers whose mark
I feel every day of my life and to a few brilliant men
whom I never met, but who have taught me more
than they could ever have conceived.

To those who taught me

at Albright College
William Bishop
Ellery Haskell
Charles A. Raith
Paul Rusby

and

at Princeton University
Edgar S. Furniss
Leon Gordenker
Marion J. Levy, Jr.
Harold Sprout

To those whom I have never met
Norman Graebner
Louis Halle
George Kennan
Henry Kissinger
Hans Morgenthau
Frederick Schuman
Nicholas Spykman
Adam Ulam

About the Author

Stanley Michalak graduated magna cum laude from Albright College in 1960 and received his Ph.D. in politics from Princeton University in 1967. Between college and graduate school, Professor Michalak served as legislative assistant to Congressman George M. Rhodes of Pennsylvania.

He is the author and coauthor of numerous books and articles including *The United Nations Conference on Trade and Development* (1983), *American Foreign Policy since Détente* (1984), and *Competing Conceptions of American Foreign Policy: Worldviews in Conflict* (1992).

Professor Michalak joined the government department of Franklin&Marshall College in 1967 and served as chairman of the department from 1973 to 1976. In 1975 he was awarded the Christian R. and Mary Lindbeck Award for Distinguished Teaching. He has also been a visiting scholar at the Foreign Policy Research Institute in Philadelphia and an author and consultant on United Nations affairs for the Heritage Foundation and the U.S. Department of State.

ACKNOWLEDGMENTS

Thanks to the following, who have read and commented on drafts of this manuscript, and to the patient participants who listened to my ideas and quizzed me thoroughly in the spring of 1999 at five seminars on power politics held under the auspices of Beacon, a continuing education program for senior citizens, Lancaster, Pennsylvania:

Dr. Robert J. Bresler, The Pennsylvania State University

Dr. Robert C. Gray, Franklin&Marshall College

Dr. James Sofka, University of Virginia

Dr. C. Alan Bruns, Franklin&Marshall College

Tim Langan, gifted student and invaluable Hackman Fellow

Sarah Michalak

Beverly Michalak

Franklin&Marshall College students who have taken my classes and seminars in international politics

CONTENTS

PREFACE

This primer seeks to provide a clear and jargon-free introduction to humanistic political realism. While underscoring the importance of anarchy, power, and structure, humanistic realism also emphasizes purpose and limits—limits to the power that states can husband, limits to the utility of force, limits to reason, and limits to principles ungrounded in experience. Thus, this book is heir to the writings of such scholars and diplomats as Theodore Roosevelt, Frederick Schuman, Winston Churchill, E. H. Carr, Nicholas Spykman, Dean Acheson, Hans Morgenthau, Arnold Wolfers, George Kennan, Kenneth Thompson, Louis Halle, and Henry Kissinger.

The need for such a book seemed obvious to me very early in the post–Cold War era. Although the United Nations succeeded in rolling Saddam Hussein out of Kuwait, George Bush's new world order never materialized, and the United Nations failed "to take over," as the head of the American branch of the United Nations Association urged. Nor did principle replace power and interests as the basis of America's foreign policy as Roger Morris proposed at the beginning of the 1990s. President Clinton's "assertive multilateralism" lasted hardly a year, and what followed was perhaps more futile uses of military force than have ever been undertaken by any American president. Although Colin Gray may be going much too far when he refers to the current era as the "interwar period," clearly, power politics is alive and well.

However, in all the literature in the field of international politics, no contemporary work exists that students or members of the public can turn to for a basic grounding in the oldest intellectual tradition in the discipline. Earlier introductions such as George Schwarzenberger's *Power Politics,* James Payne's *The American Threat,* and Martin Wight's *Power Politics* are all out of print. Hans Morgenthau's *Politics Among Nations* is lengthy and difficult for many of today's college students to read and understand and has not been updated since the 1980s. Although E. H. Carr's *The Twenty Years' Crisis* remains a classic, it is now more than sixty years old.

In addition to reaching students, I have written this book for members of the general public. Over the past thirty-five years, I have led two lives—a professional life as a teacher of international politics and a personal life as a citizen, community member, neighbor, and relative. In each of these lives, I have had innumerable conversations about questions of international politics and foreign policy, and what has continually struck me is how, on issue after issue—from Vietnam to Bosnia—the nonspecialists were, all too often, more sensible and more realistic than scholars who had spent their working lives studying such questions.

Few people in the academic world write for the general public anymore. Consequently, there is a widening gap between research and reality as scholars and citizens live in separate worlds. This primer seeks to help bridge that gap by giving members of the public greater confidence that their fundamental instincts are sound and that they should not feel embarrassed by their lack of expertise in international politics in the face of experts or professionals. My purpose is not to instruct the general public but to confirm what many intuitively know on the basis of their experience.

Obviously, my framework and much of what I say need to be qualified, as is true of any elementary text—and I have tried to point out exceptions and present qualifications throughout the work. If I have simplified and abstracted, it is because my first target is the student who will never take another course in international politics or the citizen who will never read another book on the subject. Nevertheless, since I consider this primer very much a work in progress, I welcome the comments of my readers—students and fellow citizens as well as professors.

Finally, one point must be made absolutely clear: *Nothing in this primer should be considered an endorsement or glorification of power politics, violence, or amorality.* My purpose is neither to blame nor to applaud but to understand—a purpose well stated by the Dutch philosopher Benedict Spinoza in his Tractatus Politicus more than 300 years ago: "When I have applied my mind to politics . . . I have taken my best pains not to laugh at the actions of mankind, not to groan over them, not to be angry with them, but to understand them."*

Stanley Michalak
Professor of Government
Franklin&Marshall College
Lancaster, PA 17604-3003

---

*Benedict de Spinoza, *Tractatus Politicus*, in *A Theoretical-Political Treatise and A Political Treatise*, trans. R. H. M. Elwes (New York: Dover Publications, 1951), 288.

INTRODUCTION: WHY A PRIMER IN POWER POLITICS?

America's Shattered Dreams and Enduring Post–Cold War Realities

As the Cold War came to an end, many envisioned a new era in international politics—an era in which peace and security would be maintained on the basis of the United Nations Charter, rather than on the vagaries of transient national interests, political ideologies, and Great Power "balances." The grounds for this optimism lay in a set of rather remarkable developments. In a sudden and welcomed surprise, the United Nations brought closure to a series of conflicts that had plagued the superpowers for more than a decade. In Afghanistan, Angola, Cambodia, El Salvador, Nicaragua, and Southern Africa, the United Nations compiled a superb, almost unbelievable, record. Then, when the world organization rolled Saddam Hussein's forces out of Kuwait, euphoria reigned. Speaking before the United Nations General Assembly in September 1992, George Bush claimed: "With the cold war's end, . . . we have a unique opportunity to go beyond artificial divisions of a first, second, and third world to forge instead a genuine global community of free and sovereign nations: a community built upon respect for principle, peaceful settlements of disputes, fundamental human rights, democracy, and free markets."[1]

Such sentiments were widely echoed among scholars and publicists. As early as 1990, in fact, Thomas Weiss, a leading authority on the United Nations, and Merrily A. Kessler, a specialist in Soviet affairs, wrote, "The waning of the Cold War provides an unparalleled opportunity for superpower cooperation at the U.N.," and "[raises] the possibility that the U.N. might function more among the lines that its founders intended. . . ."[2] In the aftermath of the Gulf War victory, Edward Luck and Toby Trister Gati, the president and senior vice president of the United Nations Association, called for the United Nations system to just "take over." The time had come, they argued, for "a system of collective responsibility that would engage the international community in tasks ranging from preventive diplomacy, to economic sanctions, and to joint military action as needed to maintain international peace and stability."[3]

Perhaps no one expressed the dream better than foreign policy analyst Roger Morris. According to Morris, victory has freed the United States from the "Faustian choice between ideals and interests, principle and pragmatism" that all too frequently led expediency to trump "right" during the Cold War. In the post–Cold War era, Morris claimed, principles would become pragmatic and "not only affordable but essential."[4] Such, then, was the dream: After more than forty years of Cold War rivalry, the United Nations would at last operate as its founders intended. The permanent members of the Security Council would secure justice and world peace by basing their foreign policies on the principles and procedures outlined in the United Nations Charter. Principle—supported by the power of the international community—would govern relations among nations.

New Dreams Confront Old Realities

It did not take long before reality began to diverge from the dream. When Slovenia, Croatia, and Bosnia-Herzegovina seceded from the former Yugoslavia, Serbian leader Slobodan Milosevic sought to forge a greater Serbia by supporting Serbian insurgents in the newly created states. Slovenia managed to escape the Serbian net, but the newly emergent state of Bosnia quickly found itself besieged by internal Croatian and Serbian forces that engaged in genocidal ethnic cleansing. The goal of these forces was clear: to create ethnic enclaves in Bosnia that, in time, would become annexed to Serbia and Croatia.

Elsewhere, disorder and violence mocked a seemingly impotent United Nations. In Somalia, UN peacekeepers huddled together in defensive garrisons hiding from a tough and strong-willed warlord who had intimidated American and other UN forces into either leaving Somalia altogether or remaining on his terms. In Cambodia and Angola, the losers of UN-monitored elections reverted to civil war. In Afghanistan, a UN-brokered peace that allowed Soviet troops to withdraw gracefully was quickly followed by chaos and disorder. The world looked on as genocide occurred on a massive scale in Rwanda. A few years later, the North Atlantic Treaty Organization (NATO) bombed gingerly as Milosevic's Serbian forces ferociously "cleansed" Kosovo of its Albanian population. When Milosevic relented after almost two months of bombing and pulled Serbian forces out of Kosovo, the NATO allies moved into a morass.

Past Dreams/Past Failures
The League of Nations/The Kellogg-Briand Pact/The United Nations

These post–Cold War failures will not destroy the United Nations as similar failures doomed the League of Nations—and for reasons that will be examined later in the pages of this primer. But these failures underscore enduring realities that should have made them perfectly predictable to both policymakers and analysts. These failures also underscore the persistent gap between American dreams and international realities that has endured since America sought to become a major actor for peace in the international system.

On three occasions since the end of World War I, the United States sought to create a new world order that would replace national interests and the balance of power politics with moral principles and legal agreements. In each case, the effort failed—and predictably so. At the Paris Peace Conference, Woodrow Wilson tried to create a new world order based on "a community of power" rather than "a balance of power." The U.S. Senate, of course, decided to have nothing to do with Wilson's creation, and when put to the test in the 1930s, the League failed.

During the 1920s, the United States pursued world peace through self-abnegation or self-denial—"just say 'no' to war." In 1928, American secretary of state Frank B. Kellogg and French foreign minister Aristide Briand passed around a foot-long gold pen, and delegates from almost every nation on earth ultimately signed their Pact for the Renunciation of War, better known as the Kellogg-Briand Pact.[5] By signing the pact, the signatories renounced war as an instrument of policy and pledged to resolve all international disputes only by peaceful means.

There were, of course, loopholes. States could resort to war in self-defense, and no nation was willing to restrict "self-defense" to wars fought in defense of national borders. President Coolidge and Secretary of State Kellogg always coupled their support with clear stipulations about the right of the United States to protect the lives and property of its citizens *anywhere*. Yet, even with these assurances, the Senate added a reservation to the treaty that placed any efforts by the United States to enforce the Monroe Doctrine under the category of self-defense. Great Britain entered an even more sweeping reservation, claiming for itself liberty of action in "certain regions of the world, the welfare and integrity of which constitutes a special and vital interest for our peace and security."

States were also permitted to use force in fulfillment of League obligations and in response to signatories who waged war in breach of the pact; however, *no nation was obligated to lift one finger to enforce the pact or even provide assistance to a victim of violation*. The Kellogg-Briand Pact fared no better than the League of Nations. When the pact was broken in the 1930s, none of the signatories came to the aid of victim states except for leaky and inadequate sanctions adopted in the case of Italy's invasion of Ethiopia. The only thing the pact might have prevented were formal declarations of war.

During World War II, the United States conjured up yet another scheme that would abolish power politics and usher in a world of lasting peace. While having cocktails with Soviet foreign minister Vyacheslav Molotov in June 1942, Franklin Delano Roosevelt unveiled his scheme for a regime of four "policemen"—the United States, Great Britain, the Soviet Union, and, perhaps, China—who would maintain world peace after the defeat of the Axis powers.[6] In a slightly modified form, these four policemen, plus France, formed the core of the United Nations Security Council, which was authorized *to enforce* the peace in the postwar world.

As history quickly revealed, the wartime president's design for peace rested on a number of questionable assumptions, the most fatal of which was his expectation that the policemen would always agree on the what and how of keeping the peace in the postwar world. At the very first meeting of the council, the United States and the Soviet Union found themselves wrangling about the presence of Soviet troops in Iran. Rarely in the Cold War did the policemen act in harmony and comity. For almost fifty years, the United Nations served not as a directorate of the Great Powers but as a forum for a traditional balance-of-power struggle between the United States and the Soviet Union.

Given this experience, many believed that the failure of the United Nations stemmed largely from Cold War rivalry, rather than from any inherent weakness in the approach to world peace embodied in the organization's charter. When Mikhail Gorbachev began to articulate the Soviet Union's "new thinking" in the realm of foreign policy, such beliefs seemed confirmed. For not only did Gorbachev cast aside Lenin's class-based and uncompromisingly revolutionary approach to relations among nations, he also rejected balance-of-power politics as well.

Claiming that world peace would be inconceivable without the United Nations, Gorbachev told Indian parliamentarians that "peace is indivisible and integral, which also means that conflicts and explosive situations in any given region must be settled in the interests of the entire community, [because] a fuse smoldering in one part of the globe might cause an explosion that would tear our planet apart."[7] In countless speeches, Gorbachev propounded a new international order centered on the United Nations, a place where nations would work together to resolve conflicts peacefully and tackle the larger problems of mankind, such as economic development, armaments, hunger, energy, population growth, and environmental degradation.

Once again, however, the dream has eluded the dreamers. Nations are again engaging in war, violence, and threats of force, and as before, nations with little interest in these conflicts are ignoring their obligations to assist and fight on behalf of the principles of the UN Charter. National interests, fear, and an unwillingness to sacrifice even a few youths for high principle have become business as usual. And, as in the League era, many small countries engage in moral posturing, knowing full well that when the time comes to use force against an aggressor, they would provide little, if anything, to a common effort. The quip of British Prime Minister Stanley Baldwin seems as true today as it was in his time: Collective security amounted to Britain providing the security while others stood on the sidelines and cheered.

In response to these post–Cold War realities, the same old remedies of the past seventy years are being trotted out again. Pleas are made for institutional reforms that will perfect the United Nations and, thereby, make it more reliable and effective. Such proposals range from "democratizing" the Security Council by adding new permanent members, such as Japan and Germany, and one or more "significant regional actors," such as India, Brazil, Nigeria, or Egypt, to proposals for creating a standing UN army that would operate under the secretary general. Presumably, if the members of the Security Council will not fight for principle, an international or supranational army will do the job for them. Others see the failings of the United Nations not in its organizational structure, but in a lack of will on the part of its leading members.

Such proposals will have little effect even if they are accepted. The problem with peace through international organization will not be solved by organizational tinkering—adding permanent members will most likely increase the prospect of *immobilisme* in the Security Council. Seeing the problem as one of will begs the question of why a lack of will exists—that is, why do nations lack the will to sacrifice their treasure and young men by intervening in violent conflicts, such as that in Bosnia, where their direct interests are not involved? Phrased this way, the question answers itself.

In the years ahead, the United States will confront a much more disorderly world, and it will need a new compass, or set of criteria, to make decisions. A compass based on a nonexistent Holy Grail of peace through international organizations or toothless treaties will create unrealistic expectations about how we and others will behave, and when those expectations are dashed, many may leap foolishly into the equally illusory dream of American security through isolation.

The Purpose of This Primer

As the United States faces a world increasingly like that of the nineteenth and early twentieth centuries, there is a need for a short guide that explains how and why nations act as they do in the international arena. If nations do not live up to the promises and principles embodied in the charters of international organizations or the codes of conduct embodied in international agreements, these questions—and others—require attention:

- What factors motivate states to behave as they do in international affairs?
- What kinds of international objectives do states seek and under what conditions?
- How do states go about getting what they want, and what are the most probable responses of other states to their efforts?

- When and why do states resort to the use of force, and what are the uses and limits of force in conflicts among nations?
- What can we realistically expect from the United Nations, the World Court, arbitration panels, and other peaceful settlement techniques?
- What role do morality, ethics, and world public opinion play in the international interactions of nations?

In 1936, Professor Harold Lasswell aptly framed the discipline of political science in the pithy title of his classic work, *Politics: Who Gets What, When, How.*[8] In so doing, he moved political scientists away from asking how the political world ought to be and directed attention to understanding how that world actually worked and why. *A Primer in Power Politics* provides some tentative answers to Lasswell's questions based on more than two hundred years of writings by diplomats, policy-makers, historians, philosophers, and political scientists. However, the word *primer* must be emphasized. This book is what the fifth edition of *Webster's Collegiate Dictionary* defines as "an elementary text." Still, an understanding of the five elementary lessons that frame the chapters of this book will make comprehensible a great deal of the conflict among nations and provide a basis for further study.

Politics is not a science; it is an art, and a very difficult art to master at that. Understanding how nations operate requires a great deal of study—of history, of situations, of the limits and uses of force, and of norms of behavior. Moreover, because every situation is unique, the hasty application of analogies from past situations to current ones must be avoided, and every effort should be made to look for differences between current situations and past analogies.

Still, as this primer seeks to show, the behavior of states is neither random nor completely unpredictable. A careful study of this little book should yield a set of realistic expectations about what states probably will or will not do in the pursuit of peace, order, and justice in the international system. And such knowledge is "not for nothing," to use the colloquial expression of my Pennsylvania Dutch homeland. As a wise sage once quipped, "Before you try to change something, be sure you understand how it works."

Notes

1. *Weekly Compilation of Presidential Documents* (Washington, DC, 1992), 28 (September 28, 1992), 1697.
2. Thomas G. Weiss and Merrily A. Kessler, "Gorbachev's U.N. Policy," *Foreign Policy* 79 (Summer 1990), 109.
3. Edward Luck and Toby Trister Gati, "Whose Collective Security?" reprinted in *America's National Interest in a Post Cold War World*, ed. Alvin Z. Rubinstein (New York: McGraw-Hill, 1994), 268.
4. Roger Morris, "Towards a Policy That's No Longer Foreign," *New York Times*, February 5, 1992, 23.

5. The few nonsignatories included Argentina, Bolivia, El Salvador, and Uruguay. The following mini-states were not invited to sign: Andorra, Monaco, Morocco, Liechtenstein, and San Marino.

6. FDR first revealed this scheme to Soviet Foreign Minister Vyacheslev Molotov when he was visiting the United States and having cocktails with the president in June 1942. For FDR's presentation and Molotov's stunned and perplexed response, read the fascinating transcript of this meeting in U.S. Department of State, *Papers Relating to the Foreign Relations of the United States 1942* (Washington, DC, 1961), 3: 568–69. You may find it in your library's stacks under the call number JX 233.A3. If it is not there, ask your reference librarian to help you locate it in the government documents section of your library. Further citations of this series will be cited as *FRUS* followed by the appropriate year and volume number.

7. Speech to Indian Parliament, November 27, 1986. Mikhail S. Gorbachev, *Toward a Better World* (New York: Richardson & Steirman, 1987), 378.

8. New York: McGraw-Hill Book Company, 1936.

CHAPTER ONE

International Politics Is Primarily about Order and Interests; It Is Only Secondarily about Justice and Moral Principles

What is, however, absolutely certain, is that wars are the fate of mankind, the inevitable destiny of nations; and that eternal peace is not the lot of mortals in this world.
— German Field Marshal K. von der Golz,
The Nation in Arms, 1906[1]

Intternational politics is pimarily about order and interests for a very simple reason: there is no government standing above nation-states to guarantee their safety, their security, or their survival. Leaders can and do resort to force whenever they are inclined to do so and reckon they can get away with it. Thus:

- Teddy Roosevelt "took" the Panama Canal Zone "and let Congress debate," to use the president's own words.
- North Korean dictator Kim Il Sung ordered an invasion of South Korea in 1950.
- Nikita Khrushchev sent Soviet troops into Hungary in 1956 to overthrow a government that was withdrawing from the communist camp.
- Ho Chi Minh supported guerrilla fighters in South Vietnam when elections to unify his country were not held.
- Lyndon Johnson ordered the bombing of North Vietnam and sent hundreds of thousands of American troops to South Vietnam when Ho's guerrillas appeared on the verge of success.

1

- In January 1979, communist China sent several hundred thousand troops into communist North Vietnam to punish that country for its invasion of Cambodia late in 1978.
- In 1982 an Argentine military junta ordered an invasion of the Falkland Islands to liberate two thousand subsistence sheep farmers and their families who did not want to become Argentineans;
- Ronald Reagan invaded Grenada to rescue that country from communism.
- George Bush sent American troops into Panama to capture that nation's leader, Manuel Noriega, and bring him back to the United States for trial in American courts.
- Saddam Hussein invaded Kuwait and turned that tiny country into the thirty-first province of Iraq.
- In 1993, Bill Clinton ordered a peaceful invasion of Haiti to restore democracy to that poverty-stricken country.

In each of these cases, and countless others, leaders were dissatisfied with some existing state of affairs and calculated that the benefits of using military force would exceed the costs. Some of these calculations later proved correct, and others proved incorrect. Some of these decisions proved wise, but others proved less wise. However, the following is clear: *nothing stands in the way of states seeking to use force if their leaders think they can get away with it at a reasonable cost.*

Moreover, for hundreds of years, force was considered a legitimate technique of diplomacy, albeit a regrettable one. When states disagreed over territorial or even commercial issues, war was traditionally considered the *ultimo ratio*, or final arbitrator, of such disputes. Only since World War I has the use of force lost its legitimacy as an instrument of diplomacy—at least at the level of rhetoric. Although states probably resort to violence no more or less than they have in the past, leaders are now much more likely to try to legitimize their use of force by portraying it as "defensive" or claiming it to be in pursuit of such unexceptionable values as self-determination or national liberation.

The Reality of International Anarchy

Thus, the first fact of life about international politics: The international system is a system without government. According to the great German sociologist Max Weber, government is that institution in a given territorial limit that has a legitimate monopoly on the use of violence.[2] Within the international political system, states can count on no institution standing above them to call lawbreakers into account, to protect the weak, or to enforce the law. We live in a world in which nations are restrained in their use of force only by varying degrees of *satiation, self-restraint, fear*, and *calculations of the costs and benefits* that might result from using violence—calculations that are regrettably, and all too frequently, in error.

2

Ultimately, national governments must rely on their own resources and those of whatever allies they can muster for both survival and security. As Professor Joseph Grieco has noted, "international anarchy is the principal force shaping the motives and actions of states," and "the international environment severely penalizes states if they fail to protect their vital interests or if they pursue objectives beyond their means."[3]

In fact, given the anarchic nature of the international system, even sheer survival can be at stake in the game of international politics. In the late eighteenth century, Russia, Prussia, and Austria engaged in three separate partitions of Poland, which led to the extinction of that ancient nation until the three partitioning states collapsed at the end of World War I. Poland's resurrection was short-lived, however, for, in 1939, Joseph Stalin and Adolph Hitler engaged in a fourth partition of Poland. After World War II, Poland quickly became an outpost within a new Russian empire. With the collapse of communism and the Soviet bloc, Poland returned to life as a fully independent state; to maintain its new-found independence, Polish leaders sought, and then gained, membership in NATO as insurance against a resurgent and imperialist Russia.

While the extinction of states within the international system has been fairly rare, even a cursory examination of the following maps for the years 1648, 1812, 1815, 1914, 1919, 1942, 1955, and 2000 will quickly reveal the rise and fall of both states and empires. Such changing maps are graphic reflections of the struggles for survival, security, order, status, and hegemony that have pervaded the international system since its founding at the Peace of Westphalia in 1648.

On the other hand, the international system is not a Hobbesian world where life is poor, nasty, brutish, and short. Most of the time, states do obey international law; most of the time, they do get along with their neighbors; and most of the time, they do cooperate on countless issues and problems. According to Hans Morgenthau, author of the most influential textbook on power politics in the postwar period, "during the four hundred years of its existence international law has in most respects been scrupulously observed."[4] In addition, international organizations ranging from the International Monetary Fund to the International Cocoa Council regulate important aspects of economic intercourse among nations. Nations also work together through bodies such as the United Nations Educational, Scientific, and Cultural Organization (UNESCO) and the World Health Organization (WHO) on all kinds of cooperative projects, from saving ancient monuments to organizing international research on the treatment and possible cure of AIDS. No student of power politics could take exception to the statement that "morality, law, and international organization can form the basis for relations among states; that human nature is not evil; that peaceful and cooperative relations among states are possible; and that states can operate as a community rather than merely as autonomous self-interested agents"[5]—so long as that statement is qualified with the phrase, "on most issues or most of the time."

It is also true that states are increasingly interrelated in myriad and complex ways through trade, travel, economic activity, and the revolution in communications and information. Yet, despite all of the order in the world and the increasing interrelationships among peoples and nations, states can and do resort to force at times, and they also engage in actions that threaten the interests and values of others. When leaders of states confront situations that they do not like—a coup in Haiti, thefts of food relief supplies in Somalia, the development of nuclear weapons by North Korea, the invasion of Kuwait by Saddam Hussein, or Serbia's support for secessionist Serbian rebels in Bosnia—they have the same three choices that statesmen have always faced over the past four hundred years: *acquiesce in whatever they do not like, diplomatic negotiation and bargaining*, which might involve sanctions and threats of force, or *war*. If states choose to look the other way when a stronger state uses force against a weaker one, the victim has only two choices—to resist or to surrender.

Diplomacy, War, Threats of Force, and the Fate of Nations

The myriad changes in the following maps record the results of diplomacy, war, and threats of force—all motivated by changing distributions of power, inanimate social forces, and ideas.

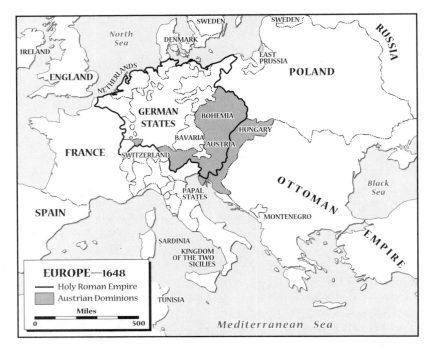

Map 1.1. Europe in 1648

International politics as we know it today has its origin in the Peace of Westphalia, which closed the Thirty Years' War and founded the system of sovereign states. Thus, this map provides the baseline for international politics over the past four hundred years. Note the vast size of Poland and the absence of any great German power in the center of Europe. The Germany that created so much havoc and destruction in the twentieth century was then a sea of free cities, church territories, and small states. Romania, Bulgaria, Serbia, Bosnia, Albania, Greece, and much of Hungary were all under the control of the Muslim Ottoman Empire.

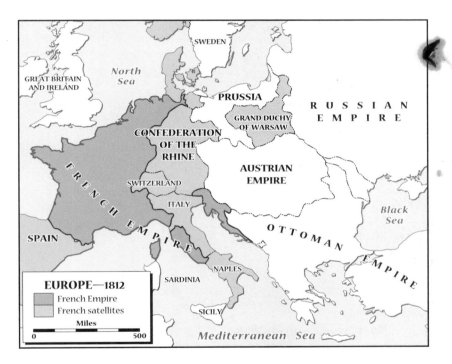

Map 1.2. Europe in 1812 at the Height of Napoleon's Hegemony

The French Revolution energized France, and within fifteen years, Napoleon Bonaparte controlled the continent of Europe, something that neither Charles V, Philip II, nor Louis XIV had come even close to achieving.[6] With the exceptions of Portugal, Sardinia, and Sicily, all of the former states of Europe were either incorporated into France directly, reduced to the status of satellites, or turned into compliant "allies" of France through defeat on the field of battle.

"For fifteen years," the British historian Alfred Cobbean notes, "France and Europe were . . . at the mercy of a gambler to whom fate and his own genius gave for a time all the aces."[7] Napoleon himself openly

5

boasted that he could extinguish Austria and Prussia at any moment of his choosing and that he could immediately summon enough men to prevent Russia, his nominal ally, from doing anything of which he disapproved.[8] "Except for Turkey, Europe is but one province of the world," Napoleon quipped as early as 1802. "When we make war," he said, "we make civil war."[9] The competitive system of sovereign states had been replaced by a continental French hegemony.

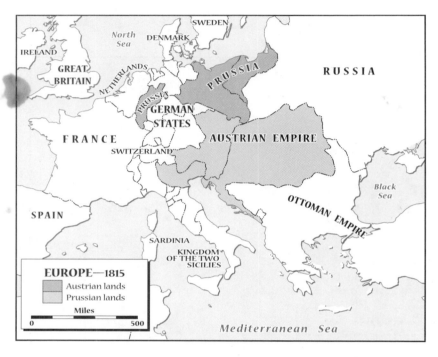

Map 1.3. Europe in 1815 after the Vienna Settlement

By invading Russia in 1812, Napoleon failed the supreme test of power politics—knowing when to stop. As diplomatic historian Paul Schroeder noted, "Durable success in power politics depends less on expanding one's power than on knowing where and how to stop and consolidate it."[10] However, the coalition that brought Napoleon down sought neither a punitive nor a vengeful peace. What they sought—and largely attained— was a peace designed to prevent any great power from securing European hegemony. The territorial settlement brokered in Vienna carefully balanced power among France, Russia, Prussia, and Austria and restored legitimate rulers to their old regimes, including the Bourbons in France.

Legitimacy was attained because the territorial settlement was a consensual one, which meant that none of the Great Powers left Vienna harboring resentment or fears for its security. Finally, restoration of the old regimes that had been deposed by Napoleon provided significant middle states with a stake in the settlement. By combining power *and* legitimacy, the architects of the Vienna settlement created a peace that would last almost one hundred years.

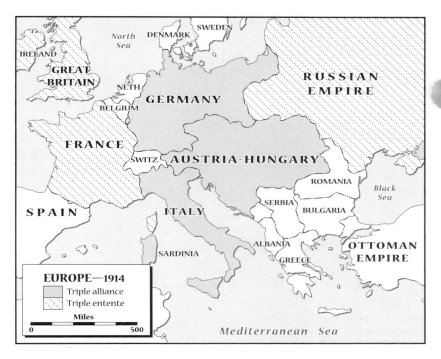

Map 1.4. Europe in 1914 after the Unification of Italy and Germay

By the mid-nineteenth century, liberalism and nationalism were challenging the monarchical regimes and the boundaries set at Vienna. In 1859, Sardinia, with the support of France, waged war to unify Italy, costing Austria-Hungary the province of Lombardy. A decade later, Bismarck embarked on three wars that unified Germany and gained Venetia for Italy, further reducing the size of Austria-Hungary. Meanwhile, the declining power of the Ottoman Empire led Russia to support the forces of Balkan nationalism, which threatened the multinational Austria-Hungarian empire.

Still, peace regined for almost twenty years after the unification of Germany because Bismark pursued a conciliatory nonexpansionist foreign policy and sought to conciliate the conflicting aims of Russia and Austria-Hungary. When Kaiser Wilhelm dismissed the Iron Chancellor, Germany embarked on a policy of Weltmacht, or world power, which threatened and united France, Russia, and Britain. When the Kaiser gave Austria a blank check to deal with Serbia after the assassination of Archduke Ferdinand, Russia mobilized. Germany responded by invading France through Belgium under its Schlieffen Plan. Britain then came to the aid of France, and Europe plunged into World War I.

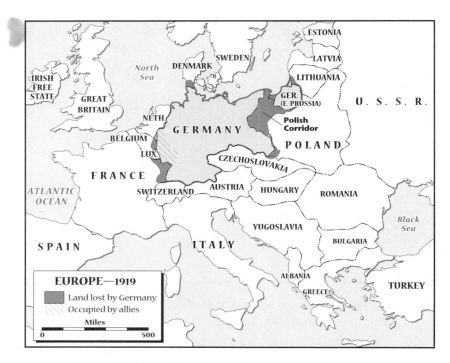

Map 1.5. Europe after the Paris Peace Settlement in 1919

World War I led to the collapse of four empires: the Russian, the German, the Austrian, and the Ottoman. In wake of the collapsed empires, new states were founded on the principle of national sefl-determination, including Estonia, Latvia, Lithuania, Poland, Czechoslovakia, and Hungary. The Ottoman Empire became a secular Turkish state, and a tiny, German Austria was all that remained of the former Austro-Hungarian empire. Unlike the allies of Vienna, the victors imposed a harsh and punitive peace on

Germany that violated the canons of national self-determination that guided the settlement elsewhere. Germany was to remain disarmed and pay heavy reparations, the Rhineland was occupied, a Polish corridor cut Germany in two, millions of Germans were placed under foreign rule, most notably in the Sudeten areas of Czechoslovakia, the Ruhr and the port of Danzig were placed under international control, and Austria was forbidden from ever uniting with Germany.

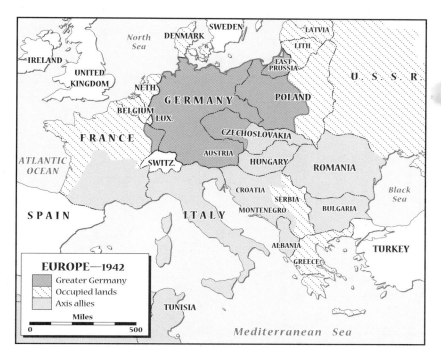

Map 1.6. Europe in 1942 at the Height of Nazi and Axis Power

By the time Adolf Hitler came to power, many in the victor states thought that the Versailles settlement was unfair, shortsighted, and illegitimate. Elites in Britain felt especially guilty about the settlement, and Neville Chamberlain sought peace not through enforcement of the Versailles settlement but through the appeasement of Hitler—as long as changes were made peacefully. Too weak to act alone and beset by weak allies in the East, France followed along behind Chamberlain. While Russia sought to create an anti-German coalition through the League of Nations in the mid-1930s, Chamberlain's appeasement policies led Stalin to make his own peace with Hitler. After signing a pact of neutrality with Stalin, Hitler launched his invasion of Poland, which led Britain and France to declare war. By 1942, Hitler's European hegemony bettered Napoleon's. All of Europe was under the control of Hitler; his junior partner, Mussolini; and assorted henchmen in eastern and central Europe. Like Napoleon, however, Hitler did not know where to stop, and his invasion of Russia brought him down, just as it did the Emperor of the French.

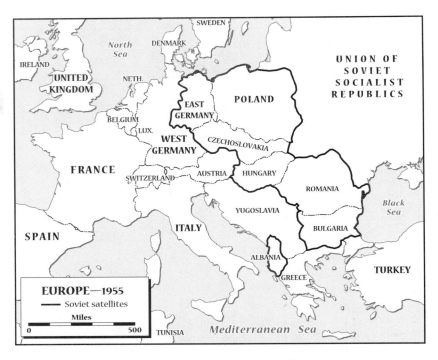

**Map 1.7. Europe between East and West in 1955:
The Soviet Bloc and the NATO Powers**

World War II led not to a thousand-year Reich, as Hitler had promised, but to the utter defeat of Germany, its unconditional surrender, and its division into a communist and a noncommunist state. East Germany became part of a great Russian empire, and West Germany became part of the NATO alliance, which united Western Europe with the United States. Europe was divided into two camps, each presided over by a colossal superpower. Thus, the great powers of Europe were trumped by two nuclear superpowers, and the world was divided into two vast blocs until decolonization brought about a "Third World." Finally, a Eurocentric international politics was replaced by world politics.

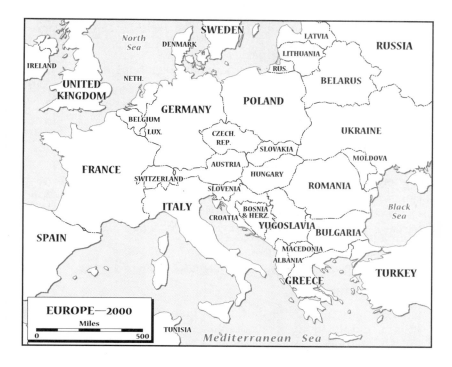

Map 1.8. Europe in 2000

The collapse of the Soviet Union created a new map in Europe and Eurasia. Germany was reunified as a democratic, market-economy state, and the members of Stalin's east European bloc proclaimed their independence and repudiated communism. The Union of Soviet Socialist Republics disappeared, and members of the union, such as Estonia, Latvia, Lithuania, the Ukraine, Armenia, and Georgia, struck out on their own as new nation-states. Russia proper had less territory in 2000 than it had had in 1810.

Sovereignty as a Confounding Consequence of Anarchy

Given that states have no legitimate authority standing above them, the concept of sovereignty is a logical corollary. States that make up the international system are sovereign states, and as such they are bound only by those laws and treaties to which they freely consent. Moreover, if the circumstances under which an agreement was signed change substantially, a state may release itself from the agreement. When differences arise over the interpretation of agreements or whether the conditions under which they were negotiated have changed substantially, each state makes the final decision for itself. In sum, each state is its own legislator, executive, judge, and jury—at least as far as its power will allow. As George Schwarzenberger put it, "In international politics, there is always an alternative to law—the appeal to power and force."[11]

If states fail to live up to international obligations they have freely undertaken, the only recourse of injured parties are acquiescence, diplomatic negotiation and bargaining, or military force. If two states have different interpretations of an international agreement or principle of international law, any of the following can result: (1) the states may negotiate a new treaty; (2) they may mutually agree to stop abiding by the treaty and go their separate ways; (3) they may seek an arbitrator or mediator; (4) the weaker party may resign itself to the views of the stronger party; or (5) the stronger party may seek to impose its will on the weaker party. All these points are well illustrated in the following three cases drawn from quite different historical periods.

CASE STUDY
America Concedes Its "Rights" for Peace in the Early Republic

On February 1, 1793, revolutionary France declared war against Britain, and the implications of that decision for American security quickly became apparent. Under the Franco-American Alliance of 1778, the United States was obligated to secure—"forever against all other powers"—French possessions in the West Indies. If the United States fulfilled that obligation and allied with France, the cost might have been devastating.

Because the United States had no navy at all—its last ship from the Revolutionary War had been sold in 1784—entry into the war on the side of France would have made its merchant ships easy prey for the British navy. Moreover, since the British were still occupying forts in the Northwest Territory in violation of the Peace of Paris, they were in a perfect position to instigate Indian wars all along the young Republic's western frontier settlements. In addition, Spain loomed as a potential threat since that country was allied with Britain. By closing the lower Mississippi to American commerce, Spain could deny western farmers a vital outlet for the export of surplus crops and prevent the entry of vital finished goods. Finally, Britain was the young republic's most important trading partner, taking more than 50 percent of its exports and supplying around 90 percent of its imports, which consisted mostly of finished goods that the French could not supply. In addition, duties on British goods provided more than 90 percent of the federal revenues![12]

President Washington and his cabinet were all agreed that the United States should remain neutral in the war, a decision that was also very much in the French interest. By standing on the international legal principle of "free ships carry free goods," America's large merchant marine would be able to carry provisions between France and its colonies without hindrance from British warships. Little wonder that France preferred America as a neutral rather than an ally. The "free ships carry free goods" principle meant that American ships could negate the British advantage on the high seas.

After France opened its ports to American ships, Britain's Privy Council quickly issued a set of orders that put the world's greatest naval power at loggerheads with the young Republic. Operating under the ancient doctrine of *consolato del mare*, the council affirmed the right of British vessels to seize enemy goods on neutral vessels. "The Principle of Free Ships Make Free Goods," Lord George Grenville wrote to his minister in America, "is one which has never been recognized by this Country, and . . . undoubtedly will not be allowed in the present case." Were Britain to do so, Grenville noted, France would secure, "those means of Subsistence, and of carrying on the war, from which the nature of their present situation, and of the Force employed against them, they must be otherwise unable to procure."[13]

Even more vexing, the council defined contraband to include all things "of such a Nature as to enable the Enemies of this Country to carry on the War against Us." When George Hammond, Britain's diplomatic envoy, explained that this definition included corn, flour, and meal, even the pro-British Alexander Hamilton was irate. That the British government would purchase food so seized was of little consolation to the young republic's sense of outrage.

Finally, the council invoked the Rule of 1756 against American shipping. First invoked during the Seven Years' War, this rule stipulated that ports closed to outsiders in peacetime could not be opened in time of war. Since trade between most French ports had been closed to non-French ships during peacetime, the Rule of 1756 meant that neutral ships carrying goods to or from such ports could be seized and confiscated.

On November 6, the council went even further and issued an order authorizing the seizure of all American shipping in the West Indies, and it did so without a timely warning to the American government. Within a matter of months more than 250 American ships had been detained and 150 condemned. Since trade between American and French West Indian ports had been open to trade during peacetime, this decision violated Britain's own definition of neutral rights under the Rule of 1756.

Clearly, Britain and America had two different views about the rights of neutrals under international law:

- America believed that it should be at liberty to transport French goods under the free ships doctrine, but Britain considered such trade open to seizure under the doctrine of *consolato del mare;*
- America defined contraband as items explicitly useful for making war, whereas Britain's definition could include almost anything;
- America believed that its ships should be able to carry goods anywhere without fear of seizure, but Britain would respect trade only between ports that had been open to neutrals before the war began.

Given the situation, the young Republic had three choices:

- It could go to war with Britain to vindicate its rights;
- It could yield and get its shippers to behave according to British mandates; or
- It could bargain with Britain in the hopes of persuading the British to revise their policies.

Making the issue more complex was the fear that if the United States gave in and accepted Britain's conception of neutrality, French privateers might begin seizing American merchant ships bound for Britain. In fact, French naval officers had already begun seizing American ships headed for England in retaliation for the failure of American merchant ships to flee or resist on encountering British warships.

Discussions within President Washington's cabinet were heated, involved, and at times confusing, but, in the end, the president decided that peace was his predominant aim. Thus, he dispatched Chief Justice of the Supreme Court John Jay to negotiate with the British. The result was Jay's Treaty, a monument to the young Republic's desire for peace. Under Articles 17 and 18 of the treaty, the United States agreed that enemy goods could be taken from neutral ships, that naval stores were contraband, that foodstuffs could be seized albeit with compensation, and that ports closed to trade in peacetime could not be opened in time of war. In return for America's surrender of its conceptions of neutral rights and contraband, the British agreed to leave the forts they had previously pledged to evacuate in the Treaty of Paris—no concession to the young Republic at all. In regard to British violations of their own Rule of 1756, a commission was created to adjudicate claims and grievances.

Fearing a public outcry, President Washington kept the treaty secret for several months, and when details leaked out, demonstrations and castigation broke out everywhere. Jay, himself, commented humorously that he could probably travel across the entire country at night by following his burning effigies. When Alexander Hamilton rose to defend the treaty in New York City, he was pelted with stones. Cries went out for Jay's impeachment from every corner of the nation, and Washington began to have doubts about putting his name to the document.

In the end the country had no recourse but to yield if it wanted to avoid a war with Britain, the supreme naval power of the time and a nation on whom the young Republic relied for 90 percent of its imports and most of its federal revenue. As one historian of the incident concluded:

> *Jay was obliged in effect to renounce the freedom of the seas. The maritime principles which the United States had bound itself to uphold in its previous treaties with foreign powers—free ships make free goods, neutrals are entitled to trade freely with belligerents in noncontraband goods, and the contraband list must be confined to a few war-making articles—were jettisoned by Jay as the price of Anglo-American harmony. In their place, the British conception of belligerents' rights was written into the treaty: naval stores were held to be contraband; provisions, under some ill-defined circumstances, could not be carried to enemy ports, and the United States acquiesced in the so-called "Rule of 1756" in which trade with enemy countries prohibited in times of peace could not be legalized in times of war.*[14]

The two nations held two conceptions of "right," and each conception was largely in consonance with each nation's economic, political, and military interests. As Immanuel Kant noted in 1795, when such conflicts arise, "states do not plead their cause before a tribunal; war alone is their way of bringing suit." But, as he also noted, "By war and its favorable issue in victory, right is not decided. . . ."[15] Although war did not result in this case, power and potential costs determined the issue—and easily in Britain's favor. America's principles may have been "valid" principles, but without the power and a willingness to go to war in defense of them, President Washington had little choice but to defer to the will of superior military and economic power.

The strong do not always win in conflicts among nations, as we shall see. But when a Great Power's vital interests are at stake and the power differential is overwhelming, as in this case, "right does not make right."

CASE STUDY
Hitler Announces Rearmament in Violation of the Versailles Treaty

On March 10, 1935, Hermann Goering revealed to a British journalist what everyone in the diplomatic community already knew but no one wanted to acknowledge publicly: Germany had built an air force in violation of the disarmament clauses of the Versailles Treaty. One week later, on Saturday, March 16, Adolph Hitler decreed a law establishing universal military service, which would lead to an army of about five hundred thousand men. Suddenly and clearly, Hitler had thrown down the gauntlet and openly defied the strictures of the Versailles Treaty.

In response, Italian dictator Benito Mussolini, hosted a meeting with British and French leaders at the city of Stresa, a favorite resort for diplomatic conferences. There, the three powers condemned the German action and referred the matter to the League of Nations. At Geneva, an extraordinary session of the League Council unanimously censured Germany and appointed a committee to study what steps might be taken *the next time* any state endangered the peace by unilaterally repudiating its international obligations.

Having been reprimanded only on paper, Hitler began rearming Germany at breakneck pace. In November 1935, 596,000 German young men were called up for training. Of the League's paper diplomacy, Winston Churchill made the following observation in the first volume of his war memoirs: "How vain was all their voting without the readiness of any single Power or group of Powers to contemplate the use of force even in the last resort."[16] What Churchill had in mind was made clear a few pages later when he drew the following conclusions about the incident:

All that was done [by the Germans] up to 1935 fell far short of the strength and power of the French Army and its vast reserves, [to say nothing of] its numerous and vigorous allies. Even at this time a resolute decision upon the authority, which could easily have been obtained, of the League of Nations might have arrested the whole process. Germany could either have been brought before the bar at Geneva and invited to give a full explanation and allow inter-Allied missions of inquiry to examine the state of her armaments and military formations in breach of the Treaty; or, in the event of refusal, the Rhine bridgeheads could have been reoccupied until compliance with the Treaty had been secured, without there being any possibility of effective resistance or much likelihood of bloodshed. In this way the Second World War could have been prevented or at least delayed indefinitely.[17]

Words alone would not stop Hitler's accumulation of swords, but the alternative to words was not total war, as Churchill rightly pointed out. However, the failure of France, Britain, and Italy to put teeth into the resolutions of the League led Hitler to conclude that the League of Nations was a mere talking shop and that the three Great Powers could easily be cowed and intimidated.

At the time, Churchill was an outcast in his party. In fact, when the Conservatives won the 1936 election by a huge margin, Prime Minister Stanley Baldwin refused to include Churchill in his cabinet, in part for fear of alienating Hitler!

Hitler had tossed the disarmament clauses of the Versailles Treaty into the wastebasket. If those clauses were to be pulled out and Hitler made to abide by them, no "international government" would do that. Only those powers that benefited from those clauses could do so, and in this case, they chose words instead of action.

CASE STUDY
Ronald Reagan's Star Wars (Strategic Defense Initiative) and the Antiballistic Missile Treaty

Like most postwar American presidents, Ronald Reagan was appalled when he realized that if the nation's nuclear deterrence policies failed, there was no hope for the survival of the American people. What consolation would a genocidal retaliation be to a population devastated by nuclear war?

Horrified by this same reality in the late 1950s and early 1960s, the Soviet leadership sought to develop and construct an antiballistic missile system to protect their capital city and vital military assets. The American response, under then Secretary of Defense Robert McNamara, was not to match the Soviet defensive efforts but to negate them by building enough offensive missiles to overwhelm any defensive system the Soviets might build. The logic was simple: Since it cost much less to build an attacking missile than a defending missile, an arms race between defensive and offensive missiles was one that the defensive side could only lose *given the technology at the time.* Seeing the futility of such defensive efforts, the United States and the Soviet Union signed an Antiballistic Missile (ABM) Treaty in 1972, which limited each side to the deployment of small ground-based systems at only two sites, which were later reduced to one.[18]

By the 1980s, however, new technologies had led a number of leading American scientists to believe that a space-based defense system might be feasible. Such a system would have the advantage of being able to destroy Soviet missiles just as they were leaving the launching pad and before they had unleashed their thousands of independently targeted warheads. Spurred by his desire to shield American and Soviet civilians from the horrors of nuclear war, Reagan quickly became the major proponent and supporter of a space-based defensive system. On March 23, 1983, the president closed a televised address on "defense and national security" by announcing that he was ordering "a comprehensive and intensive effort to define a long-term research and development program to begin to achieve our ultimate goal of eliminating the threat posed by strategic nuclear missiles." Thus, the Strategic Defense Initiative (SDI), more commonly called "star wars," was born.

Obviously, the scientific feasibility and the larger military-political implications of such a system were highly debatable.[19] What concerns us here, however, is a different obstacle to the president's realization of his dream: the extent to which the existing ABM Treaty might constrain the development and testing of such a system. The president said he would pursue his research program "consistent with our obligations [under] the ABM Treaty," but just what those obligations were seemed quite clear from Article 5: "Each party undertakes not to develop, test, or deploy ABM systems or components which are sea-based, space-based, or mobile land-based." Accordingly, the Soviets insisted on a strict interpretation of the treaty, arguing that research, development, and testing of the president's ideas could take place only in the laboratory. In their opinion, the treaty prohibited any testing at all in the field or in space. The Reagan administration, on the other hand, argued that the treaty allowed any kind of testing and development, inside or outside the laboratory, as long as no deployment took place. This *broad interpretation* of the treaty would allow the United States to develop its system much more cheaply and with much greater confidence than "in the laboratory" testing would allow.

Clearly, the interpretation of a treaty is a legal issue, but neither the Soviet Union nor the United States had any intention of submitting their legal differences to an international court for one obvious reason: The political stakes were just too high for both sides. Although the ABM Treaty itself was of unlimited duration, either side had the right to withdraw from the treaty after giving six months notice. Given this six-month breakout clause, the basis for the Soviet fears was clear. If extensive testing in space proved that the SDI was feasible, the United States might "break out" of the treaty under the six-month-notice clause and rapidly deploy its system. Were that to happen, the United States might confront the Soviets with a nuclear first-strike capacity. Even without an actual breakout, the fear alone of such a breakout might lead to a new arms race in offensive weapons.

The legal position adopted by each side clearly reflected its political interests. The Soviets were behind in the new technologies, and they could ill afford the costs of competing in a new realm of nuclear weaponry. Reagan, on the other hand, wanted to escape the nuclear sword of Damocles inherent in the nation's deterrence policies, and he wanted to move ahead with the exploration of space-based defensive systems as quickly as possible.

The possible outcomes were four:

1. the Soviet Union would get the United States to accept the narrow interpretation through bargaining on the basis of inducements or threats;
2. the United States would get the Soviets to accept the broad interpretation also through bargaining on the basis of inducements or threats;

3. having failed to work out an agreement, both sides would accept the broad interpretation and compete in developing their separate spaced-based systems; or

4. the United States would hold to its broad interpretation and the Soviets would hold to its narrow interpretation—the least likely alternative of the four.

A great deal of bargaining on this issue took place just before and during the abortive Reykjavik Summit in October 1986. The main Soviet goal was to get rid of SDI altogether, but failing that, their fall-back objective was to put the deployment of any such system as far off as possible by amending the treaty to include a longer breakout period.

In an exchange of letters before the summit, Soviet leader Mikhail Gorbachev proposed that both sides agree not to withdraw from the treaty for fifteen to twenty years during which no space system could be deployed. Then, there would be an indefinite time frame for negotiations about what would follow the revised treaty. By extending the breakout period from six months to fifteen-to-twenty years, the Soviets would gain time to develop their own system while preventing American deployment. By accepting Gorbachev's proposals, the United States would gain little from testing under its broad interpretation, and the Soviets would have time to catch up with the Americans.

Reagan countered with a seven-and-a-half year breakout clause. However, to allay Soviet fears about any unilateral American breakout, he made the following proposal: The side that wanted to deploy a defensive system would have to both *share the technology of the system with the other side* and *eliminate its own offensive weapons before deploying its system.* In this way, the Soviets' first-strike fears could never materialize.

When they met at Reykjavik, Gorbachev proposed a nonwithdrawal term of not less than ten years followed by a follow-on negotiating process of three to five years. During this ten- to fifteen-year period, deployment would not be permitted, and the Soviets' narrow interpretation of testing—"research and testing in laboratories and not outside of them"—would be followed. In response, Reagan made a counteroffer: Soviet representatives could be present at all American tests, and if a space-based defensive system should prove feasible, the United States would be obligated to share the system with the Soviets and eliminate its ballistic missiles before deployment.

The conversation then moved as follows:

Gorbachev: The pursuit of SDI will necessitate a buildup of strategic arms.

> *Reagan:* We are accused of wanting a first-strike capability, but we are proposing a treaty that would require the elimination of ballistic missiles before a defense can be deployed; so a first strike would be impossible.
>
> *Gorbachev:* You will take the arms race into space and could be tempted to launch a first strike from space."
>
> *Reagan:* That's why I propose to eliminate ballistic missiles and share SDI with you."
>
> *Gorbachev:* If you will not share oil-drilling equipment or even milk-processing factories, I do not believe that you will share SDI."
>
> *Reagan:* We will eliminate all ballistic missiles before SDI is deployed, so a first strike would be impossible."

After a discussion of particulars produced no agreement, Gorbachev tried to induce the president to accept the narrow definition of testing by substantially accepting the American position on a related issue of intermediate nuclear missiles in Europe (the so-called zero option) and by proposing that both sides cut their offensive strategic missiles by 50 percent during the first five years of a ten-year nonwithdrawal period and the remaining 50 percent over the next five years. Gorbachev was offering to cut his strategic offensive weapons by 100 percent over a ten-year period if Reagan would accept a ten-year nonwithdrawal period and agree to test only in the laboratory—an incredible offer!

But Reagan remained unmovable. When he refused the offer, Gorbachev stood up and simply said, "It's the 'laboratory' or good-bye," whereupon Reagan stood up and said good-bye. The Reykjavik Summit was over. The American president would not yield.

This issue over testing was never resolved to the satisfaction of either side during the Cold War. Once the Soviet-American conflict ended, fears about nuclear weapons declined drastically, as did concerns about the need for arms-control agreements in general. Consequently, the issue was allowed to drop when the Cold War ended, illustrating Winston Churchill's admonition that "It is the greatest mistake to mix up disarmament with peace. When you have peace you will have disarmament."[20]

The purpose of presenting these three cases is neither to affirm nor criticize the position of any of the parties. Rather, it is to underscore a simple point about the nature of the international political system: If a state engages in an action that another state finds threatening to its interests, the latter has only three alternatives—*acquiesce, diplomatic negotiation and bargaining, or military force.*

The author of a leading textbook on international politics subtitled his chapter on international law with the phrase "Right Makes Right."[21] Yet, as these three cases make clear, right and law are frequently more a reflection of interests and power than any abstract notions of justice and morality. In the dispute between Britain and the young American Republic, each side's conception of neutral rights strongly coincided with its political interests, and in the case of Britain, its military interests. In the German rearmament case, Hitler was clearly challenging the core of the Versailles settlement. If the British, French, and Italians were unwilling to force Germany to comply with its obligations under the treaty, the structure of peace embodied in the Versailles treaty would be seriously transformed—and to their disadvantage. In the disagreement between Reagan and Gorbachev, the crux of the matter was the extent to which the ABM Treaty served each side's interests.

But Why Not "Take Them to Court"?

Since legal issues were involved in each of these cases, why did the contesting parties choose not to submit their disputes to an arbitration panel or international court and thereby obtain a relatively impartial settlement of the issue? International courts have been available to states for almost a hundred years. However, these courts have always been viewed as discretionary third-party alternatives that states could choose to turn to when traditional diplomatic methods failed. As President Calvin Coolidge so succinctly put it, the Permanent Court of International Justice was a place "to which we could go but not be brought."[22]

The first international court, created by the Hague Peace Conference in 1899, was not a sitting court. Rather, the Permanent Court of Arbitration amounted to a list of jurists from which contending states could choose a neutral panel to sort out the legal aspects of a dispute between them. A Permanent Court of International Justice was created under Article 14 of the Covenant of the League of Nations in 1920. However, although the world now had a permanent, sitting court, acceptance of its jurisdiction was completely voluntary. No state could be obliged to appear before it, and the court would take cases only if both parties agreed to appear before it and pledged to abide by its verdict.

There was, to be sure, an Optional Clause in the Charter of the Permanent Court whereby states could agree to accept compulsory jurisdiction in *legal* disputes with other states that also accepted the article. Fifty-nine states eventually signed the clause, but most acceptances were hedged with exceptions and conditions. In the end, only nine states ever ratified their acceptances. Still, during its twenty years of existence, the court heard thirty-one cases and issued twenty-seven advisory opinions.

With the founding of the United Nations, the Permanent Court was succeeded by the International Court of Justice or, as it is more commonly called, the World Court. Again, jurisdiction is compulsory only under two conditions: if a treaty explicitly mentions the Court as arbitrator of disputes over interpretations of its clauses (so-called promissory clauses) or if states have accepted compulsory jurisdiction under the Optional Clause. In the former case, states cannot unilaterally refer a question involving the interpretation of a treaty to the Court. When such differences arise, both parties must consent to submitting the dispute to the Court. Thus, states frequently have a veto over compulsory jurisdiction, even when treaties contain promissory clauses. In regard to compulsory jurisdiction, Article 36 of the Permanent Court's charter was incorporated without change into the new Court's charter, and acceptances of compulsory jurisdiction during the League period were considered operative in the postwar period. Although more states have accepted compulsory jurisdiction under Article 36, most acceptances are still hedged with conditions and reservations.

The United States, for example, accepted the Optional Clause in 1946 but only with a set of reservations embodied in the Connally Amendment. Through this amendment, the United States explicitly excluded "disputes with regard to matters which are essentially within the domestic jurisdiction of the United States of America *as determined by the United States of America;* or . . . disputes arising under a multilateral treaty, unless (1) all parties to the treaty affected by the decision are also parties to the case before the Court, or (2) the United States of America agrees to its jurisdiction." In debating these reservations, members of the Senate expressed fears that the Court might concern itself with such questions as American immigration laws, tariffs, Puerto Rico, the Panama Canal, and race relations. But underneath was a simple wariness about making an open-ended commitment to adjudicate any legal dispute at any time in the future.

The only "teeth" that the charter gave to the court in regard to its jurisdiction is contained in Article 36, clause 6: "In the event of a dispute as to whether the Court has jurisdiction, the matter shall be settled by the Court." However, as we shall see, while the Court may have the legal right to settle jurisdictional disputes on paper, it has no power to compel a disagreeing party to accept its decisions. Given all these roadblocks, *the World Court has not been a very busy place.* Between 1945 and 1981, it heard only forty-two cases; between 1976 and 1981, only one new case appeared on the Court's docket.

On the other hand, the *Court's record has been excellent in resolving those cases that disputants have freely chosen to place before it.* Only once in the history of both courts has a party failed to abide by the court's ruling in such cases. While no examples are typical, the following indicate the kinds of questions that disputing countries have asked the two courts to resolve:

- In 1935 the Norwegian government issued a decree that reserved an exclusive fishing zone for its own nationals four miles from its coast. Although it did not oppose the creation of a zone as such, Great Britain protested the base from which the zone was drawn. British diplomats argued that the baselines should begin at the innermost parts of the fjords that shape the Norwegian coast. The Norwegians, on the other hand, drew their baselines from the outermost points on the mainland and relevant off coastal islands. The Court decided that both the method employed by the Norwegians and the baseline they drew were in conformity with international law. Britain went along with the Court's decision.
- In 1949 Columbia and Peru put two questions before the Court: did a state granting asylum in its embassy have the final authority to decide whether the grantee was a political refugee or a criminal, and did the state in which the embassy was situated have an obligation to guarantee that the refugee could leave its territory safely?
- In 1952 the Court was asked to decide whether licensing controls imposed by French authorities in the Moroccan Protectorate could be applied to American nationals who claimed that such controls were in violation of the treaty between the United States and Morocco of 1836 and the General Act of Algeciras of 1906.
- In 1953 England and France asked the Court to decide which one of them had more convincing proof of title to the Miniquiers and Ecrehos, two groups of islets situated between the British island of Jersey and the coast of France. In the same year the court was asked to decide whether Liechtenstein deserved restitution and compensation on behalf of one of its citizens of German nationality who resided in Guatemala and whose business property was seized by that government during World War II.
- In 1960 Nicaragua and Honduras asked the Court whether Nicaragua was obligated under an 1894 convention to accept the king of Spain's arbital decision of 1906 on disputed boundary areas between them.
- In 1969 the Court was asked to decide whether the boundary lines in the North Sea Continental Shelf between the Federal Republic of Germany, Denmark, and the Netherlands had to be drawn on the basis of equidistance.

As these examples indicate, most of the cases coming before the Court are of a legal and technical nature and seldom involve significant national interests of the countries in question. Since the early 1970s, however, the Court has involved itself in a number of cases in which one of the sides has denied its jurisdiction. In those instances, the side denying jurisdiction has usually refused to participate in the judicial proceedings. Whenever the Court has gone on to hear the substance of such cases, the results of its involvement have not varied—the state denying jurisdiction has ignored both the court's proceedings and its decision.

THE BRITISH-ICELANDIC CODFISH DISPUTE. In 1972 Iceland announced that it was expanding its exclusive fishing zone from twelve to fifty miles. Because British seamen had fished in those waters for centuries, Britain brought the dispute before the Court, claiming that Iceland's unilateral action was contrary to international law. The court immediately issued a temporary order prohibiting Iceland from excluding British fisherman from the new zone. Iceland denied the Court's jurisdiction, ignored its temporary prohibition, and began seizing British fishing ships. In response, the British government ordered warships to accompany and protect its fishing fleets. While the Court was working on the case—without Iceland's participation—British and Icelandic negotiators hammered out a temporary agreement largely on Iceland's terms.

In 1974 the Court issued its ruling: Iceland could neither extend its zone unilaterally nor exclude British fisherman. Iceland ignored the Court's decision, and when a "codfish war" broke out, it severed diplomatic relations with Britain and threatened to withdraw from NATO. When negotiations resumed, Britain, under pressure from its American NATO ally, agreed to terms set largely by Iceland.

Unlike the case of "little" America versus "Great" Britain in 1793, tiny Iceland won this dispute for several good reasons. First of all, the balance of "saliencies" lay in favor of Iceland. While the fish in Iceland's waters were crucial to the economy of three British fishing ports—Hull, Grimsby, and Fleetwood—the reduced quota of fish that Iceland set for Britain would have little impact on the British economy overall. In fact, the difference between the quota that Iceland was offering to Britain (117,000 tons) and the quota that Britain was holding out for (between 145,000 and 130,000 tons) amounted to no more than $10 to $15 million dollars. On the other hand, cod amounted to 40 percent of Iceland's exports, and unless drastic conservation measures were undertaken, Icelanders feared that the species might disappear just as herring had in the 1960s, resulting in a 16 percent loss of per capita income between 1966 and 1968. Overall, 80 percent of Iceland's export income came from fish and fishery products as opposed to .2 percent for Britain.[23]

In addition, legitimacy also ran in favor of Iceland's position. That Belgium and West Germany had accepted the quotas allocated to them also weakened the position of Britain, especially since British officials agreed that immediate conservation steps were necessary. Finally, Iceland's threat to withdraw from NATO and break its bilateral treaty with the United States put at risk a NATO surveillance station and an American naval base at Keflavík, two facilities that were vital for intelligence gathering, antisubmarine warfare, and protection of the North Atlantic sea-lanes. Thus, tiny Iceland with a navy of only six gunboats bested Great Britain, even though "the law" and the World Court were on the side of the giant. Although power counts in international politics, the powerful do not always win for reasons that will be made clear in later chapters.

FRANCE'S NUCLEAR TESTING IN THE SOUTH PACIFIC. In May 1973 Australia and New Zealand instituted proceedings to prevent France from carrying out nuclear tests in the South Pacific. The Court quickly issued an interim judgment: France should refrain from any nuclear testing that could produce atmospheric fallout on New Zealand or Australia pending the outcome of the case. France denied the Court's jurisdiction in the matter and refused to appear at any of its hearings. As the Court deliberated, France tested. After testing, France issued a statement that it would test no more. In December 1974, the court decided not to render a judgment because France's announcement that it would not test again had rendered Australia and New Zealand's application moot.

THE IRANIAN HOSTAGE CRISIS OF 1979–80. As part of its strategy to free the diplomats taken hostage by Iranian "students," the United States filed a complaint with the Court on November 29, 1979. In its brief, the United States sought release of the hostages, monetary reparations, and prosecution of those responsible for taking the hostages. On December 10, the Court heard oral arguments from American attorneys, who requested provisional measures pending the outcome of the case.

Five days later, the Court issued a provisional order directing Iran "to ensure that the premises of the United States Embassy, Chancery, and Consulates be restored to the possession of the United States authorities under their exclusive control." In addition, the Court ordered that "the Government of Iran should ensure the immediate release, without any exception, of all persons of United States nationality who have been in the Embassy of the United States of America or in the Ministry of Foreign Affairs, or have been held hostage elsewhere." Iran ignored the Court's orders.

On May 24, 1980, the Court handed down two unanimous judgments in the case: Iran was to release immediately every American and other nationals being held under unlawful detention, and Iran was ordered not to subject any diplomatic or consular staff member to any form of judicial proceedings. In other rulings that were not unanimous, the Court declared that Iran was violating its obligations to the United States under various international conventions, that it was obligated to make reparations to the United States, and that if the parties could not agree to the form and amount of the reparations, the Court would set the terms. Having refused to participate in any of the Court's deliberations, Iran gratuitously tossed off the whole effort as "meaningless."

NICARAGUA VERSUS THE UNITED STATES. In the early 1980s, the Reagan administration supplied and armed rebel Contra forces that were seeking to destabilize and overthrow the Marxist Sandinista regime that had routed dictator Anastasio Somoza. In March 1984, CIA-supported operatives of the Contras mined three Nicaraguan ports, damaging seven Nicaraguan ships and six ships from other states.

In response the Sandinista regime hired Harvard law professor Abraham Chayes, who helped the Marxist regime to bring a suit against the United States on April 9, 1984. In filing its petition with the Court, Nicaragua asked for $370.2 million in damages. Nicaragua argued that the Court had jurisdiction over the case because both Nicaragua and the United States had signed the Optional Clause in Article 36, and in Nicaragua's opinion, none of the reservations embodied in the Connally Amendment appeared applicable.

The Reagan administration argued that the Court lacked jurisdiction, claiming, first, that the dispute was a *political* one and not a legal one and, second, that Nicaragua had never filed its acceptance of the Optional Clause when it so declared in 1929. In addition, the United States argued that compulsory jurisdiction was not applicable because the United States had withdrawn its acceptance of the Optional Clause, albeit three days before Nicaragua filed its suit.

In November 1984 the Court ruled against the United States on every count. The Court had decided that the dispute was a legal one and not a political one; it announced that Nicaragua's mere *declaration* of acceptance was sufficient to establish its adherence to the clause; and it announced further that the Reagan administration's decision to withdraw from Article 36 did not apply to the current case because the required six-month period had not elapsed between the administration's announcement of intent to withdraw and Nicaragua's petition to the Court.

Two months after the Court's ruling on the issue of jurisdiction, the United States withdrew from the case, claiming that the Court was being used for political purposes. Nevertheless, the Court heard Nicaragua's arguments, and on June 27, 1986, it ruled against the United States on several counts. According to the Court, the United States was not acting in collective self-defense in Central America; rather, it was guilty of intervening in Nicaragua's internal affairs, interrupting peaceful maritime activity, and threatening the sovereignty of Nicaragua. The Court condemned the United States for using illegal threats and uses of force, for embargoing trade with Nicaragua, for mining Nicaragua's ports, and for ignoring general humanitarian principles embodied in customary international law. It also concluded that the United States owed Nicaragua reparations in an amount to be decided by the United States and Nicaragua. The Reagan administration ignored the Court's decision.

All four of these contentious cases illustrate well the conclusion drawn by Hans Morgenthau about prospects for strengthening the World Court through efforts to secure compulsory jurisdiction: "In the field of adjudication . . . it is still the will of individual nations that is decisive in all stages of proceedings."[24] The question of whether Iceland, France, Iran, or the United States *should* have abided by the Court's ruling is not at issue here. What matters is how states actually behave.

The lessons to be drawn from a century's experience with international courts are clear:

- When both parties freely agree to adjudicate, they invariably accept and comply with he Court's decisions.
- When one of the parties objects to adjudication and the Court involves itself in the case anyway, the objecting party will ignore the Court's decision if it favors the other side.
- States—large or small—will not submit disputes involving their vital interests to international legal tribunals if they have any power to determine the matter at all.

As Professor David Forsythe concluded in *The Politics of International Law*, "legal claims often are not enforced by adjudication; they are implemented in a political process based upon power."[25] This "fact of life" may be neither "right" nor just, but it will remain a fact of life so long as no power stands above states that can compel them to submit even their legal disputes, let alone their political disagreements, to third-party adjudication.

The International Political System Is an Oligarchy

Although all states may be equal in the eyes of international law, decision making in the international system is in no way democratic. Oligarchy is the political reality. States have always varied vastly in their power, and the strongest states have traditionally dominated and prevailed in significant conflicts of interest. Although there are always qualifications and exceptions, Thucydides was not totally off the mark when he quipped that in any system of independent states, "the strong do what they have the power to do and the weak accept what they have to accept."[26] Or, as George Schwarzenberger noted more recently:

> The [growth of the nation-state system] has been accompanied by the growth of an international oligarchy from its ranks. The powers which, at any time, form this inner ring have arrogated to themselves the function of exercising supreme control over affairs within international society. Every one of its members considers itself entitled to concern itself with all of the major issues of an international character, irrespective of whether they directly affect its own interests. . . . At the same time, they have to watch each other and take care that none of them will be so strong as to threaten the existence of the oligarchy itself.[27]

States have traditionally been denoted as great, medium, and minor or small powers. The expression "Great Powers" was first coined by Foreign Minister Robert Castlereagh of Britain, who sought to keep the negotiations at the Congress of Vienna solidly in the hands of those six powers "most considerable in population and weight," namely, Britain, Russia, Austria, Prussia, Spain, and the defeated France. After World War I, all of the major decisions were made by America, Britain, France, Italy, and Japan. When the smaller powers protested, French foreign minister George Clemenceau replied that the authority of the Great Powers rested on twelve million soldiers.[28] During World War II, the major postwar decisions were made by the Big Three in conferences at Tehran, Yalta, and Potsdam. During the Cold War, summit diplomacy was increasingly confined to the two superpowers.

Small states become significant actors only if they become clients or allies of a major power. During the Cold War, Soviet support enabled Cuba to play a major role in making and breaking governments in Africa and Central America during the 1970s and 1980s. With the dissolution of the Soviet Union and the end of Soviet subsidies, Cuba's international influence and significance evaporated rapidly.

The Great Powers have frequently ignored wars among small powers unless their individual or collective interests were involved. As Martin Wight has noted, "the quarrels between Small Powers seldom harm anybody except themselves, and they have never in history occasioned a major war."[29] That the Great Powers looked on for so long as war and ethnic cleansing dragged on in places such as Bosnia or Rwanda should have surprised no one.

But power alone does not always lead to membership in the oligarchy. After the defeat of Napoleon and his replacement by a restored Bourbon monarchy, France was "readmitted" to membership in the councils of the Great Powers. However, after World War I and World War II, defeated Germany was not so favored. Through the Peace of Versailles, Germany was forced to disarm and was excluded from the League of Nations. After World War II, Germany was divided up and occupied by the victorious powers. After the Bolshevik Revolution, the Soviet Union was treated as a pariah state for more than fifteen years by Britain and France. During the same period, Mussolini sought to move Italy into the ranks of the Great Power clubs, but, at best, he attained the status of a parvenu in the eyes of Britain and France. America, of course, would have been welcomed into the oligarchy, but it refused to participate, preferring isolation.

During the Cold War, the United States sought to deny the legitimacy of Mao's Zedong's victory in China by refusing to recognize his government diplomatically, by working hard to isolate it, and by seeking to keep it out of China's seat in the United Nations. Trade was embargoed, and Americans, from journalists to tourists, were forbidden to enter China. When the Geneva Conference met in 1954 to settle the future of Korea and Indochina, U.S. secretary of state John Foster

Dulles refused even to shake hands with Chinese foreign minister Chou En-lai.

Fourteen years later, President Richard Nixon decided to develop a rapprochement with China in order to wean that country from the Soviet bloc. According to Henry Kissinger, Nixon had decided that "[if] the Soviet Union and China were more afraid of each other than they were of the United States—an unprecedented opportunity for American diplomacy would come into being."[30] Knowing full well what Dulles had done at Geneva, Nixon saw a simple handshake as the most powerful way of symbolizing America's acceptance of China as one of the Great Powers.

Of his "historic handshake," Nixon later wrote as:

> At the head of the waiting delegation was Zhou Enlai, his frail frame covered by a heavy overcoat. Years earlier, at the Geneva Conference in 1954, Zhou had been deeply offended when he extended his hand to John Foster Dulles at a public gathering and Dulles refused to shake it. This had been one of those small ceremonial slights that may seem justified, even necessary, at the time, but can rankle for years afterward and even have substantial diplomatic consequences. I was determined that my first act on arriving in China would be to undo the act of omission. As I came down the ramp, Zhou began to applaud. I returned the gesture, and then, as I reached the bottom step, I stretched out my hand to Zhou. When he took it, it was more than a handshake. We both knew it was a turning point in history.[31]

The Institutionalization of Oligarchy in the United Nations Charter

The UN Charter enshrines the principle of sovereign equality in its General Assembly, but it nods to the reality of oligarchy in its Security Council. Resolutions of the General Assembly are adopted by majorities consisting of two-thirds of the members present and voting, on a one-nation-one-vote basis. However, the assembly's resolutions are merely *recommendations,* and no state is obligated to comply with them *including states that vote in favor of them.* To the Security Council, on the other hand, members of the United Nations "confer . . . primary responsibility for the maintenance of international peace and security, and agree that in carrying out its duties under this responsibility the Security Council acts on their behalf (Article 21, Chapter V: author's emphasis)."

Of course, any of the five permanent members can prevent the Security Council from exercising this responsibility merely by exercising its veto power, a veto power that acknowledges the reality of oligarchy. In fact, the United Nations was explicitly designed so that it would be unable to act against any of the permanent members or even against their pleasure. The embodiment of oligarchy in the Security Council is particularly well illustrated in the case of Nicaragua versus the United

States discussed earlier in this chapter. After the World Court ruled against the United States and the Reagan administration ignored the Court's ruling, Nicaragua exercised its right under Article 94 (2) of the UN Charter, which reads: "If any party to a case fails to perform the obligations incumbent upon it under a judgment rendered by the Court, the other party may have recourse to the Security Council, which may, if it deems necessary, make recommendations or decide upon measures to be taken to give effect to the judgment." In July 1986 the council considered Nicaragua's complaint and voted in favor of a resolution calling on the United States to comply with the judgment of the Court. The resolution failed, however, because the United States vetoed it.[32]

However, whenever the oligarchy is in agreement, it has the power *and the legitimate authority* to act decisively. Technically, it is possible for a majority of the ten nonpermanent members to block a resolution sponsored by the oligarchy. Were that to occur, a united oligarchy would never allow a paper resolution to stop them. More likely, they would merely do what they wanted to do outside the organization.

Small and neutral countries have frequently played a vital role in UN observation and peacekeeping operations in many troubled areas over the past fifty years. But when major breaches of the peace occur, it is not the Swedes or the Pakistanis or the Costa Ricans who rush to defend the victims of aggression; if anyone runs to defend of a victim of aggression, it is, instead, the soldiers of one or more of the Great Powers—usually, America in the postwar period. Moreover, when members of the oligarchy do respond to breaches of the peace, those responses are more a reflection of those members' interests than a reflection of any self-abnegating loyalty to the principles outlined in the organization's charter.

The most important thing to bear in mind about the League of Nations and the United Nations is that these organizations are not independent entities or embryonic world governments. They are, instead, creatures of their member states, and what they do or fail to do is largely determined by the wishes and interests of their most powerful members. These facts will never change as long as states are sovereign.

The Centrality of Positionality

Given the anarchic nature of the international system, a central concern of all states, and especially the Great Powers, is their *positionality*—their power and status relative to others. States seeking to have more influence in world affairs can do so only by increasing their power and status relative to others. Conversely, those seeking to maintain their influence at the top must pay attention to the rising power and status of those below them. As Professor Joseph Grieco has noted, "states are acutely sensitive to any erosion of their relative capabilities, which are the ultimate basis for their security and independence in an anarchical, self-help international context."[33]

Even among friendly, democratic states, matters of relative power and status can matter. For example, over the past fifty years, the forces of international interdependence and integration have been operating more in Western Europe than anywhere else in the world. Yet, some European nations are reluctant to take the final steps toward economic, political, and social integration, and, in part, this reluctance stems from fears about their positionality relative to each other.

Consider the case of the French. At the beginning of the postwar period, European integration was a vehicle through which French governments sought to reign in and harness German industrial, economic, and political power. As Germany has increasingly become the preeminent center of the European Economic Community, many Frenchman have become reluctant to proceed with further integration. What they fear is seeing their country become the junior partner of a reunified German colossus. In his campaign for the French presidency in 1995, Jacques Chirac said the following about establishing a common European currency: "The core of the problem is not whether we surrender this or that bit of sovereignty, but whether we do so on the same terms as Germany does. We cannot proceed with a change of this magnitude," he added, "from a position of weakness vis-à-vis Germany."[34]

On the other hand, concerns for security and positionality can lead to even greater insecurity at times. As one nation increases its power and position, other nations may become increasingly insecure. Onlookers may wonder what the "real" motives of the rising power might be, or they may worry about how that increased power might be used. As Thucydides noted in *The Peloponnesian Wars*, Sparta went to war because Athens had become too strong. War occurred not because of what Athens had done with her power but because of that power itself, which Sparta feared. While states must be concerned for their positionality, power, and status, they must also think about how they and their efforts are perceived by other states.

The Sorry Record of the Nation-State System

Obviously, the record of the international system in maintaining peace, order, and security has not been a particularly good one. All too frequently, states do not do a very good job of perceiving their own interests, of reading the intentions or resolve of other nations, or of recognizing the limits of their own power. In fact, most states seek to avoid international conflicts, and when conflicts break out among other nations, bystander states usually look the other way or pass inconsequential paper resolutions, as the League of Nations did when Japan invaded Manchuria.

Even when their values and interests are involved, states can be hesitant, slow, and incremental in responding to the actions of other states. When change-seeking states carry on menacing activities, make demands, threaten to use force, or engage in violence, the easiest responses are to do nothing, to procrastinate, to seek to conciliate the aggressor, or to accommodate themselves to the changes. The unwillingness of the victors of World War I to stand up to Hitler is just one notorious case study. During the Kuwait crisis, those so-called rising economic giants, Germany and Japan, flinched when Saddam Hussein made his move, despite their vital interest in access to foreign sources of oil. As Charles Krauthammer put it, when the shooting started, Germany and Japan hid under the table.[35] More recently, members of the oligarchy hesitated to act when Serbian forces took UN peacekeepers hostage in Bosnia and defied Security Council resolutions with brazen impunity. Only with great reluctance did they threaten retaliation if the Serbs did not desist.

What is worse, some states even join the predators. Shortly after Hitler came to power, Polish leaders became doubtful of French support in the event of either German or Soviet moves against them. Consequently, they signed a Friendship Pact with Germany, figuring that a subtle dissociation from France would lead Germany to befriend Poland and, perhaps, in the event of a German invasion of Russia, reward it with Lithuanian or Ukrainian territory. In fact, the Nazi regime encouraged such thinking. In a trip to Poland in January 1936, Hermann Goering broached an anti-Soviet alliance and a joint attack on the Soviet Union after which the Ukraine would go to Poland and northwestern Russia would go to Germany. Although Polish leaders were skeptical of such propositions, relations between the two governments became steadily closer in the years that followed,[36] and the benefits to Germany were not negligible. When the Sudetenland crisis arose, Poland completely disassociated itself from French and British diplomacy and announced that it would not allow Soviet troops to cross Polish soil in order to aid the Czechs if they and the French decided to resist a German invasion.

As we now well know, Poland's hopes of gaining either Hitler's friendship or spoils in a future conquest of the Soviet Union were completely illusory if not delusory. Hitler merely used his Friendship Pact to deceive and neutralize Poland while his attention was devoted to taking Austria and Czechoslovakia. When he decided to turn against Poland, he had no compunctions about resuming his verbal threats and denunciations, and he had no qualms in conspiring with Stalin to divide Poland in two. After Poland was extinguished, Hitler's neutrality pact with the Soviet Union allowed him to invade France and engage in an air war against Great Britain. With France and the rest of continental Europe in his control, Hitler then invaded the Soviet Union, the last sitting duck in Europe.

However, as the foregoing example makes clear, states are not people. States never act; leaders act, and individual leaders vary on a whole range of characteristics. As Professor Janice Gross Stein pointed out, "analysis of the individual leader is the critical starting point."[37] Leaders all too often overestimate their own power and underestimate the will, tenacity, and power of their adversaries. At other times, they may underestimate their own power and overestimate the power of their rivals. Miscalculation and wishful or over pessimistic thinking are rife in the arena of international politics, to say nothing of emotionally biased or emotionally infused thinking, which also degrade decision making.

Policy making is also difficult because most foreign policy problems are ambiguous and unstructured. In many situations, objectives or interests are multiple and difficult to define precisely. Trade-offs are hard to measure, and constraints—which often include fear of the unknown—loom large. While choices may be clear, the consequences of these choices may be incalculable or even unknowable. Finally, most foreign policy challenges do not immediately threaten a nation's physical security. For all these reasons, the presumption lies all too frequently in waiting or doing nothing—or "giving peace a chance," as it is euphemistically expressed in America.

Consider the following random examples of major miscalculations drawn from the past century of world politics:

- During the mobilizations that ultimately led to World War I, Kaiser Wilhelm and his advisers believed that Britain would remain neutral if Germany invaded France. On a yachting expedition on the very day of the Austrian ultimatum, the king of England's brother—also the kaiser's cousin—assured the German monarch that England would never go to war if Germany invaded France. To make matters worse, the British prime minister at the time believed that threats of war merely brought on war. Therefore, when German diplomats asked if Britain would go to war in the event that Germany invaded France, they never received a clear answer.

  Consequently, the kaiser thought he had a green light to invade France. He concluded wrongly, of course, and British intervention in support of France resulted in the slaughter of more than three hundred thousand soldiers in the fields of France.

- Before the fighting began, all the participants in World War I assumed that war among the Great Powers would be like the recent Franco-Prussian and Prusso-Austrian wars—short, decisive engagements by professional military establishments that did little civilian damage. They were wrong. The war dragged on for almost four years, and one conservative estimate of the military toll claims that ten million men were killed and twenty million were wounded.[38]

- Given all the horror of World War I, many idealists believed that world public opinion would rein in aggressors in ways that military power could not. According to Lord Robert Cecil, the principal British spokesman for the League of Nations: "[In dealing with military aggression] by far the most powerful weapon at the command of the League of Nations is not the economic or the military weapon or any other weapon of material force. By far the strongest weapon we have is the weapon of public opinion."[39]

  Lord Cecil and the many who agreed with him were completely wrong. When the dictators committed their acts of aggression, they were supported unreservedly by public opinion in their own countries while the publics of other nations responded with indifference at best and fear or resignation at worst. If anything, public opinion—or the fear of it—prevented the members of the League from living up to their obligation to defend victims of aggression.

- Despite eighty-four separate warnings, most of which came to his attention in the spring and summer of 1941, Joseph Stalin refused to believe that Hitler was preparing to attack the Soviet Union. Stalin and his minions were so convinced of Hitler's benign intentions that the general in charge responded to the officer reporting the attack with an incredulous, "You must be crazy!"[40] At the same time, Hitler believed that his conquest of the Soviet Union would be completed before the leaves began to turn in the fall of 1941. Both were wrong.

- Immediately after the Yalta Conference of February 1945, President Roosevelt reported to Congress that the decisions taken by the three wartime allies "ought to spell the end of the system of unilateral action, the exclusive alliances, the spheres of influences, the balances of power and all the other expedients that have been tried for centuries—and have always failed."[41] He, too, was wrong. In fact, as FDR spoke, Stalin was unilaterally imposing puppet governments in Poland and Romania and carving out a sphere of influence in Eastern Europe.

- In the early spring of 1950, Kim Il Sung, the communist leader of North Korea, asked Stalin's permission to invade and conquer South Korea. When Stalin replied that the United States would "never agree to be thrown out" of Korea or "to lose their reputation as a world power," the North Korean assured the Soviet leader that his forces would be victorious in three days time, well before the United States could even respond to the planned lightning strike. After hearing this assurance several times, Stalin reluctantly gave his permission for the invasion to go ahead, albeit with one caveat; the Soviet dictator told Kim, "If you get kicked in the teeth, I shall not lift a finger."[42]

Contrary to Kim Il Sung's best-laid plans, the United States did respond in time. Moreover, because the United States saw Stalin as the initiator of the war, it responded by sending ground troops to Europe and extending its structure of containment to Asia.

- After pushing the North Korean troops out of South Korea, the United States decided to march northward and liberate all of Korea. Despite repeated warnings from the Chinese communists that they would enter the war if American or South Korean troops crossed the thirty eighth parallel, the United States dismissed such warnings and moved ahead. As U.S./UN commander Douglas MacArthur quipped at the time, "If the Chinese tried to get down to Pyongyang [the North Korean capital], there would be the greatest slaughter."[43]

American policymakers and their military commander were also wrong. The Chinese did intervene in November 1950, and within months the Chinese "volunteers" had mauled American troops so badly that Washington decision makers began making plans to surrender all of Korea to the Chinese and evacuate American troops to Japan.

- In 1956 Prime Minister Anthony Eden of Britain believed that a secretly planned preemptive military strike would quickly unseat the Egyptian dictator Gamal Abdel Nasser and return the Suez Canal to British control. However, the strike—planned in concert with France and Israel, who had their own grievances against Nasser—was overly complex, ill-conceived, and badly executed. In the end, it was not Nasser's government that fell but Anthony Eden's.

- Believing that President John F. Kennedy was "too liberal to fight," Soviet premier Nikita Khrushchev began secretly installing nuclear weapons in Cuba. When the weapons were discovered, Kennedy imposed a naval blockade and threatened to go to war. Khrushchev was wrong about Kennedy, and his risky gambit cost him his job as Kremlin leader when he was "retired" in 1964.

- In 1993, Saddam Hussein thought that a "Vietnam syndrome" would prevent America from using military force to roll back his invasion and incorporation of Kuwait. He, too, was wrong.

Such miscalculations and fiascoes have been studied extensively by historians, political scientists, and psychologists. Of the wealth of studies resulting from such research, the following two books are essential reading for anyone interested in understanding international politics and foreign policy decision making: Irving Janis, *Victims of Groupthink: A Psychological Study of Foreign Policy Decisions and Fiascoes*,[44] and Ernest May, *Lessons of the Past: The Use and Misuse of History in American Foreign Policy*.[45]

The people who made the miscalculations in the foregoing examples were all highly intelligent, generally well educated, and, in many cases, experienced men, and that fact alone should give all of us some humility whenever we want to sneer at the foibles of policymakers. Nor is the problem a lack of information, which exists in abundance in governments and foreign ministries.

The great difficulties of foreign policy making stem from the complexity, interrelatedness, and open-ended nature of the problems that decision makers face. They lie in the limits of what can be done about most of the problems that policymakers confront. They lie in the hard trade-offs and risks involved in different alternatives. They lie in the uncertainties about the probable consequences of various alternatives. They also lie in the constraints of public opinion and, yes, the limits of human intelligence itself.

Sometimes states have no recourse other than the use of force to defend or secure their interests. However, most situations are ambiguous, and many decision makers, especially those in democracies, have an aversion to using military force. Consequently, for many decision makers, the easiest way out of unpleasant situations is to let things slide, to minimize the stakes, to rationalize, to negotiate, to talk, to accommodate, to appear "reasonable."

However, there is much more to international politics than misperception and miscalculation. Many conflicts between and among nations stem from incompatible objectives, and on some issues, compromise is extremely difficult if not impossible. Many conflicts are zero sum in nature—situations in which only one nation can win. America's President Polk did not have a dispute with Mexico about which the two countries could compromise; the expansionist president wanted about half of Mexico, pure and simple. Similarly, in the 1960s, the problem caused by France's desire to retain Algeria and Algeria's desire to be independent of France could not be resolved by compromise. To cite a final example, Kim Il Sung did not have a dispute with South Korea; he wanted South Korea.

Without Order, Justice and Morality Cannot Prevail

Given the preceding "facts of life," the following should now be obvious: International politics is more about interests and order than morality or justice, because order is a prerequisite for morality and justice to exist, and order has frequently been in short supply within the international system. As Henry Kissinger put it, "Any serious foreign policy must begin with the need for survival. . . . All serious foreign policy therefore begins with maintaining a balance of power—a scope for action, a capacity to affect events and conditions. Without that capacity a nation is reduced to striking empty poses."[46]

Decision makers do not enter into a world of their choosing, and the quest for security may frequently require unenviable choices. For example, when Hitler invaded the Soviet Union in June 1941, Winston Churchill quickly decided to embrace Joseph Stalin, a dictator whose record for tyranny and murder rivaled that of the German dictator. Was it moral for Britain to ally with a tyrant probably unsurpassed by Hitler?

For Churchill, the answer was an easy one. As he told some of his closest associates just before the Nazi invasion, "If Hitler invaded Hell I would make at least a favourable reference to the Devil in the House of Commons."[47] Immediately after the invasion, Churchill laid out the logic of his position to the British people in a radio address over the BBC:

> No one has been a more consistent opponent of Communism than I have been for the last twenty-five years. I will unsay no word that I have spoken about it. But all this fades away before the spectacle which is now unfolding. The past, with its crimes, its follies, and its tragedies, flashes away. . . .
> . . . We have but one aim and one single irrevocable purpose. We are resolved to destroy Hitler and every vestige of the Nazi regime. From this nothing will turn us away. . . . Any man who fights on against Nazism will have our aid. . . . That is our policy and that is our declaration. It follows, therefore, that we shall give whatever help we can to Russia and the Russian people.[48]

However, Churchill also revealed that his decision was no act of sentimental charity. The self-interested nature of his decision was clearly spelled out:

> when I spoke a few minutes ago of Hitler's blood-lust and the hateful appetites which have impelled or lured him on his Russian adventure, I said there was a deeper motive behind his outrage. He wishes to destroy the Russian power because he hoped that if he succeeds in this he will be able to bring back the main strength of his army and air force from the East and hurl it upon this island, which he knows he must conquer or suffer the penalty of his crimes. His invasion of Russia is no more than a prelude to an attempted invasion of the British Isles. . . .
> The Russian danger is, therefore, our danger and the danger of the United States, just as the cause of any Russian fighting for his hearth and home is the cause of free men and free peoples everywhere.[49]

In international politics, compelling interests in survival and order impel decision makers to base their moral decisions on the situations in which they find themselves. Situations in which only one moral or legal principle is appropriate are extremely rare. In any situation, decision makers must establish priorities among equally worthy moral principles and choose among them—not always an easy task.

Moreover, the distinction between national interests and morality is often a facile one as is the dichotomy between the pursuit of international order and the pursuit of morality. The pursuit of peace and order, even through warfare, can be a profoundly moral enterprise, for only after order and security have been attained can leaders move on to other moral tasks. For example, many people believe it is immoral for democracies to support dictatorships—or even to trade with them on a normal basis. Yet, was Churchill's decision to aid Russia really immoral? Would it have been more moral to allow the Soviet Union to fall and, in so doing, enable Hitler to use the vast natural resources placed at his disposal to construct a better war machine with which to defeat England?

To cite more recent examples, should the United States have allowed Saddam Hussein to incorporate Kuwait because Kuwait was not a democracy? Should the United States refuse to buy Saudi Arabian oil because that country is a traditional Islamic monarchy that does not accord women the same human rights that exist in America? And for that matter, should the United States withdraw its pledge to defend that country from an invasion by the likes of a Saddam Hussein for the same reason?

In most decision making situations, states have multiple interests, and when such interests conflict, decision makers are usually reluctant to sacrifice concrete benefits for abstract moral principles, especially when sacrificing the concrete interests may not ensure the triumph of the moral principles. During his first year in office, Secretary of State Warren Christopher warned Chinese leaders that unless they changed their human rights practices, the Clinton administration would withdraw the lucrative Most Favored Nation (MFN) status for their exports to the United States. In response, Prime Minister Li Peng replied, "China will never accept the U.S. human rights concept," adding that "History has already proven that it is futile to pressure the Chinese."

When the day of reckoning came, President Clinton renewed China's MFN status and announced that he was abandoning his effort to use trade as a lever to force Beijing to alter its human rights policy. As a *New York Times* headline put it, "Profit Gets the Nod." According to the *Times,* "the President, instead of imposing sanctions as promised, junked his threat and today gave what was surely the most eloquent defense of the Bush administration's China policy [that has] ever been uttered at the White House, even by President Bush."[50] Was Clinton's decision immoral, or did it merely recognize the limits of American power? Had he withdrawn the MFN status, China's economy would have continued to boom, and the human rights situation in China would not have changed one bit.

Even when moral values are clear, their attainment may not come cheaply, especially when the target of those policies chooses to resist. While trade boycotts and the denial of loans by international lending institutions may be fairly cheap as instruments of disapprobation, they seldom work. Far too many decision makers have learned the hard way that moral forces, interdependence, and world public opinion have little influence on leaders who abuse the human rights of their people, initiate civil wars, or use force and threats of force to get what they want.

Finally, when it comes to morality and the use of force, even people with impeccable religious credentials can disagree. At a panel on the nature and morality of modern warfare, the chaplain of the U.S. Army War College, Colonel Tom Norton, argued that military force must always be the last resort. According to Reverend Norton, nations should resort to force only after political, economic, and psychological efforts have failed.[51]

Consider, on the other hand, an alternative view offered by another religious leader with equally impeccable credentials—Pope Pius XI. Shortly after Hitler occupied the Rhineland in 1936, His Holiness bluntly asserted the following to François Charles-Roux, the French ambassador to the Holy See: "If you had at once moved 20,000 men into the zone re-occupied by the Germans, you would have done the world an immense service." Taken aback by the Pontiff's comment, the ambassador replied that France's inaction had been motivated solely by France's deep attachment to peace. To this profession of high moral principle, the Pontiff unflinchingly gave the following response: "Yes, and that's commendable on your part. Moreover, you doubtless reckoned that you would not be followed by the English, and still less by the Italians. But I say again, had you done that, you would have rendered everyone a very great service."[52] As the Pope's comments reveal, the controversy over the morality of using force is not a controversy between religious leaders and secular officials. Even religious people of the same faith differ on this issue.

As the veteran diplomat Charles Burton Marshall once noted, *the easiest part of foreign policy making lies in proclaiming a set of desirable, idealistic goals.* The real test of a nation's diplomacy, he maintained, lies not in the righteousness of those goals, but in the nation's steadfastness in shouldering the burdens imposed by them. According to Marshall, goals imply costs and the amount of resources available to attain them is always limited. "The hard part," he claimed, "is deciding what to do in circumstances where one can only do part of what one may wish to do."[53] Learning the difference between high ideals and foolish expectations is a starting point for any sound diplomacy.

Factoring morality into foreign policy making is not a process of picking high-sounding moral principles and basing decisions on those alone. Rather, it requires an examination of alternative solutions to particular problems and assessing the moral consequences of each—a task that rarely leads to a self-evident conclusion. In all too many situations the moral course of action is not self-evident. As Professor Kenneth Thompson has remarked, "In foreign relations particularly, every attempt to conceive political ethics in absolute terms has floundered on the shoals of circumstance. Broad moral principles seldom if ever can be said to furnish a direct, precise, and unambiguous guide to action."[54] Similarly, John Quincy Adams once wrote, "Principles are not self-applying. They do not tell you what to do. They require prudence and judgment for their application. Prudence is not self-sufficient either; it requires principles for guidance."[55]

Foreign policymakers will never have the luxury of being able to make moral choices without having to think about consequences. As Lyndon Johnson put it in his State of the Union Address in 1965, "the choice that presidents face is not deciding between the right thing or the wrong thing, but knowing what the right course of action really is." The alternatives that decision makers face are frequently all too clear to them. What is unclear, if not frequently incalculable, are the consequences that will result from each of those alternatives—and from such incalculable consequences moral judgments about particular courses of action are not easy to make.

Summary of Salient Points

International politics is primarily about interests and order; it is only secondarily about justice and moral principles

1. The international political system is a system without government: no institution with a legitimate monopoly on the use of force stands above nation-states to guarantee their safety, their security, their just desserts, or their survival.
2. Because no authority stands above them, states in the international system are sovereign and, as such, are bound only by laws and treaties to which they freely assent. As far as its power will allow, each state is its own legislator, judge, and jury.
3. Leaders can and do resort to force whenever they are inclined to do so and reckon they can get away with it.
4. Nations are restrained in their use of force only by varying degrees of satiation, self-restraint, fear, and calculations of the costs and benefits that might result from using violence.
5. Still, the international system is not a Hobbesian world where life is poor, nasty, brutish, and short; most of the time, most nations obey international law, live up to their international agreements, get along with their neighbors, and cooperate on a wide array of international issues and problems.
6. In regard to the great issues of war and peace, the international political system is an oligarchy of the Great Powers, which is institutionalized in the United Nations Charter, and positionality, or relative status rankings among the oligarchs, is an important value.
7. If states fail to live up to their international obligations, the only recourse injured parties have are acquiesence, diplomatic negotiation and bargaining, or military force.

8. The International Court of Justice lacks any enforcement powers. As President Calvin Coolidge put it, the Court is a place "to which we could go but not be brought." Consequently, the Court has compiled a fine record in dealing with disputes freely submitted to it by litigating parties; it has had little success in resolving disputes when one of the parties has refused to accept the Court's jurisdiction.

9. The record of the state system in maintaining peace, order, security, and justice has not been a very good one—states do not do a good job in perceiving their own interests, reading the intentions and resolve of other nations, or recognizing the limits of their own power.

10. However, states never act; individuals act, and policymakers frequently make costly miscalculations because of errors of misperception, incomplete or conflicting information, emotionally biased or emotionally charged thinking, and the unstructured and ambiguous nature of many foreign policy problems.

11. Still, all international conflicts are not the result of folly, misunderstanding, or misperception; incompatible objectives and interests lie at the root of major conflicts between and among nations.

12. International politics is more about interests and order than morality and justice, for one simple reason: Order is a prerequisite for morality and justice to exist, and order has frequently been in short supply in the international system. Compelling interests in survival and order frequently impel decision makers to base their moral decisions on the situations in which they find themselves, rather than on abstract moral principles.

13. Learning the difference between high ideals and foolish expectations is the starting point for a sound diplomacy.

Notes

1. From an excerpt in Evan Luard, *Basic Texts in International Relations* (New York: St. Martin's Press, 1992), 253.
2. Max Weber, "Politics as a Vocation," in From *Max Weber: Essays in Sociology*, ed. H. H. Gerth and C. Wright Mills (New York: Oxford University Press, 1958), 78.
3. Joseph M. Grieco, "Anarchy and the Limits of Cooperation: A Realist Critique of the Newest Liberal Institutionalism," *International Organization* 42, no. 3 (1988), 488.
4. Hans Morgenthau, *Politics Among Nations* (New York: Alfred A. Knopf, 1985), 295.
5. Joshua S. Goldstein, *International Relations* (New York: Harper Collins, 1994), 271.
6. Ludwig Dehio, *The Precarious Balance: Four Centuries of the European Power Struggle* (New York: Random House, 1965), 172.
7. Alfred Cobban, *A History of Modern France: Volume 2: 1799–1871* (Baltimore: Penguin Books, 1961), 19.
8. Paul Schroeder, *The Transformation of European Politics, 1763–1844* (Oxford: Clarnedon Press, 1994), 417–148.

9. Christopher J. Herold, *The Age of Napoleon* (New York: American Heritage Publishing, 1963), 265.
10. Schroeder, *The Transformation of European Politics, 1763–1848*, 583.
11. George Schwarzenberger, *Power Politics: A Study of International Society* (New York: Frederick A. Praeger, 1951), 91.
12. See Paul A. Varg, *America from Client State to World Power: Six Major Transitions in United States Foreign Relations* (Norman: University of Oklahoma Press, 1990), 36.
13. Taken from Jerald A. Combs, *The Jay Treaty: Political Battleground of the Founding Fathers* (Berkeley: University of California Press, 1970), 139.
14. John C. Miller, *The Federalist Era, 1789–1801* (New York: Harper & Row, 1960), 165–66.
15. Immanuel Kant, *Perpetual Peace* (Indianapolis: Bobbs-Merrill, 1957), 18.
16. Winston Churchill, *The Second World War: The Gathering Storm, volume 1* (Boston: Houghton Mifflin, 1961), 131 [Churchill's italics].
17. Ibid., 131 [my italics].
18. The Soviet Union constructed its site around Moscow; the United States never deployed a system.
19. For the kinds of political and strategic issues that the initiative raised within Reagan's own administration, see Chapter 17 of then-Secretary of State George P. Schultz's memoirs, *Turmoil and Triumph* (New York: Charles Scriber's Sons, 1993).
20. Churchill, *The Gathering Storm*, 92.
21. John T. Rourke, *International Politics on the World Stage*, 5th Edition. (Guilford, CT: Dushkin Publishing Group, 1995).
22. Cited in Thomas M. Franck, *Judging the World Court* (New York: Priority Press, 1986), 19.
23. See William E. Hale, "Once More the Cod," *American Scandinavian Review* 61, no. 3 (Winter 1973–74), 345–52.
24. Morgenthau, *Politics Among Nations*, 307.
25. David Forsythe, *The Politics of International Law* (Boulder, CO: Lynne Rienner Publishers, 1990), 20.
26. From Thucydides, *The Peloponnesian War*, Book 5, ch. 7, as excerpted in *Basic Texts in International Relations*, ed. Evan Luard (New York: St. Martin's Press, 1992), 120.
27. Schwarzenberger, *Power Politics*, 113.
28. Martin Wight, *Power Politics* (London: Royal Institute of International Affairs, 1946), 19–20.
29. Ibid., 33.
30. Henry Kissinger, *Diplomacy* (New York: Simon and Schuster, 1994), 722–23.
31. Richard Nixon, *The Real War* (New York: Warner Books, 1980), 136–37.
32. To follow Nicaragua's progress read the following issues of the *UN Chronicle* (April 4, 1984), 11–16; (May 5, 1985), 16; and (November 9, 1986), 83.
33. Grieco, "Anarchy and the Limits of Cooperation," 489.
34. Craig R. Whitney, "Chirac Assures Kohl on Europe's Monetary Policy," *New York Times International*, May 22, 1995, A3.
35. Charles Krauthammer, "The Unipolar Moment," *Foreign Affairs* 70, no. 1 (1991), 24.
36. Alan Bullock, *Hitler: A Study in Tyranny* (New York: Bantam Books, 1961), 285–86.
37. Janice Gross Stein, "Political Learning by Doing: Gorbachev as Uncommitted Thinker and Motivated Learner," *International Organization* 48, no. 2 (Spring 1984), 182.
38. The estimate comes from Peter Teed, *Dictionary of Twentieth-Century History, 1914–1990* (New York: Oxford University Press, 1992), 506.
39. Cited in E. H. Carr, *The Twenty Years' Crisis, 1919–1939* (London: Macmillan, 1946), 35.
40. John Stoessinger, *Why Nations Go to War* (New York: St. Martin's Press, 1993), 38, 44.
41. Taken from James MacGregor Burns, *Roosevelt: The Soldier of Freedom* (Harcourt Brace Jovanovich, 1970), 582.
42. These quotations are taken from Sergei N. Goncharov et al., *Uncertain Partners: Stalin, Mao, and the Korean War* (Stanford, CA: Stanford University Press, 1993), 145
43. Cited in Stoessinger, *Why Nations Go to War*, 72.
44. Boston: Houghton Mifflin, 1972. Other works well worth reading are Ernest May and Richard E. Neustadt, *Thinking in Time* (New York: The Free Press, 1986); Barbara Tuchman, *The March of Folly: From Troy to Vietnam* (New York: Alfred A. Knopf, 1984), and Yuen Foong Khong, *Analogies of War: Korea, Dien Bien Phu, and the Decisions of 1965* (Princeton: Princeton University Press, 1992).
45. New York: Oxford University Press, 1972.

46. Henry Kissinger, *For the Record* (Boston: Little, Brown, 1981), 79.
47. Winston S. Churchill, *The Second World War: The Grand Alliance, volume 3* (New York: Bantam Books, 1962), 313.
48. Ibid., 315.
49. Ibid.
50. *New York Times*, May 27, 1994, A1.
51. Laura Chandler Ritter, "War Is Hell—Is It Moral?" *The Valley* (Lebanon Valley College: Lebanon, Pennsylvania, Winter 1995), 8.
52. This interchange is reported in John C. Cairns, "March 7, 1936, Again: The View from Paris," in *European Diplomacy Between Two Wars*, ed. Charles Gatzke (Chicago: Quadrangle Books, 1972), 186–87.
53. Charles Burton Marshall, *The Limits of Foreign Policy* (New York: Henry Holt, 1954), 17.
54. Kenneth W. Thompson, *Political Realism and the Crisis of World Politics: An American Approach to Foreign Policy* (New York: John Wiley & Sons, 1960), 160.
55. Cited in Greg Russell, "John Quincy Adams and the Ethics of America's National Interest," *Review of International Studies* 19, no. 3 (1993), 25.

CHAPTER TWO

Revisionism Is the Driving Force in International Politics

L ike all politics, international politics involves conflicts between those who want to keep things the way they are and those who want to change them. The difference between power politics and other kinds of politics is that force, threats of force, and war are frequently the instruments through which such conflicts are waged and resolved.

Because states are sovereign over territory, a good way to think about issues of war or peace is in terms of differences over territorial distributions of power and influence. In a recent study, K. J. Holsti found that more than half of the wars since 1648 involved territorial issues, and a large number of the remainder involved struggles over the political or ideological orientation of particular governments, as in Vietnam or Afghanistan.[1]

Territorial disputes are particularly vexing because states in possession of disputed territory are under no compulsion to freely cede what they already possess. Consequently, the party seeking change may have no alternative but recourse to force. As E. H. Carr noted in his *Twenty Years' Crisis,* "Normally, the threat of war, tacit or overt, seems a necessary condition of important changes in the international sphere."[2] Former Secretary of State Henry Kissinger seconded Carr's opinion when he pointed out in his *Diplomacy* that "In all of Europe's long history, it [is] not possible to enumerate many, if any, territorial changes which had been the result of anything other than force."[3]

The study of power politics is the study of how states go about seeking to change and maintain existing patterns of power, influence, status, and territory through force and threats of force. However, before going further, several caveats must be made. First, power politics is not all there is to the study of international politics. As Professors Robert Keohane and Joseph Nye pointed out more than twenty years ago, a whole domain of international political issues exists in which military force is largely irrelevant, welfare rather than security is the predominant value, and decision making takes place within international forums where one-nation-one-vote decision-making patterns prevail.[4] Issues such as global warming, human rights, the ozone layer, international migration, desertification, debt relief, and rules over trade and investment all fall into this realm of non-power politics.

Second, the "things" over which states have been willing to wage war have changed over time, as the German journalist and strategic thinker Josef Joffe pointed out:

> in contrast to past centuries, where trade routinely triggered war, and war unsheathed trade weapons like embargoes and blockades, the issue is not the strategic control over routes, resources, and markets. If there has been a paradigm shift in international politics, the evidence seems most persuasive in the economic realm. Why would Japan bomb Pearl Harbor if they can buy it? Most players have come to accept the non-zero-sum nature of the economic game . . . and so trade and flag are no longer Siamese twins. Whether it is vast imbalances (as with Japan and China) or "cultural exceptions" (as in the GATT struggle with the EU), the remedy is not cannon but conference diplomacy. And the "admixture of other means," to borrow Clausewitz, involves at worst, "anti-dumping" clauses, punitive tariffs, and deliberate neglect of the dollar.[5]

Finally, not all states are involved in power politics, and relations between and among most states are characterized by amity rather than conflict. It is almost inconceivable, for example, that the United States and Britain or the United States and Canada would ever threaten or use force if their interests came into conflict. However, just because most states have amicable relations most of the time does not mean that power politics is beginning to disappear. In his classic study, *Power Politics*, Professor George Schwarzenberger put it this way:

> In systems of power politics and of power politics in disguise the tone is set not so much by States with a record for self-restraint and law abidingness, but by States which are powerful enough to threaten the existing status quo and from which the worst must be expected. . . . It is therefore rather naive to point to the pleasing record of this or that state or even a majority of states at any given time in order to disprove a description of international politics as power politics. The essential thing is that every generation has its potential or actual black sheep which prevents the others from grazing in peace.[6]

The "playing fields" of power politics are usually set out at the ends of great wars, when peace conferences create new maps that reflect new distributions of power forged on the fields of battle. In effect, peace treaties are like constitutions in that they set the terms within which states will pursue their interests—they take territory away from some states and give it to others; they codify and seek to legitimize new configurations of power; they create new conflict resolution mechanisms, such as the Congress system after the Vienna settlement in 1815 or the League of Nations that was embedded in the Treaty of Versailles after World War I. Peace settlements set the stage, so to speak, for new rounds of conflict between states that will seek to maintain the new status quo and those that will seek to change it. The business of diplomacy, and especially the diplomacy of satisfied powers, is the business of maintaining those new orders and handling change—even violent change—in ways that do not fundamentally destabilize relations among the Great Powers.

At the end of the Napoleonic Wars, the agreements forged at Vienna in 1815 were freely accepted by all the members of the oligarchy, including the defeated power, France, which was quickly restored to membership in the oligarchy. Thus, not only did the Vienna settlement create an equilibrium of power among the Great Powers, it also abounded in legitimacy. For almost fifty years thereafter, none of the Great Powers went to war with one another. The Treaty of Versailles, on the other hand, was explicitly drafted to punish the German people and keep them down. In fact, the German delegation was not even allowed to negotiate about the terms of the settlement. After six months of hammering out a settlement among themselves, the victors merely presented the resulting treaty to the waiting German delegation for their signatures. When the German government balked, the Allies delivered an ultimatum: sign the treaty or face an invasion. Given these alternatives, the members of the Reichstag voted to accept this diktat, and the treaty was signed on June 28, 1919. The settlement lasted less than a generation.

In the closing years of World War II, Winston Churchill, Franklin Roosevelt, and Joseph Stalin met at Yalta to decide who would get exactly what after the defeat of the Axis powers. Very quickly, American principles of self-determination and democracy clashed sharply with Stalin's determination to build a sphere of influence in Eastern Europe. As a result, the big three quickly found themselves in a cold war, which arose from differences over what the postwar map of Europe would look like and the principles upon which regimes in the liberated countries would be established.

At issue in both the interwar and postwar eras was the question of legitimacy as much as power. Believing that the Versailles treaty was a punitive and unjust peace, all German governments sought to revise and wiggle out of the restrictions imposed on Germany by the Allies. Until the rise of Hitler, the treaty's stipulations were complied with only out of fear and weakness. Once Germany gained the will and the means to change the settlement by unilateral acts, threats of force, and violence, it would go about doing so—and when it did, those who imposed the peace in the first place could either seek to enforce its provisions or try to conciliate Germany with concessions.

In the postwar period, the issue of legitimacy arose among the victors rather than between the victors and the vanquished. For almost twenty years, the United States refused to recognize officially either the division of Germany or Stalin's redistribution of territory in Eastern Europe. In the era of détente, this policy changed, and at the Helsinki Conference in 1975, thirty-five members of NATO and the Warsaw Pact pledged that they would not seek to change the European postwar boundaries by force.

Diplomatic historians make their living by studying and tracing the evolution of maps created by peace conferences. Political scientists use the same historical material as a laboratory for developing and testing generalizations about the kinds of goals that different kinds of nations seek under various conditions and the kinds of strategies they employ to secure those goals—and with what varying degrees of success.

Wars and the diplomacy between those wars underscore the centrality of the problem of order in relations among states. As in any domestic system, international politics reflects changing configurations of power and interest among competing groups. And, as in all social and political life, international politics is affected by vast impersonal economic, technological, and social forces that weaken some countries and strengthen others.

Revisionist, Status Quo, and Noninvolved States

Scholars refer to an existing distribution of territory, rank, power, and values as a *status quo,* and in regard to that status quo, they classify countries as (1) *revisionist* states, (2) *status quo* states, or (3) *noninvolved* or *neutral* states.[7] Like all forms of politics, international politics is moved by states seeking change. Other states get involved in such quests for change only when their leaders perceive significant threats to important values and interests or when they believe they might help to alleviate conflicts between other nations by offering their good offices or friendly efforts at mediation.

Revisionist Powers

Revisionist powers are dissatisfied with the existing status quo and want to change it. At the most grandiose levels, nations such as Napoleonic France or Hitler's Germany sought to create vast new empires. At the other extreme, the Republic of Panama acted as a revisionist power when it demanded that the United States cede the Panama Canal after a series of violent demonstrations in 1964. And the issues are not always territorial. After decolonization, many developing countries rejected existing international laws governing the nationalization and expropriation of foreign investments. In the 1970s, a coalition of Third World states sought to replace the liberal postwar international economic order with a New International Economic Order (NIEO) that would change the existing rules on trade and investment in order to distribute more of the global economic product to developing countries. During that same decade, members of the Organization of Petroleum Exporting Countries (OPEC) decided that they, rather than the Western multinational corporations, would set the price of oil in world markets, and the results of that decision were extremely costly to billions of people in both developed and developing countries. During the 1970s, in fact, people in the industrialized states transferred more than $80 billion to OPEC countries—a proportion of national income for some West European countries that was equivalent to the reparations originally levied against, but never collected from, Germany by the Treaty of Versailles! Despite calls for military intervention, the developed countries accepted this fundamental change in power relations.

Revisionist powers tend to be strategically offensive, and it is they who frequently decide how long conflicts will continue. However, do not conjure up in your mind an Attila the Hun or Darth Vader image of a typical revisionist leader. While some leaders of revisionist states do thrive on threats, bombast, tension, and risk taking, such bluster can be dangerous, especially when the revisionist side is the weaker one. Also, such strategies might create defensive preparations and resistance from status quo powers.

In most circumstances, leaders of revisionist powers mask their demands and actions in ways that do not provoke a threatening response from status quo powers. Belligerence will frequently be accompanied with postures of reasonableness and professions of a desire for peace. Instead of presenting themselves as predators, leaders of revisionist states often portray themselves as victims of past grievances and characterize the objects of their prey as unworthy of defense or support. In discussing the Sudetenland issue of 1938, Churchill noted how Hitler was able to take a clear grievance and then blow it out of all proportion to gain legitimacy and sympathy for his demands.

One should never be surprised when revisionist leaders try to present themselves as reasonable, conciliatory, and accommodating people. Such postures are a major tactic of revisionist powers especially when they are dealing with leaders of democratic powers. Consider the following—and not untypical—remarks that Hitler made in an interview with a leading French journalist in the mid-1930s: "There is no dispute in Europe sufficiently important to justify a war. . . . I am not quite mad—a war would not settle anything; it would only make matters worse—it would mark the end of our races who are the elite of humanity, and in time, Asia and Bolshevism would rule Europe. . . . I have a great deal of work to do at home. I have restored the German's sense of honor; I want to restore his joy in life. I shall need years to restore

Germany's prosperity. Do you really think I want to upset my work with a new war?"[8]

Given this and many similar statements, it is easy to see why British elites discounted those passages in *Mein Kampf* that glorified war and sought to conciliate Hitler by rectifying the "injustices" of the Versailles treaty. After being accorded respect and conciliation, they believed, the German dictator might be content to continue his good works in Germany and leave the continent of Europe in harmony and peace. Such were the hopes; when they proved to be an illusion, Britain and France went to war on unenviable terms. France was conquered, partitioned, and occupied by the Nazis while the British men of peace lived to see their cities pelted with a rain of German bombs. Leaders of revisionist powers know well that what people in status quo countries desire most is peace—and especially citizens of democratic status quo countries. They also know full well that democracies will always be very hesitant to go to war over countries and issues that seem far removed from their own national defense.

If revisionist leaders have a failing, it lies in their not knowing when and where to stop and in not recognizing the point at which the status quo adversaries will go to war against them. Rare is the view expressed by the French general Carnot after France's striking victory over the First Coalition in 1794. Fearing that the victorious republic might want to continue fighting to unite "all the ancient territory of the Gauls," Carnot warned that, "however seductive this [goal] may be, it will be found perhaps wise to renounce it [because] France would only enfeeble herself and prepare an interminable war by aggrandizement of this kind."[9] Much more typical are the revisionist oligarchs who push their luck and wind up in disastrous wars—wars that they not only lose but from which they lose their power and even their lives at times.

As Patrick Glynn has noted, status quo powers are frequently responsible for the failure of revisionist leaders to know where to stop. By professing peaceful intentions and not resisting revisionist policies, leaders of status quo powers often bring war on themselves by sending misleading signals to revisionist leaders. According to Glynn, "World War I revealed a pattern that would pave the road to fighting more than once in the twentieth century: the systematic tendency of democracies to appear weaker and less resolute than they really are in periods leading up to war."[10]

The Roots of Revisionist Foreign Policies

In his *Power Among Nations,* Hans Morgenthau lists three inducements to a policy of revisionism: (1) defeat in war; (2) victory in war; and (3) weakness.[11]

DEFEAT IN WAR. Stories of defeated countries seeking to avenge the losses of one war through recourse to another are legion. At the end of the Franco-Prussian War Bismarck took the provinces of Alsace and Lorraine from France and sowed the seeds for a war of revenge among Frenchmen. After World War I, the two provinces went back to France, sowing seeds for a war of revenge among most Germans. When in 1925, Foreign Minister Gustav Stresemann proposed renouncing German ambitions in regard to the provinces to create a genuine peace with France, he was subjected to violent and widespread criticism ranging from German communists to German nationalists. Most ominous was the response of General von Seeckt, the person in charge of secretly rebuilding the German army in violation of the Versailles treaty: "We must acquire power, and as soon as we have the power, we will naturally retake all that we have lost."[12]

To cite another example, Hungary lost about one-third of its territory, much of it to Romania, through the Treaty of Trianon at the end of the First World War. Ever since, Hungarians have sought to undo that decision. In World War II, Hungary fought on the side of Nazi Germany, seeking to regain its lost territory and, perhaps, to add even more. During the Cold War, many Hungarians still fumed about their losses in World War I, and by the late 1980s, *communist* Hungary was near the brink of war with *communist* Romania because of the latter's treatment of Hungarians in its province of Transylvania.

Even now, in this post–Cold War era, the dream of a greater Hungary is still alive among some Hungarians. In 1990, the ears of government officials in Romania, Serbia, and Slovakia perked up when the Hungarian prime minister declared that he was working for the interests of all 15 million Hungarians—of which only 10 million lived in Hungary—and in 1992, Prime Minister Antall created a special Office for Hungarian Minorities Abroad, which was charged with monitoring the conditions of Hungarians living outside the Hungarian boundaries created by the terms of Trianon.

According to Miklos Kontra, a linguistic professor at the Hungarian Academy of Sciences, "There is a perceived desire [on the part of Hungarians] for revenge by redressing the borders that existed before World War I." But, Kontra protests, "This is a joke. There is no such desire." Perhaps, he is right; perhaps there is no such desire now. But if Hungarian minorities abroad organize and clamor and if the West's fecklessness in Bosnia and Kosovo and its wariness in policing the aftermath of those conflicts are taken as a precedent, what might Antall conclude, to say nothing of even more nationalistic politicians in Hungary?[13]

VICTORY IN WAR. Ironically, as Morgenthau points out, victory in war as well as defeat in war can lead to a policy of revision. Defensive wars frequently tempt winners to engage in revisionism by seeking buffer zones and spheres of influence as "insurance" against future revisionism by the defeated aggressor. After expelling Napoleon's armies from Russia and pursuing them all the way to Paris, Czar Alexander I decided that Russia deserved some compensation for its service to Europe. According to Lord Salisbury, the czar proceeded as follows:

> When the Congress assembled at Vienna and the map of Europe lay on the table, he laid his hand upon Poland, with the words, C'est a moi [That's mine]! He had 200,000 men in Poland and the allies might come and turn them out if they could. His throne he added, would not be safe, if, after all of his sacrifices, he came back to Russia empty handed. It was evident that his heart was set upon the acquisition, and that if he yielded at all it would only be to force. As one of his generals put it, "With 600,000 men one does not have to negotiate very much."[14]

One hundred and thirty years later, Soviet foreign policy exemplified both inducements to a policy of revision—defeat in a previous war and victory in a current one. Only this time, Russia was represented by a commissar rather than a czar. The first priority of Stalin was to regain former Czarist territories lost after World War I, most notably the Baltic countries of Estonia, Latvia, and Lithuania as well as eastern Poland, Bessarabia, and Bukovina. When his troops liberated these areas, they were quickly incorporated into the Soviet Union. As his troops liberated Eastern Europe, it became increasingly clear that Stalin's objective was not the restoration of freedom and independence for these countries but the creation of a vast Soviet sphere of influence. Defeat in World War I led Stalin to regain what Russia had lost after 1917, while victory in World War II led him to revise the prewar status quo in Eastern and Central Europe.

WEAKNESS. If history makes anything clear, it is that power vacuums seldom remain unfilled for long. No better example illustrates this inducement to a policy of revisionism than the history of the United States. Over a period of one hundred years, the American Republic fought the British, the Spanish, the Mexicans, and numerous Indian tribes to create a vast continental nation. Of course, many Americans saw what they were doing not as revisionism but as their "manifest destiny to overspread the continent allotted by Providence for the free development of our yearly multiplying millions."[15]

Declining empires and nations frequently become the prey of powers seeking to gain at their expense. At the end of the nineteenth century, the waning power of the Chinese empire led to rivalry between Japan and Russia over Manchuria and Korea. After defeating and expelling Chinese forces from Korea in 1895, Japan treated the newly independent peninsula as its own exclusive economic preserve. However, completion of the Trans-Siberian railroad at roughly the same time allowed Russian explorers, settlers, and investors to begin entering both Korea and Manchuria in sizable numbers. Hoping to avoid friction, Japan proposed a spheres-of-influence agreement in 1902, whereby Russia would get Manchuria and Japan would get Korea. The Russians responded by stringing out the ensuing negotiations while simultaneously moving settlers and troops into northern Korea in the hopes of presenting the Japanese with a fait accompli.

Thinking that Japan was too weak to challenge her, Russia contemptuously broke off negotiations in February 1904 and refused to accept Japanese dominance in Korea. In a matter of days, Japan launched a surprise attack and destroyed the Russian Pacific Fleet, which was laying at anchor in Port Arthur. Thereafter, her troops quickly won a string of stunning victories on the ground. In the peace negotiated by Theodore Roosevelt, Russia agreed to withdraw her troops from northern Manchuria and recognize Japan's exclusive rights in Korea. Japan also gained control of the Liaotung Peninsula, including Port Arthur and the southern half of Sakhalin Island.

After losing to the Japanese in 1905, Russia turned her expansionist ambitions back to the Balkans, where she hoped to obtain spoils and influence at the expense of another collapsing power, the Ottoman Empire. In this quest, Russia would find itself continually at loggerheads with the insecure and increasingly unstable Austro-Hungarian Empire, Great Britain, and later Germany, whose Kaiser Wilhelm took upon himself the mantle of friend and protector of the Ottoman Empire and the Islamic World. This rivalry later ignited the sparks that led to the First World War.

RISING POWERS AND REVOLUTIONARY REGIMES. To Morgenthau's list, one more inducement to revisionism must be added—namely, rising powers and revolutionary regimes. As indicated earlier, impersonal animate and inanimate forces lead some states to rise and others to fall. For example, industrialization in the German states led to the creation of a vast and ominous continental power once Bismarck unified them under a Prussian hegemony. Similarly, Italian nationalism led to the creation of modern Italy in the middle of the nineteenth century. Having attained the power worthy of membership in the oligarchy, both countries sought the rank, status, influence, and territorial privileges held by established members of the oligarchy. Under Kaiser Wilhelm, Germany sought "a place in the sun," which would have required a loss of territory and influence held by Britain, France, Russia, and even America. Under Mussolini, Italy sought to restore the ancient Roman Empire. Upon its industrialization, Japan initiated a similar revisionist foreign policy in Asia, seeking to create a "co-Prosperity sphere" of its own. Thomas Jefferson sought to create an "empire of liberty" across the American continent.

Revolutions also frequently lead to foreign policies of revisionism, especially when such regimes base their legitimacy on universal values. Revolutionary France sought to spread liberty, equality, and fraternity across Europe. Bolshevik Russia dreamed of transforming a world of capitalist states into a socialist commonwealth. Libyan leader Muammar al-Qaddafi has dreamed of creating a North African Arab Confederation from Egypt to Morocco. Since the fall of the shah of Iran,

Islamic fundamentalists have sought to overturn secular Arab states such as Egypt and Algeria, which had friendly relations with developed democracies. If the fundamentalists succeed, the developed countries may find oil, their the most vital natural resource, concentrated in hostile hands.

Note, however, that the above are only *inducements* to policies of revisionism; none of which always leads to policies of revisionism. As K. J. Holsti points out in his study of international wars, while almost anything might lead to war, nothing will always lead to war.[16] "Foreign policy is a purposeful activity," Holsti notes,[17] and purposes vary considerably among people—even within the same country or regime. American foreign policy underwent significant changes through the presidencies of Dwight Eisenhower, John F. Kennedy, Lyndon Johnson, Richard Nixon, Jimmy Carter, and Ronald Reagan. Part of the variation can be explained by different contexts and different agendas, but each of these individuals also left his own mark on American foreign policy. Similarly, Soviet leaders have varied considerably in the goals and objectives they set for their nation. The conservative Machiavellian, Joseph Stalin, was not the revolutionary Bolshevik that Leon Trotsky was, and the adventurous diplomacy of Nikita Khrushchev was more akin to that of Kaiser Wilhelm than his predecessor and communist mentor, Joseph Stalin. And, of course, Mikhail Gorbachev was a surprise to everyone.

Different environments create different contexts or opportunities, but different people will respond to the same contexts and opportunities differently even within the same political and cultural system. *History and situations merely provide opportunities and constraints. How states respond to those opportunities and constraints depends on the individuals who are in charge of making decisions for those states and the constraints or permissiveness set by those whom they govern.*

People and their purposes count while the anarchic structure of the international system provides both constraints and opportunities for the realization of those purposes.[18] Some nations accept defeat in war and do not seek to avenge themselves. Some nations do not seek additions to their territory when they are victorious in war. All states do not seek to expand at the expense of weak neighbors or declining countries and empires. Some rising powers do not seek territorial expansion. Some revolutionary regimes do not pursue revisionist foreign policies, and even those that do frequently lose their ideological ardor over time and begin behaving like traditional states.

THE OBJECTIVES OF REVISIONISM. In terms of objectives, revisionist foreign policies can vary along a dimension ranging from limited increments of power, status, and territory to imperial or hegemonic ambitions. The revisionist foreign policies of Bismarck or Cavour typify a limited or finite revisionism. Both of these nineteenth-century statesmen used military force to change the status quo, but their aims were largely limited to territorial consolidation of German- and Italian-speaking peoples. Their efforts were not first steps toward a regional or continental imperium. What both leaders sought was Great Power status and the rights or perquisites that went along with membership in the oligarchy.

However, the unification of Germany also mean the eclipse of France as the major power on the European continent, and the impact of that change in power relationships quickly became apparent when Kaiser Wilhelm sent Bismarck into retirement in 1890. Unlike the "Iron Chancellor," Wilhelm sought to do something with Germany's newfound power. Security and predominance on the continent of Europe were not enough for either the Kaiser or many of his subjects. What he pursued was a foreign policy of Weltpolitik, or world power, making Germany a major global competitor that would give the old imperial powers a real run for their money.

The difference between Bismarck and Wilhelm was a significant one. Bismarck pursued a nation-building imperialism similar to the nineteenth-century continental revisionism of the United States or Serbian revisionism in the twentieth century; Wilhelm's "place-in-the-sun" revisionism typified that of Japan in the first half of the twentieth century and the Soviet Union during the Khrushchev and Brezhnev years.

While the Kaiser sought status, influence, and some client states or colonies here and there, Hitler sought to create a vast colonial empire in central Europe and eastern Russia. In Hitler's grand scheme, France would be defeated in battle and reduced to a rump satellite. Russia and Poland would be conquered—their territory incorporated into the Third Reich or turned into colonies, their peoples either exterminated or consigned to slavery. The rest of central Europe would be transformed into satellites or colonies. The British would be marginalized in their islands, and the United States would be isolated in its hemisphere. Japan would exercise hegemony in Asia, and Fascist Italy would reign over the Mediterranean and North Africa.

Similarly, Napoleon sought neither French security nor continental influence nor even a position of primacy among equal Great Powers of his day; what he sought was *hegemony*. Other Great Powers would be satellites rather than peers; he, the emperor, would decide, and they would acquiesce. As early as 1802, Napoleon claimed that "Except for Turkey, Europe is but one province of the world. . . . When we make war, we make civil war."[19] Later, he would brazenly boast that he could extinguish Austria and Prussia at any moment of his choosing and that he could immediately summon enough men to prevent Russia, his nominal ally, from doing anything of which he disapproved.[20] The competitive system of sovereign states had been replaced by a continental French hegemony. As the British historian Alfred Cobban noted, "For fifteen years, France and Europe were . . . at the mercy of a gambler to whom fate and his own genius gave for a time all the aces."[21]

THE MOTIVATIONAL ROOTS OF REVISIONISM. Revisionist foreign policies can be motivated by one or both of two kinds of forces—*external-defensive* and *internal-promotional*. Given the anarchical nature of the international system, all nations have security interests that stem from their particular geopolitical situation. Consequently, some revisionist policies stem from defensive or security motivations. The defensive motivations behind Stalin's creation of a sphere of influence in Eastern Europe at the end of World War II are obvious. Russia had been invaded by Napoleon in 1812, by Kaiser Wilhelm's forces in 1914, by Poland in 1920, and by Hitler in 1941. Given this history, almost any Russian leader would have sought to move Russia's defensive perimeter into the center of Europe when German troops retreated after the battle of Stalingrad. Stalin's maneuvers at the close of World War II had as much to do with history and the fear of another German invasion as with the promotion of communism.

Promotional or offensively oriented revisionism is impelled from inside the state. Such revisionism may have its roots in the pride of a rising nation or the existence of some ideology or belief system that leaders seek to promote abroad. Kaiser Wilhelm's Weltpolitik represented the revisionism of a newly arisen power that was "feeling its oats" and seeking to revise global patterns of status and influence more in its favor. As the famous German sociologist Max Weber put it, Bismarck's unification of Germany "would have been better left undone if it was meant to be the end and not the starting point of a German policy of world power." Similarly, America's continental expansion was internally driven. America united itself from the Atlantic to the Pacific not because it had to defend itself from external enemies but because its dynamic people faced relatively weak obstacles to its drive for manifest destiny.

Defensively motivated revisionism is much easier to deal with. Once legitimate security needs are met, revisionist powers will usually settle down and calculate further expansion on the basis of cost-benefit calculations—calculations that factor in resistance that might be provided by Great Powers supporting the status quo. If status quo powers draw lines and make clear the costs if revisionist powers try to cross lines that have little to do with their security, peace is likely to be maintained.

Similarly, "place-in-the-sun" revisionism will also be tempered by cost-benefit calculations if status quo powers pose such choices. In May 1911, a rebellion broke out in Morocco and French troops entered that country for the ostensible purpose of restoring order. In response, Wilhelm sent the gunboat *Panther* to the Moroccan port of Agadir under the pretext of seeking to ensure the protection of German citizens. Assuming that the French were really out to absorb Morocco, the Kaiser's real goal was to secure compensation if the French established

Morocco as a protectorate. If the French failed to offer appropriate compensation, German forces would push them out of Morocco. When the Germans indicated that they were seeking the entire French Congo, the French stood firm, and the British stood solidly behind them. Meanwhile, Austria, Germany's major ally at the time, had no interest at all in going to war with France and England over Morocco. Wilhelm quickly found himself isolated, but with his prestige and reputation well engaged, he had committed one of the cardinal sins of diplomacy: he had gotten himself into a position from which he could neither retreat without losing face nor march ahead without entailing grave risks.[22] In the end, the French enabled the Kaiser to bow out graciously by granting him minimal strips of land in the middle of Africa.

Promotional revisionism based on belief systems frequently lack a sense of rational limits. Islamic fundamentalism, for example, is at war with both secular Arab states and the "Great Satan states" that lie beyond the world of Islam. A conquest or two, here and there, would never quench the movement's missionary goals. Even if the fundamentalists attained supremacy in the Arab World, their victory would probably only whet their appetite for further expansion. Victory in the Islamic World would merely affirm the validity of their revisionist path and spur them on to holy wars with the "enemies" of Islam.

In his *Politics among Nations*, Hans Morgenthau coined the phrase "nationalistic universalism" to denote such ideologically based revisionism. According to Morgenthau, leaders of such nations see their country "as the starting point of a universal mission whose ultimate goal reaches to the confines of the political world,"[23] and because of the universal nature of such ideologies, they can frequently find allies within target nations. Such "fellow travelers" add to the fear and disarray among intended targets. At the close of World War II and thereafter, national communists and "progressive" allies in Eastern Europe worked with Soviet forces in communizing their countries.

The universal appeals of the Soviet Union helped to make its revisionism look like the spread of progress to idealists and progressives in noncommunist countries, and in the 1960s, the high economic growth rates of the Soviet system made it attractive as an economic model for many elites in Third World nations that had recently been freed from Western colonialism. Universal ideologies provide people in other countries with dreams and hopes of better days—dreams against which the reality of their existing lives will always pale. Revolutionary revisionists who promise a new order and better lives will always have a powerful weapon against status quo states—at least until experience allows people to see how well the dream works out in reality.

Still, although revolutionary regimes create fear, mistrust, and tensions within nonrevolutionary regimes, their success rate has not been high. After studying the French, Russian, Iranian, and Chinese revolutions,

Professor Stephen Walt concluded that, "None of them spawned successful imitators during the decade after the seizure of power, and efforts to spread the revolution via propaganda or contagion only angered and alarmed other states."[24] In the end, revolutionary revisionists expand their territory and influence in the same manner as all other kinds of revisionists—by marching legions or the threat of war.

Walt's study documents well the difficulties that revolutionary regimes encounter in spreading their belief system to other countries—especially when opponents of the regime engage in containment.[25] He also documents the difficulty, if not the futility, of attempting to eradicate revolutionary regimes. *No revolutionary regime in a major power has ever been rooted out by foreign intervention short of a major war.* On the other hand, Walt's study demonstrates that efforts to appease such regimes also fail. Rather than allaying fears, tensions, and hostilities, such "olive branch tactics" merely increase suspicions among revolutionary elites who perceive such conciliatory gestures as efforts to trick or manipulate them.

The best strategy for status quo powers in dealing with such regimes, Walt concludes, is quiet containment. The rationale for the quiet part of this strategy is to avoid the kind of rhetoric that will only feed into the fears and diabolical enemy images characteristic of both revolutionary and antirevolutionary elites. As Walt demonstrates, quiet deterrent strategies can work. Despite its militant rhetoric, Iran has pursued its revisionist aims by relatively low-risk strategies—anti-American and anti-secular rhetoric, support for terrorist forces, and the provision of weapons and other aid to allies abroad. In the twenty years since the fall of the shah, Iran has failed to add one country to its hoped-for new fundamentalist order, although it did come close in Algeria, where more than eighty thousand people had died by the end of 1999, and its support for fundamentalist forces wreaked great havoc in Egypt.

In time, the frustrations engendered by quiet containment policies will wear down the ideological fervor of the regime and lead it to turn inward. The experience with ideological revisionists since the French Revolution indicates that, over time, revolutionary fervor burns out as new power structures arise within the revolutionary society and people in those new power structures seek to get on with their daily lives. Within France, the revolutionary fervor of the regime burned out within a decade; the Soviet Union's revolutionary fervor ended in 1927 when Stalin announced his program of "Socialism in One Country." Richard Nixon's visit to Mao's China in 1974 marked the end of the that country's career as a "revolutionary," revisionist state.

The end of ideological-based revisionism may not mean the end of more traditional revisionism, however. Revolutionary changes frequently revitalize and enhance the power of a state, and this revitalization and newly found power can lead to more traditional imperialist aims. During the 1970s, Leonid Brezhnev ferried Cuban troops into

Angola and Ethiopia to secure victories for Marxist factions in those countries, and he supported Marxist forces in Central America that were waging war against traditional right wing dictatorships. However, these maneuvers were more akin to the "target of opportunity," "fits and starts revisionism" of Kaiser Wilhelm than the revolutionary strategies proposed by the early Bolsheviks. And in every case, Soviet and Cuban victories had more to do with military might and common interests than with revolutionary ideals or principles.

Some revisionist foreign policies can be based on both external and internal motivations. Given her lack of natural resources, Japan's quest for the natural resources in Korea and Manchuria at the turn of the twentieth century stemmed largely from defensive orientations. On the other hand, continual racial slights from Western powers engendered among the Japanese a racial and cultural pride that also led them to seek the erosion of Western power and influence in the Pacific.

Status Quo Powers

Status quo powers are more or less satisfied with the existing distribution of territory, power, and influence. Like conservatives within a domestic political system, status quo powers are beneficiaries of the existing configurations of resources, status, and influence. Status quo Great Powers have a place in the sun, and they frequently believe that their place is not only well-deserved but natural. At the same time, because they benefit from the status quo, they have a stake in preserving it. *If a given status quo is to be preserved when it is under challenge, only the status quo powers will do the preserving.*

Obviously, maps and political life cannot be frozen, but if peace is to be maintained, status quo powers must learn how to deal with powers seeking change. However, precisely because they are satiated, status quo powers are frequently unwilling to engage in policies that might risk or jeopardize their comfort—particularly when violence erupts in areas that do not clearly appear to be vital to their survival. When status quo powers lack the will or power to deter and resist demands for change, then, clearly, both the map and its attendant status and power rankings will change accordingly.

If status quo states have a "typical failing," it amounts to underestimating threats to their status and interests, and not knowing where, when, and how to draw lines—a question that will be addressed extensively in the next two chapters of this primer. While status quo powers have seldom been initiators of major wars, their policies frequently have been responsible for them. All too often, the paralysis and appeasement policies of status quo powers have led revisionist states to believe that status quo states would prefer "peace" to war when confronted by threats of force or the employment of force.

After discussing a number of wars of miscalculation, James Payne drew the following conclusion in his book, *The American Threat*, which was written in the 1970s:

> *A war lost by the aggressor who initiates it is a war of miscalculation. . . .*
>
> *Wars of miscalculation have been the scourge of the twentieth century [and] another such war threatens to destroy civilization. It is therefore critical that we understand how they come about. The key is, of course, the fundamental misjudgment that the aggressor makes about his opponents: he underestimates their willingness and ability to resist.*
>
> *. . . Instead of looking toward aggressors to explain misjudgments, it turns out that we must look at defenders. An examination of each of these cases of miscalculation reveals that it was the defenders who played the significant role in causing the aggressors to underestimate them. These defenders practiced "appeasement," that is, they allowed aggressors to take away rights and territories unopposed. From their inaction aggressors drew the reasonable but incorrect conclusions about their willingness and ability to resist.*[26]

The following table summarizes the major polarities involving status quo and revisionist powers.

Status Quo Powers	Revisionist Powers
Seek Stability	Seek Change
Want "Peace"	Want "Justice"
Defensive	Offensive
React	Initiate
Cautious	Take Risks
Restrained	Unrestrained
Fear Escalation	Threaten Escalation

Noninvolved or Neutral States

Noninvolved or neutral states seek to stay out of the struggles for power, status, and influence among the Great Powers. Switzerland has been a neutral nation for almost two centuries and its neutrality has largely been respected. "Largely been respected," of course, is the key point. Consider the case of Belgium.

Through the Treaty of London of 1839, the Great Powers of Europe recognized the independence of Belgium as a European state and pledged to guarantee the country as "an independent and perpetually neutral state." This pledge notwithstanding, Germany violated Belgium's neutrality twice and at great cost to the neutral country and others. In August 1914, German troops invaded France by sending its troops through Belgium. For this violation of Belgium's neutrality, Britain declared war on Germany. On hearing of the decision, German leaders were shocked that Britain would go to war "just for a word—'neutrality,' a word which in war time had so often been disregarded. . . .

Just for a scrap of paper," the German Chancellor remarked, "Great Britain was going to make war on a kindred nation who desired nothing better than to be friends with her."[27]

Having been burnt once, Belgium cast aside its neutrality after World War I and entered into an alliance with France against Germany. When French forces marched into the Ruhr in 1923 because of chronic German defaults on deliveries of in-kind reparations, Belgian troops and technicians accompanied them. However, when the French and British faltered in their will to enforce the restraints of the Versailles treaty after Hitler announced rearmament in 1935 and then marched into the Rhineland one year later, Belgium abrogated its alliance with France and returned to its prewar status of neutrality. As the American journalist John Gunther explained at the time, "The Belgian case was simple: [they] didn't want to be the cockpit of the next war."[28]

Hitler was delighted with Belgium's return to neutrality. Knowing that France and Britain would never violate Belgium's neutrality, Hitler could be confident that any moves he made in Eastern Europe would not lead to an attack against Germany in the West. His Siegfried line would deter any French invasion across the Franco-German border, and France's respect for international law in general and Belgian's neutrality in particular would insure against a French invasion of Germany through Belgium. On the other hand, since Hitler fully intended to attack France through Belgium, a neutral Belgium relying on only its own limited military capabilities would render his invasion and conquest of France easier and quicker.

Not surprisingly, Hitler went out of his way to assure King Leopold that Germany would never violate Belgium's neutrality so long as Belgium would not threaten Germany. To underscore his point about Belgium's never threatening Germany, Hitler usually accompanied his pacific assurances with dire threats of what would happen if Belgium ever abandoned her "independent" status and began working with Britain and France. To enhance the credibility of his pacific assurances, Hitler forbid the German press from even mentioning the territories of Eupen and Malmédy, which Germany had lost to Belgium at the end of World War I. These would be seized easily enough once Belgium was invaded.

In return, King Leopold went out of his way to underscore his disassociation from Britain and France. In addition to the usual peaceful rhetoric, the monarch refused to allow British and French military experts to undertake an analysis of his country's defenses. But none of Leopold's well-meaning efforts were of any use. Once Hitler was ready to move against France, Belgium's neutrality proved no refuge from war. When the invasion came on May 10, 1941, King Leopold surrendered immediately and became a German prisoner. Fort Eban Emael, Belgium's main obstacle to invading German forces, was taken out of commission in less than an hour, and all of Belgium was gone in less than three weeks.

Having observed Hitler's respect for Belgium's neutrality, those other two venerable European neutrals, Switzerland and Sweden, quickly bent to German pressure and supplied Hitler with vital materials that he needed to wage war. However, Switzerland buttressed its policy of benevolent neutrality by building a military force capable of "punitive resistance," and by the end of World War II, the neutral country possessed a well-equipped army of fifty divisions as a deterrent to any German thoughts about violating its neutral status.[29]

Noninvolvement and Neutrality Are More Often a Condition Than a Choice

The key to any neutral country's security and survival lies in its awareness of why it enjoys the luxury of being aloof from regional, continental, or global struggles. As Walter Lippmann pointed out in his 1943 classic, *US Foreign Policy: Shield of the Republic*, the isolationism America enjoyed in the nineteenth century stemmed not from "our geography, our inherent virtues, and our own isolated military" but from sheer "historical accident." According to Lippmann, "Asia was dormant, Europe divided, and Britain's command of the seas unchallenged."[30]

Once German submarines wreaked havoc on American shipping and its conception of neutral rights during World War I, America had the same choice it had in the 1790s when Britain began to enforce its Orders in Council of 1756: It could yield to the challenger's conditions; it could fight; or it could negotiate. At first, President Wilson chose to ignore Germany's dictum that "all ships" in all waters from the North Sea to the eastern Mediterranean would be sunk. Then, when Germany sunk three American ships on March 18, 1917, he called a special session of Congress, which assembled on April 2. After two days of debate, the Senate declared war by a margin of 82 to 6 and four days later, the House declared war by a vote of 375 to 50.

Similarly in Asia, when British naval power could no longer contain the Japanese during the interwar years, America could either acquiesce in Japan's quest for hegemony in Asia or try to do something about it. After the Japanese invasion of Manchuria in 1931, President Hoover fruitlessly sought to contain Japan with words of disapprobation. Ten years later, when the Japanese moved into French Indochina, the United States froze Japanese assets and thereby cut off the source credit that enabled Japan to purchase aviation fuel for its industry and war machine. When Japan sought to negotiate an "unfreezing" of its assets, Secretary of State Cordell Hull insisted that Japan pull back not only from Indochina but from Manchuria as well. Rather than give in to this demand, Japan's leaders chose war. On December 7, 1941, her naval forces devastated the American Pacific fleet based at Pearl Harbor, and America's days of isolationism and neutrality were over again.

Throughout the nineteenth century and well into the twentieth century, most Americans were unaware of the real basis on which their security rested. Typical was the view expressed in a speech by a twenty-eight-year-old Abraham Lincoln in 1837: "All the armies of Europe, Asia, and Africa combined, with all of the treasure of the earth (our own excepted) in their military chest, with a Bonaparte for a commander, could not take a drink from the Ohio or make a track on the Blue Ridge in a trial of a thousand years. . . . [*Danger*] *cannot come from abroad. If destruction be our lot we must ourselves be its author and finisher.*"

Yet, less than twenty-five years earlier, a fairly small contingent of British troops invaded Washington almost unopposed and burned down the Capitol and the White House. This the British did at a time when they were preoccupied with Napoleon's armies on the continent. As Louis Halle points out in his insightful book, *Dream and Reality: Aspects of American Foreign Policy:* "mere detachments of British forces, all alone, without the armies of Europe, Asia, and Africa, and with a Bonaparte in opposition rather than in command, had little trouble doing what was substantially more revealing of our vulnerability than making a track in the Blue Ridge or sipping water from the Ohio."[31]

It was not the Atlantic or Pacific Oceans that allowed America the luxury of its isolation. It was a friendly British navy that ruled supreme on those oceans. When Britain's supremacy on the seas ended, so would America's isolationism.

Nations with Mixed Foreign Policies

While general observations can usually be made about a country's foreign policy posture, some nations pursue different strategies in different areas. During the nineteenth century, the United States pursued a policy of non-involvement in regard to Europe, while behaving as a revisionist power on the American continent. By conquering Indian nations, purchasing Louisiana and Florida, threatening war with Britain over Oregon, and gaining half of Mexico through conquest and purchase, the American states built a vast continental nation. During the Cold War, America's NATO allies took a status quo posture in regard to Europe while their posture toward American efforts to resist communist expansion in Asia and Central America was largely one of noninvolvement or aloofness. Many Europeans were frequently critical of American policies in those areas.

CASE STUDY
Mussolini's Fears and Dreams

Mussolini's Italy is a notable and instructive example of a state with mixed aims. At the Paris Peace Conference, Italy gained the South Tyrol, a former part of the Austro-Hungarian Empire, that contained two hundred thousand German-speaking people. Obviously, keeping this territory safely within the Italian fold would be much easier if Germany remained weak and Austria remained an independent buffer state between Italy and Germany. Italy's interest in supporting the status quo created by the Versailles settlement in central Europe was strong and clear.

When French and Belgian forces invaded the Ruhr in 1923, Mussolini gave the venture his blessing. Two years later, he also agreed to guarantee the "western" part of the Versailles settlement through the Locarno agreements. Meanwhile, Italian subsidies to ideologically sympathetic Austrians turned that country into a compliant Fascist satellite by the time Hitler came to power. As the American journalist John Gunther put it in 1936, Mussolini had become "to all intents and purposes, the Lord High Protector of Austria."[32]

The triumph of Hitler presented the European status quo with a major challenge to the entire structure of power and paper that had been created in the 1920s to secure it. The first test came in July 1934 when Hitler's Austrian followers tried to seize power as a first step toward uniting Austria with Germany. When the revolt broke out, Mussolini quickly ordered his Fascist allies in Austria to move against the insurgents, and he marched one hundred thousand troops up to the Brenner Pass as an insurance policy in case Hitler tried to intervene with German troops. If the Austrian Nazis had counted on German military intervention to rescue them, they were sadly mistaken. Facing the prospect of a military conflict with Italy, Hitler stepped back in humiliation. Mussolini's show of force was designed to keep the Versailles settlement intact, and it succeeded.

While solidly supporting the status quo against German revisionism, Mussolini had revisionist ambitions in the Mediterranean, Africa, and Asia. In a speech to the Italian people in March 1934, Mussolini sketched out his long-term diplomatic objectives:

> Let us calmly consider a plan that reaches the nearby millennium, the year 2000. It is only a question of sixty years. The historical objectives of Italy have two names: Asia and Africa. South and East are the cardinal points that should excite the interest and will of Italians. There is little or nothing to do towards the North and the same towards the West, neither in Europe or beyond the ocean. These two objectives of ours are justified by geography and history. Of all the large Western Powers of Europe, Italy is the nearest to Africa and Asia. A few hours by sea and much less by air are enough to link up Italy with Africa and with Asia.[33]

In the mid-1930s, the status quo and revisionist strains in Italian diplomacy came into conflict and, ultimately, the revisionist side triumphed. After Hitler announced his plans to rearm Germany in March 1935, Mussolini insisted that the Stresa Declaration applied only to "[the] unilateral repudiation of treaties which may endanger the peace of Europe." The implication was clear: Mussolini expected compensation for his support of the status quo in Europe—namely, a free hand in regard to Ethiopia.

The Italian dictator's expectations were not off the mark. In January 1935, Prime Minister Laval of France concluded an agreement with Mussolini to defend the independence of Austria. In discussions leading up to this agreement, Laval led the Italian leader to believe that France was indifferent to the fate of Ethiopia. In fact, Laval may even have promised to provide Mussolini with financial aid for his Ethiopian venture.[34]

Nor were the British averse to appeasing the Italian dictator. Two months after the Stresa Declaration, British foreign minister Anthony Eden visited Italy and presented a proposal whereby Ethiopia would cede all of its southern province of Ogaden to Italy and grant undefined economic concessions elsewhere. On spurning this "half-a-loaf" proposal, Mussolini responded with umbrage at Eden's implication that Italy would have to engage in negotiations to do what the British had previously done in Egypt and the French had done in Morocco solely on their own initiatives. Still, he felt confident that Britain and France would allow him a free hand one way or another.

Mussolini began seriously contemplating the conquest of Ethiopia in 1933, and the following year, he set in motion preparations for military action. In December 1934, the pretext that he needed occurred. A contingent of Italian troops wandered into Ethiopia from Italian Somaliland and was fired upon by Ethiopian forces in the little village of Walwal. On hearing of the incident, the Italian government immediately demanded a formal apology and financial compensation. Ethiopia responded by appealing to the League of Nations.

When the League Council met in January 1935, the Italian delegate minimized the incident, claiming there was no need for the League's involvement at all. The incident, he said, was not "likely to affect the peaceful relations between the two countries." The Italian government, he claimed, was eager to settle the dispute peacefully through arbitration or conciliation as provided in a treaty that Italy and Ethiopia had signed in 1928. Under this agreement, both countries pledged "constant peace and friendship" and promised that all disputes between them would be submitted to a "procedure of conciliation and arbitration." On hearing the Italian delegate's conciliatory statement, the council adjourned the question.

Once the dispute was placed in limbo, the Italian government strung out the process of selecting the arbitrators to gain time for its military forces to group and prepare for their invasion. Two months after the council's adjournment, an arbitration team had yet to be created. When Ethiopia again appealed to the League, the Italian delegate made more conciliatory remarks. On hearing these professions, the council tabled the dispute for a second time, and Italy began the process of assembling an arbitration team. Six months later, in September 1935, the team reached a unanimous conclusion: Neither government could be held responsible for the incident.

Italy rejected the report, and Mussolini prepared to launch his long-planned invasion. By professing peaceful intentions and a willingness to arbitrate under the terms of the 1928 treaty, the Italian dictator bought almost a year of free time to ready his forces. When the invasion came, on October 2, 1935, Britain and France decided to oppose his action, much to Mussolini's surprise, rage, and hurt feelings. Six days later, the League Council voted that Italy had "resorted to war in disregard of its obligations under Article 12 of the Covenant." One week later, a coordinating committee of the council called on all members of the League to engage in economic sanctions, and on November 18, the sanctions went into effect.

Several months after the imposition of sanctions, Hitler's troops marched into the Rhineland in violation of both the Treaty of Versailles and the Locarno treaties, which Hitler himself had pledged to respect after announcing the rearmament of Germany the previous year. In signing the Locarno accords, Britain and Italy had promised to intervene militarily if either France or Germany sent military forces into the demilitarized zone. The time to deliver on the guarantee had arrived. Mussolini offered to reconstitute the Stresa Front and rally to the defense of Locarno, but his willingness to defend the status quo in Europe had a price—the League's sanctions against Italy would have to be dropped. Britain and France declined the offer, and Hitler was able to negate the linchpin of the Versailles settlement without firing a shot.

From that time on, Mussolini began his movement into the camp of Hitler, a man whom the Italian leader feared, loathed, envied, and disliked. Immediately after the Rhineland crisis, Mussolini wrote in his diary:

> Germany will not stop at the occupation of the Rhineland. Germany marches, nobody manages to stop her, either with war nor with peace. The Germans are headstrong and Hitler is . . . hard and ruthless.
>
> The Germans are never able to establish relations of accord and friendship with anyone. Never.[35]

Nevertheless, having concluded that Britain and France would never stand up to Hitler, Mussolini decided to make his peace with the Nazi dictator; he would trade the status quo in the north of Europe for a free hand in the Balkans, the Mediterranean, and Africa—a typical and "time honored" spheres-of-influence arrangement. In making his peace, Mussolini risked having to cede the South Tyrol to Germany, but, happily, Hitler was content with Austria alone.

Mussolini's accord with Hitler cost Italy virtually nothing because the revisionist aims of Italy and Nazi were fully complementary. Germany sought to crush France and then move into Central Europe and Russia to create a continental colonial empire for resources and *lebensraum*. Mussolini, on the other hand, sought to build an empire in the Mediterranean, Africa, southeast Europe, and the Middle East. Nowhere did their aims really clash.

Cooperation began when the two dictators supported the fascist side in the Spanish Civil War during the summer months of 1936. By that year's end, the announcement of a Rome-Berlin axis changed the geopolitical configuration of Europe. If the status quo powers would not act to stop one of them acting alone, how would they stop the two dynamic powers united in a Pact of Steel? The revisionist side of the Italians triumphed over the status quo side— and much to the disadvantage of France and Britain, whose leaders faced German revisionism in central Europe, Italian revisionism in North Africa and the Mediterranean, and Japanese revisionism in Asia.

Types of Situations in the International Political System

At any given time, the political relations among members of the Great Power oligarchy will fall into one of the following categories:

1. *Situations of Stability and Legitimacy among the Great Powers: Conflicts* within *a Given Status Quo.* There have been periods when relative peace and stability have reigned in the international system. Although changes may occur in such systems, the changes are marginal or incremental, posing little challenge, if any, to the status or core interests of the oligarchs.

One such period existed from the Congress of Vienna in 1815 until 1890 when the Kaiser dismissed Bismarck. Although there was conflict and even warfare during this period, none of the Great Powers had hegemonic aims, and conflicts were handled through the give-and-take of diplomacy, which included, at times, summit meetings of diplomats from the Great Powers.

By the mid-1990s, such a situation existed among members of the post–Cold War oligarchy. While civil strife has been rife since the end of the Cold War and rogue states like Iran, Iraq, and North Korea have been minor irritants, none of the major powers has belied any major revisionist goals. According to

Terry Deibel, professor of national strategy at the National War College:

> For the first time in virtually anyone's memory, Americans may be entering a period of world politics when none of the most powerful states harbors aggressive intent, and all are therefore freed of critical threats to their security. Of course, the great powers will continue to compete. . . . Nor will the post–Cold War world be free of violence; too many signs in the formerly socialist and Third World points in the opposite direction, and some of these conflicts (as the Gulf crisis warned) may well threaten the West's vital interests. But fear of forceful domination on a global scale does seem to have ended for the foreseeable future, and with it the distinguishing feature of international politics of the twentieth century.[36]

A few years later, George Kennan, the father of America's Cold War containment strategy, seconded Deibel's observation. For the first time in centuries, Kennan noted in a *New York Times* essay, Great Power rivalries no longer threatened the peace of the world. "We must do all in our power," he cautioned, "to see that things remain that way."[37]

Given the collapse of the former Soviet and czarist empires, a future Russian government might seek to regain some of its losses. But as of this writing, Russia is busy enough with the difficulties of making the transition to a stable democracy and a viable market economy. However, a major goal of Western diplomacy should be to help the Russians succeed in this quest and keep that country among the ranks of satisfied nations. Such will be one of the diplomatic challenges of the twenty-first century.

Another diplomatic challenge of the twenty-first century will involve the future of China. A burgeoning economic powerhouse with a resourceful people and a proud heritage, China is the riddle of post–Cold War diplomacy. Will it become a great trading state like Japan, or will it become a revisionist state seeking a place in the sun like Wilhelm's Germany? This question has engaged a great deal of discussion and debate. How decision makers in America and other Great Powers answer that question will have significant implications for their foreign policies and the prospect for peace.[38]

2. *Situations in Which Major Struggles among the Great Powers Are Taking Place: Conflicts Seeking to Overturn an Existing Status Quo.* Throughout the history of the international system, leaders of status quo powers have frequently failed to recognize the "real ambitions" of revisionist powers until they find themselves fighting on unenviable terms. In 1939, Britain and France did not go to war with Germany for the

least defensible part of the Versailles peace treaty—the Polish corridor and Danzig—as the British historian A. J. P. Taylor suggests; they went to war because they believed that Hitler's ultimate aims jeopardized their own survival. Similarly, the Great Powers learned of Napoleon's ambitions too late to stop him with a diplomacy backed by force.

3. *Ambiguous Situations.* The most difficult situations are those in which it is unclear whether revisionist states are seeking fundamental changes of the status quo or merely changes within a status quo that all parties largely accept as legitimate. The reason for such ambiguity is a simple one: Revisionist leaders seldom identify themselves as incrementalists, regionalists, or hegemonists; in fact, they, themselves, may not even know what their ultimate goals may be, for their appetite may increase with the eating.

In the early 1930s, Japan's aims in Asia probably did not extend much beyond the physical control of Manchuria and the reduction of China to a quiescent satellite state. When the Western powers responded to Japan's behavior with mere words, her response was increasingly one of both irritation at the carping and contempt for the fecklessness of the Western powers. To be sure, Japan did ally with Hitler in the Anti-Comintern Pact, but that alliance had a largely defensive aim—deterring the Soviet Union from challenging it in Manchuria. In fact, it is not clear that Japan had any intentions of moving against Western colonies in Asia during the early 1930s. As William R. Nester notes in his study of American relations with Japan, "There was no grand plan for Japanese imperialism in the 1930s and early 1940s. . . . Tokyo," he concludes, "simply took advantage of opportunities that arose to enhance Japan's national interests as they were then understood."[39] What spurred Japan on was Hitler's defeat of France and Holland, Britain's preoccupation in Europe, and America's economic embargo of vital war materials.

No Status Quo Should Be Considered Sacrosanct

While revisionism is in fact the driving force in international politics, one caveat must be entered: *Never confuse any status quo with justice or morality*—the territory that most nations possess they possess as a result of previous uses of force, or "aggression," if you will. As Martin Wight pointed out in his *Power Politics*, "The distinction [between defense and aggression] is usually a matter of centuries and not morals, for the dissatisfied Power is often seeking to take what the satisfied Power took by aggression previously."[40] In his *Twenty Years Crisis*, E. H. Carr even goes so far as to claim that there is no such thing as a defensive or an aggressive war.

What makes revisionist demands so disarming for defenders of the status quo is the simple fact that any status quo is filled with "injustices," and status quo powers frequently benefit from those injustices. For example, on the basis of what moral principle could the United States criticize Japan's invasion of Manchuria given America's invasion of Mexico and its acquisition of about one-half of Mexico's territory? On the basis of what moral principle could the British and French oppose Mussolini's use of military force to colonize Ethiopia, the last bit of independent territory in Africa?

Revisionist leaders have frequently tied leaders of status quo powers in moral knots by arguing from moral principles or dwelling on moral consistency. During the Czechoslovakian crisis in 1938, Neville Chamberlain was aghast at the very idea that Britain might go to war in opposition to the principle of self-determination! To cite another example, on the basis of what principle could the United States insist that the Soviet Union withdraw nuclear missiles from Cuba while it had nuclear missiles aimed at the Soviet Union in Turkey?

As we shall see in Chapter 4, what is important is neither the "justness" of the status quo nor moral consistency—for neither will ever exist on this earth. What matters are the implications that changing configurations of arms, influence, and territory will have on existing distributions of power and influence. The task for status quo members is not to attain Academy Awards for moral rectitude or moral consistency, but to determine what interests are vital for their security and to ensure that they have the armaments to secure those interests through deterrence at best and war if necessary.

If there is only one "never" in thinking about and making foreign policy, it is this: never even think of trying to secure consistency of principle, moral or otherwise, in foreign policy decision making. Consider the two cases of North Korea's invasion of South Korea and India's invasion of Goa in 1961. Under Article 51 of the United Nations Charter, states are limited to the use of force only in self-defense. All other uses are proscribed and considered breaches of the peace, and the job of the Security Council is to stop all breaches of the peace. The theory underlying the United Nations can be succinctly put: State A invades the territory of State B. In all such instances, the members of the UN Security Council are obliged to support B through sanctions or force if diplomacy fails to settle the issue.

Such would be a foreign policy and international politics based on principle rather than interest or power. Obviously, neither states nor international organizations ever respond in such an automatic manner— they never will, and they never should. In addition to considering what the UN Charter or international law stipulates, decision makers will always consider their nation's interests and power in a given situation. In the Korean case, a North Korean victory would have dealt a significant blow to the prestige and credibility of the United States and added another territory to the Soviet bloc.

Tiny Goa, on the other hand, had been a Portuguese colonial possession since 1510 and, as such, was the last remaining vestige of colonialism on the Indian subcontinent. When repeated discussions between India and Portugal failed to bring about the colony's independence, India decided to resort to force, and in less than forty-eight hours, Goa and two other tiny Portuguese enclaves lay under Indian flags. Adlai Stevenson, the U.S. ambassador at the United Nations, condemned the invasion as a blatant act of aggression in the Security Council: "Let us be perfectly clear what is at stake here gentlemen. It is the question of the use of armed force by one state against another and against its will, an act clearly forbidden by the Charter. We have opposed such action in the past by our closest friends as well as by others. We opposed it in Korea in 1950, in Suez and in Hungary in 1956, in the Congo in 1960, and we do so in Goa in 1961."[41]

What greatly disturbed Stevenson was that Ceylon, Libya, and the United Arab Republic all joined the Soviet Union in opposing, and vetoing, an American, British, French, and Turkish resolution calling for the cessation of hostilities, the withdrawal of Indian forces, and a resort to peaceful measures to resolve the dispute. Having been rebuffed in the Security Council, Stevenson considered taking his case to the General Assembly, "the organized conscience of mankind." His preliminary soundings of sentiment in that body brought back the disappointing news that India would have been applauded rather than condemned by the developing nations. Third World nations had no love for Portugal, a colonial power with a heinous record of atrocities in its African colonies of Angola and Mozambique. America's European allies, on the other hand, had no love for the semi-fascist dictatorship of Antonio Salazar, and they had no interest in alienating India over a relatively trivial issue.

Ambassador Stevenson stood virtually alone in his condemnation of India's aggression. In response to Stevenson's charges that India had violated the UN Charter and international law, the Indian delegate C. S. Jha called on UN members to reject "any narrow-minded legalistic, considerations of international law" in regard to the conflict over Goa. "European international law writers," he claimed, "are, after all, part of the atmosphere of colonialism."[42]

Of course, the Kennedy administration had no intention of placing sanctions against India, let alone coming to the aid of Portugal militarily. Its protest was designed to convince the world that America's foreign policy was a foreign policy of disinterested principle and to register a complaint against the use of force in diplomacy.

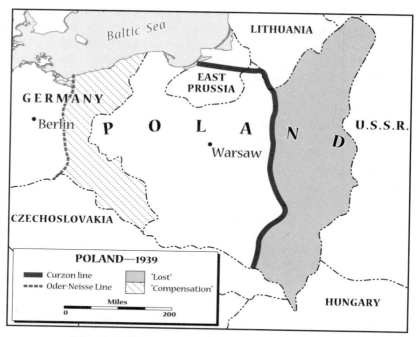

Map 2.1. What Did FDR Give Away at Yalta?

The Curzon line denotes the "ethnic" boundary of Poland based on the principle of nationality as drawn at the Paris Peace conference. The shaded area indicates former Czarist territory gained by the Poles on the field of battle and which Stalin took back when Soviet troops entered the area during the close of the Second World War. At the Yalta Conference in February 1954, Stalin offered to "compensate" the Poles for their loss by giving them German territory up to the Oder-Niesse rivers indicated on the map—land that the Poles took. None of these changes was officially accepted by the United States until the Helsinki Conference of 1975.

CASE STUDY
FDR's "Sell Out" of Poland at Yalta

Martin Wight's point about the distinction between aggression and defense being a matter of years is well illustrated by one of the most hotly debated issues during the first decade of the Cold War, namely, whether FDR betrayed Poland by seeking to appease Stalin with Polish territory at Yalta. At that conference in February 1945, FDR and Churchill agreed that the eastern boundary of Poland would be set largely along the Curzon line, which had been designated as the Russia-Poland boundary at the Paris Peace Conference after World War I. In so agreeing, Churchill and FDR assented to the

Soviet incorporation of territory that was part of Poland during the interwar period. However, Poland's possession of that territory in the first place was the result not of any right but simple military might. When Russia fell into disarray after the collapse of the czarist regime, Poland set out to conquer the Ukraine. While Poland's armies were not that successful, they did manage to gain 150 miles of territory east of the Curzon line, a conquest recorded as the permanent frontier between Russia and Poland through the Treaty of Riga in 1921.

This now seemingly minor incident illustrates well some of the central points in this chapter. After the fall of the czar and the ensuing civil war, *Russia's weakness* tempted Poland to wage war to revise the ethnic boundary set by the Curzon line. *Russia's weakness* and *its defeat in that little war* sowed the seeds of revision in the Soviet Union, and when power turned in its favor, Stalin did not hesitate to stake his claim to regain the territory lost through the Treaty of Riga. As early as December 1941, Stalin insisted that, without question, the territories gained by Poland under the Riga treaty must be "returned" to the Soviet Union. As he quipped to Churchill and FDR at the Yalta conference, "You cannot expect me to be less Russian than a British Lord," referring to Lord Curzon after whom the boundary set at Paris was named.

Spokesmen for Poland, of course, had a different view. According to the Polish ambassador of the London Government in Exile—a government that Stalin did not recognize as the government of Poland—the boundary issue had been settled in the Treaty of Riga, "a freely negotiated treaty between Poland, Soviet Russia, and the Ukraine Soviet Republic." In response to this claim, the political columnist, Walter Lippmann wrote the following in a letter to the *Washington Post:* "if the Ambassador means to imply that this eastern frontier was not conquered because the acquisition was recognized in part by the Treaty of Riga . . . , then no territory has ever been conquered. For after every conquest there is a treaty."[43]

Who, then, was giving away what to whom at Yalta? Obviously, neither Churchill nor FDR gave any Polish territory away at Yalta because neither possessed any Polish territory to give to Stalin— after all, one can only concede what one has the power to withhold. To be sure, the Polish government in exile would never have freely conceded the territory it had taken from Russia, but that government was in London. On the other hand, why would Stalin freely concede to Poland territory that the Soviet Union had lost only under the duress of war? As E. H. Carr noted, "Every treaty which brings a war to an end is almost inevitably accepted by the loser under duress."[44]

At best, FDR and Churchill acquiesced in Stalin's incorporation of these areas when persuasion failed to get the Soviet dictator to do otherwise. As Professor Robert Osgood has noted, "Russia's expanded spheres of influence in Asia and Europe [were] the direct consequence of the Red Army's sphere of operation during the war. ... Once the Red army occupied an area, whether in eastern Europe or Manchuria," he notes, "it [was] certainly unrealistic to suppose that America could have determined the fate of that area by diplomatic conversations at Yalta or anywhere else."[45] At worst, FDR and Churchill legitimized Stalin's inevitable incorporation of the territory.

Which country—Poland or Russia—had the moral right to this territory is unclear. How could or should that have been determined? According to the Atlantic Charter no territorial changes were to be made without the expressed consent of the people living in those territories. If that rule implied that a plebiscite should have decided the moral question, one thing is clear: Neither the Poles nor Russians would have allowed that to happen.

One final footnote: As a gesture of conciliation, Stalin offered the southern half of East Prussia and the German territories of East Pomerania, West Pomerania, Liegnitz, and Upper Silesia as compensation for Poland's losses, which, of course, the Poles accepted. The ethnicity of these territories was as follows: East Prussia, 92.8 percent German; East Pomerania, 99 percent German; West Pomerania, 100 percent German; Liegnitz, 100 percent German; and Upper Silesia, 57 percent German. When Stalin made his offer, no Pole raised the principles of nationality and national self-determination; in fact, to avoid having millions of Germans in postwar Poland, Polish authorities forced the German inhabitants of these territories to flee into East and West Germany as refugees. Now that the Cold War is over, some Germans from these areas are seeking compensation for their losses.

International Conflicts Can Seldom Be Viewed in Isolation

While every reader of this primer is aware of the Korean War, many are probably unaware of the Goa incident of 1961, and the reasons are obvious. The North Korean invasion had implications for international peace, while the Goa incident was a backwater affair of virtually no consequence except for the people in Goa.

When international conflicts arise, many people tend to think about them in terms of their particular merits—who wants what and why? Are the goals and means pursued by each side fair or just? Is an equitable settlement possible? While addressing such questions, foreign policy decision makers must also assess disputes within their larger context—

namely, how a particular dispute and its probable outcomes are related to their nation's power and positionality, what precedents might be set by different modes of conflict resolution, and how various outcomes might affect the power, positionality, and prestige of other members of the oligarchy.

CASE STUDY
John F. Kennedy Learns the "Linked" Nature of Conflicts

President John F. Kennedy quickly learned about the interrelatedness of seemingly isolated conflicts early in his term. Three months after taking office, the young president allowed the Bay of Pigs invasion to go down to ignominious defeat, and almost immediately thereafter, he retreated in Laos. To many, the new president looked weak, inexperienced, and indecisive.

With this record of irresolution behind him, Kennedy went off to meet Soviet Premier Nikita Khrushchev in June 1961 where he had a harrowing experience. As Richard Reeves notes in his superb history of the Kennedy presidency: "[For Khrushchev] the timing was right: triumphant in space, on the move in a half dozen countries around the world, Soviet power and influence were at a peak, and Khrushchev wanted the Americans to acknowledge that before the world."[46]

From the beginning of their first encounter, the Soviet leader threatened, demanded, and attacked, and his demeanor toward Kennedy ranged from impatient contempt to patronizing condescension. As Kennedy, himself, put it, "He treated me like a little boy. . . . Like a little boy."

The major issue at Vienna was Berlin. Hanging over the heads of the Western countries was a six-month ultimatum that Khrushchev had given them: either negotiate a peaceful withdraw of their forces from Berlin by the end of 1961 or the Soviets would unilaterally sign a peace treaty giving East Germany control over the Western allies' access to Berlin—access, which Khrushchev strongly implied, the East Germans would deny. In the latter event, the West would face the unenviable alternatives of retreating before the forces of a minor Soviet satellite or using military force to blast their way into Berlin. Were that to occur, Khrushchev made it clear that the Soviets would support the East Germans militarily. When Kennedy said, "We cannot accept that," Khrushchev responded angrily: "The USSR will sign a peace treaty, and the sovereignty of the GDR will be observed. Any violation of that sovereignty will be regarded by the USSR as an act of open aggression . . . with all the consequences ensuing therefrom. . . . If the U.S. wants to start a war over Germany let it be so. If there is any madman who wants a war, he should be put in a straitjacket. So this is the Soviet position. The USSR will sign a peace treaty at the end of this year."

With the summit about to end in stalemate, Kennedy insisted on one last, ten-minute meeting alone with Khrushchev. "We can destroy each other," Kennedy began, and then expressed his hope that the Soviet leader would not present him with situations that deeply involved and threatened American security interests. The critical American interest in Berlin was access, Kennedy explained. Khrushchev could do as he pleased in regard to East Germany, Kennedy said, as long as it did not jeopardize that interest.

"Force would be met by force," the Soviet leader retorted. And after telling Kennedy that he was preparing for war, Khrushchev was even more belligerent: "If the U.S. wants war that's its problem. It's up to the U.S. to decide whether there will be war or peace. The decision to sign a peace treaty is firm and irrevocable and the Soviet Union will sign it in December if the U.S. refuses an interim agreement."

Having been delivered about as blunt an ultimatum as one gets in the field of diplomacy, Kennedy's response was equally blunt: "Then, Mr. Chairman, there will be war; it will be a cold winter."

Of course, there was no war, albeit only after Kennedy threatened war publicly to enhance his resolve and credibility. In his address to the nation in July 1961, the beleaguered president vowed to go to war even though the West might be in an untenable position. "I hear it said that West Berlin is militarily untenable," the president exclaimed, and then quickly countered with the following: "And so was Bastogne. And so, in fact, was Stalingrad. Any dangerous spot is tenable if men—brave men—will make it so."

To back up his words, Kennedy announced a $3.25 billion increase in defense expenditures. The army would be increased by 125,000 men, the navy by 29,000, and the air force by 63,000. Draft calls would be tripled, and more reservists could be called up with extended duty tours. Beyond the raw numbers, Kennedy made clear the personal impact his commitment might have on ordinary Americans: "And let me add that I am well aware of the fact that many American families will bear the burden of these requests. Studies or careers will be interrupted; husbands and sons will be called away; incomes in some cases will be reduced. But these are burdens which must be borne if freedom is to be defended—Americans have willingly borne them before—and they will not flinch from the task now."

In the end, Khrushchev decided not to risk the war he said he was preparing for, and the crisis ended when he built his Berlin Wall to end the hemorrhaging of East Germany's most skilled and educated people. Every day, about a thousand East Berliners or East Germans walked or rode into West Berlin with no intention of ever going back to East Germany.

Kennedy and Khrushchev's confrontation over Berlin illustrates well a number of the major points in this chapter. *First, conflicts among nations, and especially conflicts among the oligarchs, can seldom be viewed or dealt with as discrete, once and done, affairs.* What statesmen do, or do not do, in seemingly discrete disputes signal possible precedents for future situations, and from such possible precedents, leaders of other nations draw inferences about will and credibility. Leaders of revisionist powers pay careful attention to how leaders of status quo powers act under challenge. As we will see in the next chapter, it is often better for leaders of status quo powers not to make threats or initiate military actions than to do so and either fail or back down.

As the confrontation at Vienna and later over Berlin make clear, both Khrushchev and Kennedy looked at the particular disputes between their countries as part of a larger pattern. Because of Kennedy's behavior in the Bay of Pigs and Laos crises, Khrushchev thought that Kennedy would back down in Berlin as he had in the past. Kennedy also came to see the issue of Berlin in a larger context, as he made clear to the American people in his address: "The immediate threat to free men is in West Berlin. . . . An attack upon that city will be regarded as an attack upon us all. We cannot separate its safety from our own. . . . But that isolated outpost is not an isolated problem. The threat is worldwide. . . . There is also a challenge in Southeast Asia, where the borders are less guarded, the enemy harder to find, and the dangers of communism less apparent to those who have so little."[47]

Second, across the entire range of topics discussed at the Vienna summit, Kennedy was continually on the defensive, and his defensiveness stemmed from more than just his diplomatic retreats. The roots of Kennedy's defensiveness also stemmed from the situation that any status quo power faces. The problem is well put in Richard Reeves' discussion of the harrowing summit meeting:

> . . . the American President's arguments did seem old and defensive. [Kennedy] was taken by surprise, caught in the web of Communist cant. He was defending traditional spheres of influence, defending colonialism, defending old-line dictators, tripped into defending ideas he did not believe in and men he despised. Balance of forces, balances of power. Defending the status quo, he had stumbled through a mirror. He was on the other side arguing against revolution, against change. The Marxist coal miner was tying him in knots.[48]

Revisionist leaders are frequently virtuosos at wrapping up their demands in high sounding principles or berating their potential victims in ways that will make them appear unworthy of support. In so doing, they engender feelings of guilt in leaders of status quo powers and make them feel that their defensive actions are immoral and unprincipled. Such tactics can be especially effective against the leaders of democratic status quo nations because they provide ammunition to citizens within those democracies who want to "give peace a chance" and are looking for reasons to do nothing in response to challenges by revisionist powers.

Revisionism as the Driving Force of International Politics

The study of international politics is the study of how states go about seeking to change and maintain existing patterns of power, status, influence, and territory. Revisionist powers drive the forces for change and the political processes within the international system. It is they who raise the issues, create new agendas, make demands, initially threaten force, or in some cases, initiate the use of violence, as is illustrated by the following incomplete list of major revisionist powers since the French Revolution makes clear:

1815–World War I: France, United States, Piedmont/Sardinia, Prussia, Russia, Japan, Serbia

Interwar Period: Poland, Weimar Germany, Nazi Germany, Italy, Hungary, Poland, Japan

Postwar Period: Soviet Union, North Korea, North Vietnam, Egypt

Post–Cold War Period: Iraq, Iran, Serbia, China (?), Russia (?)

The business of diplomacy, especially the diplomacy of satisfied powers, such as Britain and France during the interwar years and the United States during the Cold War era, is the business of maintaining order and handling change—even violent attempts at change—in ways that do not fundamentally destabilize the existing status quo. The question of war or peace lies in the hands of status quo powers.

Summary of Salient Points

Revisionism is the driving force in international politics

1. Like all politics, international politics involves conflicts between those who want to keep things the way they are and those who want to change them.
2. The study of international politics is the study of how states go about seeking to change or maintain existing patterns of power, influence, status, and territory through persuasion, diplomatic negotiation and bargaining, or military force.
3. In regard to any given status quo, scholars classify countries as revisionist, status quo, or noninvolved or neutral states.
4. Since revisionist powers are dissatisfied with the status quo and want to change it, they are usually the initiators of international conflicts.

5. The major inducements to policies of revisionism are (1) defeat in war, (2) victory in war, (3) weakness in surrounding areas, (4) rising powers, or revolutionary ideologies or belief systems.

6. Revisionist foreign policies may be motivated by external-defensive motivations or internal-promotional motivations.

7. If revisionist powers have a typical failing, it lies in not knowing where to stop.

8. Status quo powers are more or less satisfied with the existing distribution of territory, power, and influence

9. If status quo powers have a typical failing, it involves underestimating threats to their status and interests, and not knowing where, when, and how to draw lines. Although status quo powers have seldom been the initiators of major wars, their policies have often been responsible for them.

10. Noninvolved or neutral states seek to stay out of struggles for power, status, and influence among the Great Powers. The key to a neutral state's security and survival lies in its awareness of why it enjoys the luxury of being noninvolved when international conflicts arise.

11. Although general observations can usually be made about a country's foreign policy, nations will frequently reflect mixed postures in regard to different areas and issues.

12. No status quo should be considered sacrosanct; most territory that nations possess is the result of previous uses of force.

Notes

1. K. J. Holsti, *Peace and War: Armed Conflicts and International Order 1648–1989* (New York: Cambridge University Press, 1991), ch. 12.
2. E. H. Carr, *Twenty Years' Crisis* (New York: Harper and Row, 1964), 216.
3. Henry Kissinger, *Diplomacy* (New York: Simon and Schuster, 1994), 459.
4. See their now-classic study, *Power and Interdependence* (New York: HarperCollins, 1989), for a first cut in understanding the politics of "global issues" stemming from interdependence.
5. Josef Joffe, " 'Bismarck' or 'Britain?' Toward an American Grand Strategy after Bipolarity," *International Security* 19, no. 4 (Spring 1995), 99–100. © 1995 by the President and Fellows of Harvard College and the Massachusetts Institute of Technology.
6. George Schwarzenberger, *Power Politics* (New York: Frederick A. Praeger, 1951), 14–15.
7. The discussion that follows draws heavily on the excellent discussion of these concepts in Barry Buzan, *People, States, and Fear: The National Security Problem in International Relations* (Chapel Hill: University of North Carolina Press, 1983); Abdul Aziz Said et al., *Concepts of International Politics in Global Perspective*, 4th Edition (Englewood Cliffs, NJ: Prentice Hall, 1995), 34–38; Randall L. Schweller, *Deadly Imbalances: Tripolarity and Hitler's Strategy of World Conquest* (New York: Columbia University Press, 1997); and Arnold Wolfers, *Discord and Collaboration: Essays on International Politics* (Baltimore: The Johns Hopkins Press, 1962).
8. Reprinted in John Gunther, *Inside Europe* (New York: Harper and Brothers, 1936), 90.
9. R. B. Mowatt, *The Diplomacy of Napoleon* (New York: Russell and Russell, 1971), 11.
10. Patrick Glynn, *Closing Pandora's Box* (New York: Basic Books, 1992), 42.
11. Hans Morgenthau, *Politics Among Nations*, 5th Edition (New York: Alfred A. Knopf, 1973), ch. 5.
12. Louis L. Snyder, *The Weimar Republic* (New York: D. Van Nostrand, 1966), 73.

13. Carol J. Williams, "Ethnic Tension Poses Threat to Hungarians," *Los Angeles Times*, January 7, 1994, 4.
14. Quoted in Hans J. Morgenthau, *In Defense of the National Interest* (New York: Alfred A. Knopf, 1951), 84.
15. This phrase contains the first use of the term *manifest destiny*. It was written by journalist John L. O'Sullivan in an 1845 issue of *The United States Magazine and Democratic Review* 17, no. 85 (July-August 1845), 5–6.
16. Holsti, *Peace and War*, 3.
17. Ibid., 17.
18. Ibid., ch. 1.
19. Christopher J. Herold, *The Age of Napoleon* (New York: American Heritage Publishing, 1963), 265.
20. Paul Schroeder, *The Transformation of European Politics, 1763–1848* (Oxford: Clarendon Press, 1994), 417–18.
21. Alfred Cobban, *A History of Modern France: Volume 2: 1799–1871* (Baltimore: Penguin Books, 1961), 19,
22. This precept is one of the fundamental rules of diplomacy presented in Morgenthau's *Politics Among Nations*, 589.
23. Ibid., 351.
24. Stephen M. Walt, *Revolution and War* (Ithaca, NY: Cornell University Press, 1996), 335.
25. See ibid., ch. 7.
26. James L. Payne, *The American Threat* (College Station, TX: Lytton Publishing, 1981), 11–12
27. Justin Wintle, ed., *The Dictionary of War Quotations* (New York: The Free Press, 1989), 296.
28. Ibid., *Inside Europe*, 438.
29. Dean Acheson, *Present at the Creation* (New York: W. W. Norton, 1969), 61.
30. Walter Lippmann, *US Foreign Policy: Shield of the Republic* (Boston: Little, Brown, 1943), 30, 49.
31. Louis Halle, *Dream and Reality: Aspects of American Foreign Policy* (New York: Harper and Brothers, 1958), 7–9. (Lincoln quotation in preceding paragraph is also from this source.)
32. Ibid., *Inside Europe*, 277.
33. Cited in Henderson B. Braddick, "The Hoare-Laval Plan: A Study in International Politics" in *European Diplomacy Between Two Wars, 1919–1939*, ed. Hans Gatzke (Chicago: Quadrangle Books, 1972), 154.
34. See Braddick, "The Hoare-Laval Plan," 156.
35. Taken from excerpts published in the *New York Times*, June 27, 1994, A6.
36. Terry L. Deibel, "Strategies Before Containment: Patterns for the Future," *International Security* 16, no. 4 (Spring 1992), 80.
37. George Kennan, "The Failure in Our Success," *New York Times*, March 14, 1994.
38. For a quick overview of this debate see Henry S. Rowen's "Off-Center on the Middle Kingdom," which is a review of Richard Bernstein and Ross H. Munro's "The Coming Conflict with China" in *The National Interest* 48 (Summer 1997), 101–4.
39. William R. Nester, *Power across the Pacific: A Diplomatic History of American Relations with Japan* (New York: New York University Press, 1996), 38.
40. Martin Wight, *Power Politics* (London: Royal Institute of International Affairs, 1946), 33–34.
41. From Richard Stebbins, *The United States in World Affairs: 1961* (New York: Harper and Brothers, 1962), 216.
42. Ibid., 372.
43. John Morton Blum, ed., *Public Philosopher: Selected Letters of Walter Lippmann* (New York: Tichnor and Fields, 1985), 461.
44. Carr, *Twenty Years' Crisis*, 187.
45. Robert Osgood, *Limited War: The Challenge to American Security* (Chicago: The University of Chicago Press, 1957), 104.
46. Richard Reeves, *President Kennedy: Profiles of Power* (New York: Simon & Schuster, 1993). Quotations of the conversations are taken from *FRUS, 1961–1963* (Washington, DC, 1996), VI, 164–230.
47. Ibid., 201.
48. Ibid., 161.

CHAPTER THREE

Be Wary of the Itch to Use Military Force; Those Who Give In to It Frequently Rue the Day They Did So

"War is hell," said General Sherman; "[It] is cruelty and you cannot refine it." Napoleon III, the French adventurer who sought to emulate his conquering uncle, vomited and almost fainted when he saw the horror of war on the battlefield at Magenta. Even Bismarck—the man who said that Germany would be unified not by "speeches and resolutions" but by blood and iron—cringed when he witnessed the cauldron of blood and iron on the field of battle at Sadowa. "He who has once gazed into the glazed eyes of a dying warrior will think twice before beginning a war," he remarked to one of his generals during the Austrian campaign.

War is, indeed, a terrible thing, but it is also an incalculable thing that often unleashes consequences quite contrary to the expectations of those who initiate it. The great Prussian field marshal Count Helmuth Karl von Moltke repeatedly told Bismarck that nothing was ever certain in war. Similarly, Clausewitz cautioned that "War is the province of chance. . . . In no other sphere of human activity must such a margin be left for this intruder." War, he wrote, "increases the uncertainty of every circumstance and deranges the course of events."[1] Over a century later, Winston Churchill issued the same warning: "Never, never, never believe any war will be smooth and easy or that anyone who embarks on the strange voyage can measure the risks and hurricanes he will encounter."[2] Retired North Korean general Yoo Sung Chul reflected the views of his predecessors when he noted: "The Korean War was planned to last only a few days, so we did not plan anything in case things might go wrong. If you fight a war without preparing for failures, then you are asking for trouble."[3]

Many are the leaders who have been brought down by military ventures they embarked on confidently—Napoleon I's invasion of Russia,

Napoleon III's war with Prussia, Kaiser Wilhelm's invasion of France, Emperor France Joseph's declaration of war against Serbia, Adolph Hitler's invasions of Poland and Russia, Lyndon Johnson's decision to fight a land war in Vietnam, the Argentinean generals who invaded the Falkland Islands thinking that "Maggie" Thatcher would be a pushover. On the other hand, many governments have undertaken military actions that were successful—Alexander I's decision to pursue Napoleon's troops across Europe, James Polk's war with Mexico, Cavour's liberation of Lombardy, Bismarck's wars to unify Germany, Japan's decision to go to war with Russia in 1905, Ho Chi Minh's use of force to unify Vietnam.

If nothing else, this rough set of examples underscores the most important fact about war—its problematic nature. Every foreign policymaker should always be mindful of the slippery slope he descends on when he resorts to military force. While military action may be easy to start, it is often very difficult to stop, as Lyndon Johnson found out in Vietnam, as the Soviets found out in Afghanistan, as Bill Clinton found out in regard to Kosovo, and as the Russians found out in Cechnya. Yet, remaining aloof or trying to stay out of a conflict is no guarantee that a nation will avoid getting involved in a war, as the king of Belgium discovered when German troops invaded his neutral nation in 1941, as Americans found out on the day Pearl Harbor was bombed, and as Stalin learned in June 1941 when his ally Hitler unleashed the German Wehrmacht against them.

Wars are lost not because national leaders fail to calculate but because they miscalculate. Overconfidence, pride, and hubris lead decision makers to overestimate their own capacities and underestimate the will, tenacity, and power of their victim and their victim's allies. One study of war found that initiators lost two-thirds of all the wars they had begun. Victims defeat their predators because, all too frequently, they are fighting for their honor and their dignity, those intangible motivating forces that often prove much more powerful than any desire for material gain or territory.

Still, in an anarchic international system, threats of force and the employment of force are essential for a diplomacy designed to ensure peace, security, and order. Military forces are essential to deter others from infringing on a nation's interests, to defend those interests if deterrence fails, and to signal resolve and intent. Rather than serving as a role model and leading others to emulate them, nations that fail to arm or seek to "give peace a chance" may become victims or objects of prey. However well-meaning, defenseless nations seldom dissuade a motivated and well-armed revisionist power from invading them.

Three times in the last century, Americans went to war completely unprepared for the conflict they were about to embark on, and after two of those wars, the United States virtually disarmed. What happens when you are unprepared for war became readily apparent to Harry Truman in the summer of 1950.

CASE STUDY
Korea Is Outside the American Defense Perimeter

On the last Saturday in June 1950, President Truman flew into Independence, Missouri, for the first day off with his family since Christmas. As the family engaged in after-dinner conversation on their newly screened-in porch, the president was interrupted by a telephone call from Secretary of State Dean Acheson. The message was as simple as it was stark: "Mr. President, I have very serious news: the North Koreans have invaded South Korea."

That invasion was as good an example of "plate glass" aggression as one could imagine—a figurative plate glass window had been smashed, and the vandals were running into the store wrecking everything in their path. When such events occur, leaders of status quo powers must decide whether to resist or cut their losses and draw a line elsewhere. In making this decision, one obvious consideration is the map. Where is the area? How much will its loss matter strategically? A second set of questions involves resources—whether one can marshal enough resources quickly enough to resist successfully without unacceptable costs and consequences elsewhere. A third set of questions involves psychological factors—what messages will different alternatives send to allies and adversaries.

American military and political officials had already answered the first set of questions well before the invasion of South Korea. Assuming that the next war would be a total war, the Joint Chiefs of Staff affirmed repeatedly in secret findings that the Korean peninsula would be of no strategic importance in the event of a war. In consonance with this assessment, the United States had pulled the bulk of its troops out of Korea by June 1949, leaving about five hundred officers to train a force of sixty-five thousand Koreans that would be used largely for internal security.

When the ninety thousand North Korean troops spearheaded south behind one hundred heavy Russian T-34 and T-70 tanks, they encountered an ill-equipped and untrained constabulary force totally unprepared for combat. The defending forces had neither tanks, anti-tank weapons, artillery, nor air support. As Truman's biographer, David McCullough, put it, "World War II bazookas bounced off the Russian tanks like stones."[4] In the battles that ensued, the defending forces were vastly outnumbered, ranging from three to one, to ten to one, and even twenty to one at times. By the end of the month, allied forces were fighting with their backs to the sea, and General Walton Walker, the UN commander in the field, was issuing "stand or die" orders.

Not only was South Korea ill-equipped to withstand a North Korean invasion. America's decision about the unimportance of South Korea had been publicly communicated on several occasions by high-ranking American officials. In an interview with a British journalist in March 1949, General Douglas MacArthur implied that Korea was not in America's defensive network when he said that our defensive line "starts from the Philippines and continues through the Ryukyu Archipelago [and] then it bends back through Japan and the Aleutian Island chain to Alaska."[5]

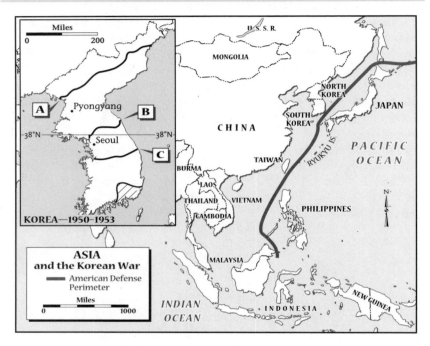

Map 3.1. Korea Is Outside the American Defense Perimeter

The solid line in the large map indicates America's defense perimeter as defined by Secretary of State Dean Acheson and General MacArthur. Note that South Korea and Taiwan are conspicuously "outside" the perimeter. Both Kim Il Sung and Mao thought they had a green light to take those areas respectively and made plans to do so. In the inset, the lined area indicates the foothold perimeter that American/UN forces occupied in July 1950 when General Walker was issuing "stand or die" orders. The thirty-eighth parallel was set as the original dividing line for Korea, but the armistice at line B reflects the results of the war. Line A across the top of North Korea indicates the furthermost advance of UN forces before the Chinese intervened and drove them back into south Korea as far as line C.

Nine months later, in some extemporaneous remarks to the National Press Club, Secretary of State Acheson similarly excluded Korea from the list of countries that the United States would defend in the event of a war. Several months after that, the chairman of the Senate Foreign Relations Committee, Tom Connally, indicated that Russia could take Korea any time it wanted to and that the United States would do nothing to stop it. In an interview with *U.S. News and World Report* in May 1950, Connally was asked, "Do you think the suggestion that we abandon South Korea is going to be seriously considered?" His answer was: "I am afraid it is going to be seriously considered because I'm afraid it's going to happen, whether we want it to or not. I'm for Korea. We're trying to help her—we're appropriating money now to help her. But South Korea is cut right across by this line—north of it are the communists, with access to the mainland—and Russia is over there on the mainland. So that whenever she takes a notion she can just overrun Korea just like she probably will overrun Formosa when she gets ready to do it. I hope not, of course." Following this response, Connally was asked, "But isn't Korea an essential part of the defense strategy?" His answer was equally blunt: "No. Of course, any position like that is of some strategic importance. But I don't think it is very greatly important. It has been testified before us that Japan, Okinawa and the Philippines make the chain of defense which is absolutely necessary. And, of course, any more territory along in that area would be that much more, but it is not absolutely essential."[6]

Since he was the most powerful member of the Senate in the realm of foreign policy, Connally's remarks greatly alarmed South Koreans. In a conversation with the U.S. Chargé in Seoul, President Syngman Rhee characterized the senator's remarks as "an open invitation to the communists to come and take over South Korea."[7] The secretary of state, the president, and other spokesmen for the administration tried to undo Connally's remarks by affirming America's support for the independence of Korea and noting America's programs of economic and military assistance. However, no one contradicted Connally's statement that the United States would not resist an invasion of the country.

Despite those clear statements of policy, President Truman did not take long in changing his mind about the tiny country's importance. When Acheson confirmed that a full-scale invasion was in progress on the following day, the president responded with an alacrity that verified his reputation for decisiveness: "Dean," he said, "We've got to stop the sons of bitches no matter what." Years later, when a television executive approached the former president about making an hour-long documentary on the decision to resist, the president was taken aback. The decision had taken about ten seconds, Truman told the executive and then asked how in the world a ten-second decision could be turned into an hour-long documentary.[8]

Clearly, Truman's decision to resist was not based on the strategic importance of Korea—that question had been decided, and the answer to it belied a flaw in the thinking of American decision makers. America's military strategists had neither contemplated nor planned for anything other than world war or global peace. According to a former commander in chief of UN forces in Korea, General Matthew Ridgway: "By 1949, we were completely committed to the theory that the next war involving the United States would be a global war, in which Korea would be of relatively minor importance and, in any event, indefensible. All our planning, all our official statements, all our military decisions derived essentially from this belief. The concept of 'limited war' never entered our councils."[9]

The nation's military strategists could offer the president only two choices when the North Korean forces stormed across the thirty-eighth parallel—initiate World War III or surrender the area and wait for the communists to initiate a global war by attacking some vital American interest such as Western Europe or Japan.

Truman quickly grasped the nature of his problem. To launch global war would be a disproportionate response. On the other hand, failure to respond might lead to more Koreas and increase the fears of West Europeans sitting right next to the huge Soviet colossus in Eastern Europe. Inaction, it seemed to Truman, would merely send the wrong signals to everyone while encouraging more Koreas or other risk-taking behavior by the Soviet bloc. Truman clearly explained his perception of the problem in the second volume of his memoirs:

> In my generation, this was not the first occasion when the strong had attacked the weak. I recalled earlier instances: Manchuria, Ethiopia, Austria. I remembered how each time the democracies failed to act it had encouraged the aggressors to keep going ahead. Communism was acting in Korea just as Hitler, Mussolini, and the Japanese had acted then, fifteen, and twenty years earlier. I felt certain that if South Korea was allowed to fall Communist leaders would be emboldened to override nations closer to our shores. If the Communists were permitted to force their way into the Republic of Korea without opposition from the free world, no small nation would have the courage to resist threats and aggression by stronger Communist neighbors. If [the North Korean attack on South Korea] were allowed to go unchallenged it would mean a Third World war, just as similar incidents had brought on the second world war.[10]

As Truman saw it, the issue was not Korea's *strategic value* but its *deterrent value*—the value of resisting to convince the Soviets that the status quo could not be nibbled away freely and to reassure America's allies in Europe and Asia that they could rely on America's resolve and support. Kim Il Sung's invasion of Korea caused a turning point in American strategic thinking.

Having decided that Korea was worth fighting for, decision makers still had to determine whether the United States had the capabilities to stop the onslaught and roll the North Koreans back across the thirty-eighth parallel. Such questions are decided by the state of one's forces and the situations within which they might be employed:

- Could they gain access?
- Did the nation possess enough of the right weapons in the right quantities?
- What would the fate of these forces be if the invader's allies joined in the conflict? Was there an exit strategy in case calculations proved mistaken?
- Would a military response draw resources away from other important areas and make them more vulnerable?

These questions were addressed on the president's return to Washington, and the answers he received were pervaded with uncertainties. How well the Koreans could do on their own was uncertain because no one knew how well-armed the enemy was, although all the evidence indicated that the situation was extremely serious if not grave. On the other hand, if the South Koreans could not defeat the North Koreans on their own, it was uncertain whether America had enough forces in readiness to make a difference. For the immediate future, American assistance would be limited to its planes and ships in the Far East and four understrength divisions that were occupying Japan.

The difficulty of addressing these questions was further compounded by the Pentagon's lack of any plans for fighting a limited war in Korea—or anywhere else for that matter. After hearing a detailed "situation report" from Secretary of State Acheson at the first meeting on his return to Washington, President Truman asked Secretary of Defense Johnson to present his department's views. Mr. Johnson curtly responded that the department had no recommendations to make because the department had no war plans for Korea! Nor did the Joint Chiefs of Staff have anything to recommend for the same reason. In the end, members of the chiefs spoke in their individual capacities, which Secretary Johnson, himself, described as "the individual, unrehearsed, unprepared, and uncoordinated statements of the several Chiefs and [Service] Secretaries. . . . "[11]

However, the chiefs were very clear about the difficulties an American response would encounter—the unsuitable terrain of the Korean peninsula as a field of battle, the difficulties in operating a five-thousand-mile supply line, the possibility that fighting in

Korea might draw down forces needed to maintain other military responsibilities, and the lack of adequate combat-ready forces. At the second meeting of the president's advisers, Generals Bradley and Collins doubted that air and sea power could turn the tide. In their opinion, only the commitment of ground troops would stop the advancing North Koreans and that would require a general mobilization. Then came more doubts: Even if the president decided to use American ground forces, the chiefs were uncertain whether they could arrive before the South Korean troops were defeated, and even if the troops that General MacArthur had available in Japan did arrive before the South Koreans were defeated, they might not be enough to forestall a North Korean victory.

Despite the president's desire "to hit those fellows hard," it was not clear whether the nation had the forces to do so. The decision to respond militarily in Korea was made under conditions of great uncertainty. As Secretary of Defense Johnson later noted, "Neither I nor any member of the Military Establishment in my presence recommended that we go into Korea. . . . The recommendation," he said, "came from the Secretary of State, but I want to repeat that it was not opposed by the Defense Department all the members of which severally pointed out the trouble, trials, tribulations, and the difficulties."[12]

Although fully aware of the military difficulties and risks that lie ahead, the president and his advisers were all agreed that inaction would be intolerable. As General Bradley would later write, "If the defense of South Korea was risking an all out war the choice was not ours, for the Communists had thrown down the gauntlet."[13] In the end, America went to war not to secure a strategic piece of real estate but to establish its credibility and enhance its ability to deter. According to Secretary of State Dean Acheson,

[The attack] was an open, undisguised challenge to our internationally accepted position as the protector of South Korea, an area of great importance to the security of American occupied Japan. To back away from this challenge, in view of our capacity for meeting it, would be highly destructive of the power and prestige of the United States. By prestige I mean the shadow cast by power, which is of great deterrent importance. Therefore, we could not accept the conquest of this important area by a Soviet puppet under the very guns of our defensive perimeter with no more resistance than words and gestures in the Security Council. It looked as though we must steel ourselves for the use of force. That did not mean in words later used by General Mark Clark, that we must be prepared "to shoot the works for victory," but rather to see that the attack failed.[14]

Thus, the United States embarked on its first limited war, a war in which neither victory nor global peace but the defeat of aggression was the goal. To make that decision clear to the members of the military establishment, one Pentagon official barked the following order to one of his generals: "Your job is to throw the North Koreans out of South Korea."[15] In less than three days, the United States had found an alternative to a military strategy that consisted of global war or doing nothing.

Limited War: The Alternative to Global War or Doing Nothing

From the North Korean invasion and the three years of warfare that followed it, a number of lessons can be drawn. First of all, any diplomatic strategy that relies on either all-out war or paper diplomacy will proceed predictably through a progression of repeated retreats followed by a major war on unenviable terms. Such was the fate of Neville Chamberlain and FDR in the interwar period. On the other hand, a diplomacy based on repeated limited wars will be politically disastrous to leaders who undertake them. President Truman left the White House in disgrace because of "Truman's war," and his successor, former General Dwight David Eisenhower, rode into the White House on the slogan of "No More Koreas." As one of his biographers put it, Truman's decision to fight in Korea "wholly rearranged the priorities of his administration, consigned the Fair Deal to limbo, left his presidency in tatters, and did grave damage to his morale."[16] Lyndon Johnson suffered a similar fate because of both his decision to Americanize the major responsibilities for fighting in Vietnam and his failure to prevail there.

Fighting a limited war may be necessary at times, but limited wars are difficult for democratic publics to accept precisely because they are limited. Fighting forces are frequently hemmed in with limits about what and where they can hit and with what weapons and when. When casualties arise, people will complain about "fighting with our hands tied behind our backs" and call on governments to either win or get out. In addition, many citizens will ask how fighting limited wars in far-off places like Korea, Vietnam, or Kuwait can have any direct relation to the nation's security at all.

Yet, the only alternatives to limited war in the nuclear age are retreat or mutual nuclear devastation. As General Matthew Ridgway put it in the concluding chapter of his book, *The Korean War:*

> A limited war is not merely a small war that has not yet grown to full size. It is a war in which the objectives are specifically limited in the light of our national interest and our current capability. A war that is "open-ended"—that has no clearly delineated geographical, political, and military goals beyond "victory"—is a war that may escalate indefinitely, as wars will, with one success requiring another to insure the first. An insistence on going all-out to win a war may have a fine masculine ring, and a call to "defend freedom" may have a messianic sound that stirs our

blood. But the ending of an all-out war in these times is beyond imagining. It may mean the turning back of civilization by several thousand years, with no one left capable of signaling the victory.[17]

The North Korean Strategy: A Military Fait Accompli

While America never wanted to fight in Korea, neither did Kim Il Sung. If there is anything that Kim did not want, it was a long drawn out war with a great number of casualties. Had Kim known that he was about to embark on three long and bloody years of inconclusive warfare, he probably never would have launched his invasion in the first place. Kim opted for war because he thought he could pull off a fait accompli—a quick strike that would be all over before anyone could do anything about it.

According to a retired North Korean general, Kim and his colleagues were convinced that, "the American people would never participate in the war. . . . We are absolutely sure of this," Kim was reported to have said, and the logic behind this conviction was simple:

- The United States had not participated in the guerrilla war in China and was willing to suffer a loss of "the giant." If America would not go to war for high stakes in China, Kim reasoned, it would certainly not participate in a small war on the Korean peninsula.
- General MacArthur and Secretary of State Acheson both explicitly excluded South Korea from the American defense perimeter.
- Finally, given the favorable military balance and his belief that widespread support for the North Korean regime existed in South Korea, Kim was certain that the war would be over before the Americans could get in.[18]

When Stalin heard these arguments in a secret meeting in March 1950, his response was equally simple: "the Americans will never agree to be thrown out of [Korea and] lose their reputation as a great power."

Several weeks later, Kim raised the question again with Stalin and stressed the military balance that lay in his favor. The North Korean forces would engage in such a massive surprise attack that the war would be over in three days and a planned uprising of more than two hundred thousand guerrillas would quickly provide personnel to rule the newly conquered territory. Even if the United States did decide to fight, Kim assured the skeptical Stalin, the war would be over before the Americans could get there. While finally agreeing to an invasion, the skeptical Stalin warned Kim, "If you get kicked in the teeth, I shall not lift a finger. . . . You have to ask Mao for all of the help."

While many in the West believed that Stalin ordered the North Korean invasion, the reality was much more complex. Clearly, the Soviet leader did not want a war with the United States, and he was doubtful that the United States, as a Great Power, would tolerate being defeated by a small country so quickly after its retreat in China. *Ironic as it may be, Stalin had a better understanding of America's situation and its probable response than both Kim Il Sung or America's own decision makers!*

Rather than initiating the Korean War, Stalin's role was one of acquiescing in the decision to invade, although Soviet generals did much of the military planning and the North Koreans were well equipped and supplied by the Soviets throughout the war. Had Stalin tried to prevent or veto Kim's invasion, he might have been seen as weak within the communist camp. As a former North Korean official explained, after Kim's "persistent assertions and requests, [Stalin] could not find any excuse for refusal." A quick victory for Kim would redound to the prestige of the Soviet camp and make Americans look like an unreliable and fearful ally. If the Koreans did get themselves into a war with the Americans, American lives and resources would be depleted in a marginal theater. If America became involved in a war with China, the already hostile relations between the two nations would probably be poisoned for decades, and with America as an enemy, Mao would be more dependent on the Soviet Union and, thereby, more "controllable."

In sum, the Korean War was largely a war of miscalculation, and to a great extent, the Truman administration was responsible for Kim's miscalculation. America's words and actions gave Kim every reason to believe that he could finish off his operation without any interference from the United States. Nor could one place much blame on Stalin. Given the withdrawal of American forces and the statements of MacArthur and Acheson, what arguments could Stalin have made against an invasion? Clearly, the North Korean's firm belief that he could pull off a fait accompli was in no way unreasonable, given the situation.

Fait accompli efforts are undertaken by both revisionist and status quo powers to create new situations and forestall action by allies of the target state. Such quick strikes are especially tempting because when they succeed, they are usually not contested. When German troops occupied the Rhineland in 1936, Hitler created a new situation that Britain and France could either accept or resort to force to undo. They chose to give peace a chance. In 1948, the Soviets engineered a communist coup in Czechoslovakia that presented the West with another satellite in Eastern Europe and few alternatives to do anything about it. In 1983, Ronald Reagan invaded Grenada and eradicated a Soviet and Cuban ally. On the other hand, George Bush's resort to military force to undo Saddam Hussein's lightning conquest of Kuwait is rare in the annals of diplomacy. The problem with fait accompli strategies is that when they fail, countries get stuck, as Kim found out in Korea and the Soviets found out after they invaded Afghanistan.

Deterrence: A Military Strategy for Status Quo Powers Seeking to Avoid the Choice between Surrender or War

If we desire to avoid insult, we must be ready to repel it; if we desire to secure peace, . . . it must be known that we are at all times ready for war.
—President George Washington

Whatever enables us to go to war, secures our peace.
—Thomas Jefferson

We shall more certainly preserve peace when it is well understood that we are prepared for war.
—Andrew Jackson[19]

For status quo powers seeking to avoid war, deterrence is the time-worn strategy. The logic underlying this strategy is well expressed by the three early presidents in the epigrams just presented. The goal is to get a potential revisionist to contain himself through the realization that any effort to revise the status quo by force would either fail or be too costly even if it succeeded.

From the Korean case, we learned how not to deter:

- You announce that you will not fight for a given piece of territory that an adversary or his ally might like to attain.
- You withdraw forces of your own that could help the threatened country to defend its territory.
- You inadequately arm the defensive forces of the target country.

While the preceding actions may not necessarily lead to an invasion, one thing is certain: the fate of that territory will remain at the discretion of the revisionist power.

The basic principles of deterrence are extremely simple:

1. The power seeking to deter must lay down a marker.
2. It must enhance the credibility of that marker by arming the potential victim's forces well enough to make any direct or indirect invasion extremely costly to the revisionist power.
3. If the ally is extremely valuable, the status quo power should put its own troops in harm's way of any potential invading forces. This step is especially important because those forces serve as hostages—if they are harmed by attacking forces, the leaders of the power seeking to deter will have little choice but to fight the revisionist's armed forces.
4. The power seeking to deter must get the potential revisionist invader to realize that if it resorts to war, the defenders will

resist and impose great costs even if the invasion succeeds. To the extent that any of these first four conditions is lacking, the status quo power will have a credibility problem, and deterrence may fail.

5. The power seeking to deter and the defending power should go out of their way to ensure that military forces are so configured and so emplaced as to make their defensive intent clear. Military professionals can usually tell the difference between troops dug in and emplaced for defensive purposes and those that are configured to engage in a first strike. By defensively positioning deterrent forces, the potential invader will be reassured that as long as it stays on its side of the line, it need have no fear of war.

Deterrence usually works for a very simple reason: Revisionist states, like all states, have geopolitical or core national interests that, once satisfied, decrease the utility of further gains and, thereby, discount the price that revisionists would be willing to pay for them. While a communist South Korea might be of high value to Kim Il Sung, it had no relation to the Soviet Union's geopolitical security at all. As Stalin told Kim after listening to his arguments, "the Korean friends should not expect great assistance and support from the Soviet Union, because it had more important challenges to meet than the Korean problem."

Deterrence works by raising the potential costs that a revisionist power would incur by seeking to expand. *The less important the gain to the expansionist power, the less the risk and costs it is likely to incur.* In the Korean case, Stalin repeatedly made it clear to Kim that "if the United States participated in the war, the Soviet Union had no intention of joining the fray."[20] While a communist South Korea might be desirable, it was under no circumstances worth a war with the United States.

When the Korean armistice was signed in July 1953, the South Korean ambassador to the United States wondered, "How we could survive with a million Chinese in North Korea?" The answer was obvious. The Chinese had been warned that if they opened the war again, the United States would bomb targets in Manchuria and most probably use tactical atomic weapons. The South Korean army had been greatly strengthened and American forces would remain. In combination, these forces had been able to halt Chinese offensives without attacking supply targets in Manchuria or using tactical atomic weapons. While the Chinese would have undoubtedly fought ferociously to defend their own territory, it was unlikely that they would have paid the price America threatened to "take" South Korea and then turn it over to their North Korean ally.

"Price signals" work in international politics as they do in free markets. The Chinese entered the Korean War only because American troops were marching up to the Yalu River, which marked the border between

China and North Korea. To prevent the creation of an American satellite along their very border, the Chinese would enter the war, and they so warned the United Nations.

The divergence of interests and the role of potential costs in the behavior of revisionist states are also revealed in the case of Taiwan, which had also been excluded from the American defense perimeter. After MacArthur and Acheson implied that they would not fight for Taiwan, Mao began making plans for an invasion of the island. Once President Truman sent the Seventh Fleet into the Formosa Strait after the invasion of South Korea, Stalin noted the signal. According to Sergei Goncharov and his colleagues, "[The Soviet dictator] stated quite bluntly that he would never risk a conflict with the United States over Taiwan and pressed the Chinese to put off their 'planned' invasion."[21]

Although *the theory* of deterrence is relatively simple, *the reality* that decision makers must deal with is not. All states have limited resources, and every piece of real estate is not of equal strategic value. Nor are all states equally defensible. Therefore, creating a deterrence strategy requires answers to three questions:

1. Which areas are vital and which are not (an extremely difficult question to answer in the abstract)?
2. What kinds of military forces would make a policy of deterrence credible, at what places, and at what prices?
3. To what extent can the threatened power impose significant costs on the invader if deterrence fails and under what conditions?

For any status quo power, or any Great Power for that matter, the world is not divided into vital areas and nonvital areas. The issue is always more or less, rather than either/or. Thus, there is a gradient of how much one is willing to spend to secure different areas. Deterrence of vital areas is seldom much of a problem because the stakes involved in the loss of such areas is obvious. For example, while the Soviets could never be absolutely certain that the United States would go to war if they invaded Western Europe during the Cold War, the consequences would have been so high if they were wrong that they would probably never have tried to invade in the first place. On the other hand, some vital areas are relatively secure because it would be difficult for a revisionist power to get to them. Japan's position during the Cold War was relatively secure because of its island position. Conventional Soviet or Chinese forces just could not get to Japan even if they wanted to, and raining bombs, conventional or nuclear, on Japan would merely have provoked retaliatory bombings or worse.

The difficult question is how to deter in areas that are of moderate interest and where there are obvious limits to the treasure and casualties that the nation seeking to deter would realistically spend to secure them. As Henry Kissinger noted many years ago, Soviet and Chinese aggressive moves were always in areas where American interests, commitments, and resources were small or insignificant, such as Korea and Vietnam.[22] *For deterrence in such areas, the most crucial factor is not the credibility or military resources of the Great Power, but the willingness and ability of the small power to resist and impose high costs on the potential invader.* A small power standing alone can frequently deter a major revisionist power if it is able and willing to impose significant costs on the potential attacker.

Consider the following extreme, but still instructive, case. During World War II, Hitler ordered his general staff to prepare plans for an invasion of Switzerland to carve out a corridor that would allow secure access between Germany and Italy. After studying the matter, his generals concluded that while an invasion and occupation would be successful, its costs would be extremely high—costs that would be imposed by a well dug in Swiss force of roughly four hundred thousand men.

Without firing a shot, the Swiss army succeeded in its most important mission, which was not to defend Swiss territory but to deter an invasion of Switzerland. As foreign policy analyst Louis Halle put it, "The Swiss Army . . . had accomplished its prime mission, which was not the active defense of national territory but the *deterrence* of any occasion to practice such defense."[23] *The success of the Swiss Army, according to Halle, lay in the very fact that it did not have to fight at all.*

To cite another example, Yugoslavia looked like an easy prey for invading Soviet forces when Stalin expelled it from the bloc in June 1948. Had Soviet forces crossed into Yugoslavia through Hungary and Bulgaria, they would not have feared confronting American or European troops. The West did nothing when Czechoslovakia was overthrown in February, and Yugoslavia's leaders viewed capitalist Britain and America as no less enemies that the Soviets.

Yugoslavia's situation looked so hopeless that Stalin was certain that he would not even have to resort to force. He would shake his little finger and Tito would fall, he reputedly said.[24] But not so: Shaking his finger did not lead to Tito's fall and neither did vitriolic denunciations, economic boycotts, subversion, attempted assassination, border incidents, and threats of military force.

When it was clear that only a full-scale invasion would dislodge the Tito regime, Stalin balked. The Yugoslavs had a well-deserved reputation as fearless partisans against Hitler. If Stalin invaded, he risked getting bogged down in a fierce guerrilla war against a well-armed and united Yugoslavian people who would be fighting not for communism but for their independence as a nation. In the end, Stalin wisely stayed his hand. As the Harvard historian, Adam Ulam noted about this successful case of deterrence: "The Communist chieftain of a primitive Balkan country with a population of 16 million said 'no' to Stalin, chased out Soviet minions, imprisoned Soviet partisans, and dared the Soviet bloc to do its worst."[25]

Coercive Diplomacy: Getting What You Want without War

But what about those cases where deterrence fails but neither limited war nor giving in seems satisfactory? What about those "in-between" cases in which revisionist states engage in actions that may not warrant war, but still cannot be tolerated or allowed to go unnoticed or unpunished? When such instances arise, decision makers feel an almost irrepressible temptation to threaten the use of military force or to employ limited, and frequently exemplary, uses of military force to warn, threaten, intimidate, punish, or to compel another power from doing what the initiating nation wants.

Scholars have studied such in-between cases under the rubric of "coercive diplomacy"—uses of military force and threats of force to persuade another country to stop doing something it is doing or to undo something that it has already done. The stocks in trade of coercive diplomacy are both "sticks" and "carrots." The array of sticks consists of veiled warnings, shows of the flag, ultimatums, threats of force, demonstrative uses of force, and threats of further escalation. To make it easier for the objects of the coercive diplomacy to yield, leaders of coercing states frequently dangle inducements or "carrots" alongside the threats and uses of force.

Perhaps the most famous (or infamous) use of coercive diplomacy was the dropping of atomic bombs on Hiroshima and Nagasaki. Certainly the bombs were not necessary to win the war, for victory was merely a matter of time. The bombs were dropped mainly to scare the Japanese into surrendering as quickly as possible to save hundreds of thousands, if not millions, of lives that would have been lost in an invasion of the home islands. The original strategy entailed only sticks: the Japanese were to surrender unconditionally or face the prospect of more atomic bombing. However, after two bombs, the Japanese would still not surrender unless they were allowed to keep their emperor, which, in the end, we agreed to allow. Had Truman given the Japanese an ultimatum that included the promissory carrot—that they could keep their emperor if they surrendered immediately—the first bomb might never have fallen.

A CLASSIC SUCCESS OF COERCIVE DIPLOMACY. At the outset of the Cuban missile crisis, President Kennedy's advisers explored a traditional military strategy of "bomb now and talk later"—take out the missiles militarily and provide the Russians with a fait accompli. When the air force acknowledged that a surgical strike might not destroy all of the missiles and that any air strike would probably incur civilian and Russian casualties, the strategy was placed in the holding file. Also sobering was the frank admission by the Joint Chiefs of Staff that only a full-scale invasion would really ensure that the missile installations were demolished.

Given the probable costs and risks of traditional military options, the members of the president's advisory committee, the ExComm (for Executive Committee), explored the option of a blockade. A blockade would show resolve, prevent the entry of more missiles and supplies, and give Soviet premier Khrushchev time to reconsider his action. If the Soviet premier did not agree to take the missiles out voluntarily, the military option could still be employed. However, the weakness of a blockade was obvious: It could not remove the missiles already there.

The major determinants of success in any effort to employ some form of coercive diplomacy are three:

1. the relative importance of the issue to the parties in conflict, the so-called balance of interests or balance of saliencies;
2. the extent to which the coercer has usable military forces;
3. the domestic and international support that each of the parties enjoys.

The more of these factors the coercer has in his favor, the more likely he is to succeed.

In terms of the balance of interests, the United States had powerful motivations to get the missiles out. If allowed to go unchecked, the Soviet actions would have made a mockery of the Monroe Doctrine, but more importantly, the missiles in Cuba would have checkmated America's nuclear advantage. On the other hand, although the Soviets had a significant interest in seeing the Castro regime survive as a communist outpost in the Western Hemisphere, securing Havana was not worth a military confrontation with the United States, especially one that might escalate into nuclear war.

In terms of usable military forces, the United States had commanding conventional superiority in the Caribbean, and it was precisely this military imbalance that affected the balance of interests. If the United States invaded Cuba with conventional forces, the Soviets had no military means of saving the Castro regime. Their only military alternatives were to fire the nuclear missiles that were operational in Cuba or to move against an area of Western vulnerability elsewhere, as in West Berlin. But neither of those acts would have done anything for Cuba. If "push came to shove," the Soviets would have to stand aside at some incalculable cost to their prestige or retaliate in ways that would only have risked a further emotional and potentially uncontrollable confrontation with the United States, which, in the end, would have done nothing for Cuba.

In terms of support, public opinion at home and abroad was solidly behind President Kennedy. Khrushchev had emplaced the missiles in stealth, and his diplomats had lied repeatedly when queried about the issue.

Despite these clear advantages, President Kennedy was still very concerned about moving Premier Khrushchev into a corner and causing him a great loss of face. To make retreat easier for the Soviet leader, he agreed to make a pledge vowing not to invade Cuba, and he promised privately to remove American missiles in Turkey after a discreet interval. By offering these "carrots," Kennedy provided the Soviet premier with an opportunity to withdraw gracefully, claiming that the threat of the missiles had persuaded the United States to agree to respect the freedom and independence of Castro's regime.

A CLASSIC FAILURE. Lyndon Johnson's use of a bombing campaign to persuade North Vietnam to stop supporting communist insurgents in the South illustrates well what can happen when factors making for success run against a would-be coercer.

The president would not even consider what might have worked—a massive and crushing attack against North Vietnam's major industrial, military, and oil facilities as proposed by the Joint Chiefs of Staff. Damage on such a scale, the president feared, might provoke the Chinese into entering the war as they did in Korea and lead to an even bigger problem than he had with the Vietcong and the North Vietnamese. Massive bombing raids also would entail massive civilian casualties, which would lead to even greater international and domestic opposition to American policies in Vietnam.

Fearing a wider war with China and further disapproval of his policies at home, the president decided to bomb below the seventeenth parallel, where there were few targets of value and none that had much military significance. The underlying logic was simple: If the North Vietnamese saw that America was willing to bomb in areas of little value, they would "get the message" that the next bombing might cause real damage.

As National Security Adviser Walt Whitman Rostow put it, "Ho has an industrial complex to protect: he is no longer a guerrilla fighter with nothing to lose." Similarly, Secretary of Defense McNamara asserted that getting the North Vietnamese to turn off the war, "[would depend] not upon the *current* level of bombing but rather upon the credible threat of future destruction which can be avoided by agreeing to negotiate or agreeing to some settlement in negotiations."[26]

Given the unfavorable military situation in South Vietnam, it would have taken a great deal to persuade the North Vietnamese to stop their support. Obviously, the bombing campaign had little impact militarily because it was not supposed to in the first place. But politically, the North Vietnamese actually benefited from the bombing. By posing as helpless victims, the North Vietnamese were able to gain support for their plight within the United States and weaken support for the president's policies at home. As the president bombed, protesters all across America began their chant, "LBJ, LBJ, how many kids did you kill today?"

By hitting targets of minimal military significance, the president signaled weakness rather than strength or restraint. As Professor Robert Osgood noted in an early autopsy on the war, "To Hanoi, U.S. [military] self-restraint confirmed the favorable balance of interests, which eventually would induce the United States to withdraw when the costs of war became disproportionate to U.S. interests."[27] Even the president's carrots—his offer of billions of dollars in reconstruction aid if North Vietnam stopped its support for the war—appeared more as a sign of weakness than of magnanimity and generosity.

In the end, rather than coercing the North Vietnamese, the president had deterred himself from taking decisive military action because of his desire to avoid civilian casualties and his fears of a land war with communist China. Consequently, President Johnson got mired into a limited and, seemingly, unwinnable war of attrition. His only hope was that if America stayed and fought long enough, the North Vietnamese would slowly wind down the war and give up in frustration.

Any such hope was easily belied by the asymmetry of interests in the war. The North Vietnamese and their allies in the South were fighting for what they saw as their national liberation, and they were amply supplied and replenished by their Communist bloc allies. On the other hand, most of the American public could not believe that the maintenance of a noncommunist Vietnam was worth the open-ended expenditure of lives and treasure that the president appeared willing to undertake. In the end, it was the United States that wound down its military efforts and gave up in frustration, an outcome confidently expected by North Vietnamese leader Ho Chi Minh who once quipped that "You will kill ten of our men and we will kill one of yours and in the end, it will be you who will tire of it."[28]

Unlike the Cuban missile crisis, none of the factors mentioned above favored the United States in its conflict with the North Vietnamese. Although the president was committed to maintaining a noncommunist South Vietnam, he was not so committed that he would risk a land war with China to secure that interest. To minimize that risk, he would neither invade North Vietnam nor bomb in ways that might provoke Chinese intervention.

Finally, unlike Korea and the Cuban missile crisis, there was no support for the bombing campaign in the United Nations or even among the NATO allies The secretary-general of the United Nations frequently criticized American policy in Vietnam, as did many foreign leaders. Within the United States, opposition to the war grew as the casualties increased. Colleges and universities became centers of the strongest antiwar movement since the Mexican War, while many, if not most, ordinary citizens felt that if we were going to fight a war, we should either fight to win or bring the boys home.

Given the ineffectiveness of their South Vietnamese allies, the Kennedy and Johnson administrations repeatedly faced the unenviable choice of either giving up and withdrawing from Vietnam or increasing American involvement and assuming greater responsibility for the direction of the war. Getting out of Vietnam was not an option for President Johnson, who vowed he would not be the first American president to lose a war. He also feared suffering the same fate of Harry Truman, who "lost" China to the communists in 1949.

Unwilling to leave, unwilling to take the war to North Vietnam, and unable to gain through negotiations what he could not win on the field of battle, President Johnson sent more than half a million men to Vietnam who became mired in a conventional war of attrition on the Asian landmass. Although the Vietcong and North Vietnamese forces could never have defeated the American and South Vietnamese forces, victory for the United States and its ally always seemed a long way off.

During his conduct of the Vietnam War, Lyndon Johnson sought to avoid three things: the "loss" of another "China"; a Korean-type limited war of attrition on the Asian mainland; and a division of the American people. The president did prevent the loss of another China, at least temporarily, but he did so only by Americanizing South Vietnam's war. This temporary success was purchased at the price he most wanted to avoid—a massive and inconclusive war of attrition on the Asian mainland. What he did avoid was a division of the American people, but not in the way he wanted. Instead of dividing over the war, the American public united against the war. The doves opposed the war because they thought it was immoral or unrelated to American security. The hawks opposed the war precisely because it was a no-win war of attrition.

The Perennial Conflict over Decisive and Limited Uses of Force

Although many military professionals are extremely skeptical about fighting limited wars, most are even more uncomfortable with coercive diplomacy. Whenever diplomats propose limited or symbolic uses of force, military professionals almost always demur. What is the military objective of the proposed action, they ask? What if the exemplary use of force doesn't work? What does one do next? At what point does one stop? How does one disengage?

Most critics of limited war and coercive diplomacy adhere to the "decisive use of force" school of thought. In their opinion, military force should be employed only if one is willing to defeat the enemy decisively through the application of massive and crushing fire-power in ways that will minimize casualties and win quickly. "When you get into war," President Eisenhower once remarked, "you should win as quick as you can, because your losses become a function of the duration of the war. . . . Get everything you need and win it," he advised. Even more vivid is the remark of Britain's first sea lord in World War I, Admiral Lord Fisher, who once quipped that "Moderation in war is imbecility." But perhaps the most memorable and simple expression of this view was General Douglas MacArthur's ringing statement made at the height of the Korean War: "There is no substitute for victory." In sum, get in to win, or don't get in at all.

The idea of fighting a war merely to hold a line, or to prevent victory by the other side, or to negotiate a peace settlement based on the status quo before the fighting begins as in Korea and Vietnam is unconscionable to the members of this school. The employment of pinprick bombings and symbolic displays of force to send a message is even more of an anathema to this way of thinking. So, too, are open-ended and escalating uses of graduated force that do not have clearly marked missions and exit strategies. Supporters of the decisive use of force doctrine point to Kuwait and Grenada as examples of how military force should be used.

While the logic of the decisive force theory may sound compelling, the realities that decision makers deal with, all too frequently, do not lead themselves to such simple "do nothing" or "go for broke" alternatives. Critics of the "decisive use of force" school point out that militarily speaking, both Kuwait and Grenada were not typical of the kinds of challenges facing diplomats. Both were isolated targets that could count on no allies to come to their aid. Iraq's forces, supply lines, and economic assets were all sitting ducks for softening by American air power, and Grenada was virtually without an army.

If a nation will use force only when the conditions of a Kuwait or a Grenada exist, critics argue, it will probably seldom use force. According to critics, exponents of the decisive use of force ignore some of the most important principles of the great military strategist Clausewitz: "War is the pursuit of politics by other means," and "The value of the [political objective in war] must determine the sacrifices to be made in pursuit of it *in magnitude* and in duration." According to Clausewitz, "Once that expenditure of effort exceeds the value of the political objective, the object must be renounced," advice that is easier to give than to follow.[29]

Experience supports the critics rather than the supporters of the decisive use of force doctrine. Presidents are extremely reluctant to use force massively when confronted with limited challenges to American interests. Even advocates of the decisive use of force theory have found it necessary to resort to less than decisive uses of force when they have been in office. General Eisenhower, for example, both contemplated and used force in moderation while he was president. When the French were failing in Vietnam, he was willing to employ limited air strikes to relieve the besieged garrisons at Dien Bien Phu until congressional leaders vetoed the idea. In 1958, he sent a small force of U.S. Marines into Lebanon with an unclear mission or exit strategy.

To cite another example, Ronald Reagan said he would never send American boys to die unless he expected them to win. Yet, when he sent American marines into Lebanon in 1982, he had no intention of victory or winning. Similarly, his ordering of U.S. fighter planes to impose pain on Muammar Qaddafi for the Libyan leader's support of a terrorist attack against American soldiers in a West Berlin disco was a perfect example of an effort at coercive diplomacy. In both of these cases, Reagan's military objective was not clear at all. In fact, Senator Ernest Hollings's critical remarks about the Lebanon venture sound exactly like something candidate Reagan would have said in the 1980 presidential campaign: "If they've been put there to fight, there are far too few. If they're put in there to be killed, there are far too many."[30]

The unresolved issues of when and how to use military force have been debated since America embarked on an internationalist foreign policy at the end of World War II. During the Korean War, these issues were clearly articulated in the Truman-MacArthur hearings. During the Eisenhower administration, the debate took place over that administration's strategy of massive retaliation. During the Reagan administration, internal debates went public in a series of speeches and statements by Secretary of State George Shultz and Secretary of Defense Caspar Weinberger. During the Clinton administration, counsels were similarly divided. When members of the military questioned proposals for punitive air strikes in Bosnia, Madeleine Albright sarcastically asked, "What's the point of having this superb military you're always talking about if we can't use it?" To which General Colin Powell immediately shot back: "American GIs are not toy soldiers to be moved around on some sort of global game board."[31]

These difficult questions exist precisely because coercive diplomacy is a political rather than a military strategy. Instead of having traditional military objectives, coercive diplomacy seeks to signal, to impress, to punish, to inflict pain, and to create fear rather than to impose one's will on an adversary. For almost any political leader, and certainly for leaders of democratic states, any alternatives to all-out war, limited war, and retreat are appealing.

CASE STUDY
Bombing for Peace and Bombing for Victory in Bosnia

During the Bosnian conflict, the Clinton administration sought to employ coercive diplomacy on three occasions. Taken separately and collectively, the president's efforts illustrate well both the limits of force and the extent to which the three factors mentioned earlier—relative salience of interests, usable military instruments, and domestic and international support—can confound the best intentioned efforts of even the world's most powerful superpower "to do good."

On taking office, the president and most of his advisers saw the Bosnian conflict as a simple case of Serbian aggression. Given this perception, the moral and legal implications were clear: Members of the United Nations were obligated to come to the aid of the victim. According to Secretary of State Warren Christopher, the destruction of Bosnia would violate the principle of the United Nations Charter "that internationally recognized borders should not be altered by force." Of the "ethnic cleansing," and the wanton rape and killing of innocent civilians, Secretary of State Christopher claimed that "Our conscience revolts at the idea of passively accepting such brutality." The president put it more bluntly: "We have an interest in standing up against ethnic cleansing."

Members of the administration also saw the credibility of the United Nations and the future of international order at stake. If the Serbs were allowed to succeed in Bosnia as they had in Croatia, they might begin ethnic cleansing in the Serbian province of Kosovo, where 90 percent of the population was Albanian, or move their troops into the former Yugoslavian republic of Macedonia, which might provoke a war with Turkey and Greece.[32] However, as members of the administration quickly found out, "doing something about Bosnia" was much more difficult than moralizing about it—thus, the following lengthy odyssey.

Stage 1. Bombing for Victory: Clinton's Abortive "Lift and Strike" Proposal (Winter–Spring 1993). Shortly after taking office, the president publicly alluded to using air strikes against Serbian positions and an end to the UN arms embargo against the Bosnian Muslims. As soon as he did, Slobodan Milosevic, the Serbian dictator and supporter of the Bosnian Serbs, began pulling in his reins and making conciliatory noises, especially in regard to the Vance-Owen Plan, which the Europeans were supporting as a way of resolving the conflict.

When nothing followed the president's comments, business "as usual" resumed in Bosnia, and when Serbian forces began savagely assaulting the Muslim town of Srebrenica in mid-March 1993, the necessity for action seemed pressing. However, the more the president and his advisers deliberated, the more they realized that, despite their desire to "do good," their options were severely constrained:

- Doing nothing, the president believed, would be unconscionable.
- Defining the situation as "a European problem" would amount to adopting the position of former President Bush, which Clinton had excoriated during the election campaign.

- Falling behind the recently negotiated Vance-Owen agreement smacked of a Balkan Munich, which recognized the fruits of Serbian aggression and ethnic cleansing.
- Sending in ground troops to defeat the Serbs would be politically unsustainable among the American people in the absence of any clear American security interest in the conflict.

Having rejected both diplomacy of the Vance-Owen variety and war on the ground, the president turned to bombing as a way of coercing the Serbs to settle the war peacefully and getting better terms for the Bosnians. Failing that, bombing would at least punish the Serbs, and it might help to even up the balance of military forces. On the other hand, while there were lucrative targets in Serbia—fuel dumps, military facilities, command and control centers, rail terminals and bridges—hitting such targets might cause considerable civilian damage. In addition, since the Bosnian Serbs were not particularly dependent on Serbia for supplies, bombing in the Republic of Serbia would probably not have a decisive impact on the battlefield.

Hitting targets closer to the lines of engagement would be difficult because of Bosnia's mountainous terrain and frequent heavy cloud cover. Also, since much of the Serbian artillery was highly mobile, the Serbs might "shoot and scoot," to quote General Powell, and thereby elude retaliatory air strikes. Intelligence assessments also noted that the Serbs could put their howitzers and mortars next to schoolhouses or churches, threatening heavy civilian casualties. Since the striking planes would be vulnerable to surface-to-air-missiles, taking out those weapons would have to be part of any bombing strategy, and the Serbs could also place these systems next to civilian locations.

Finally, there was the question that every president must face when he contemplates limited uses of force to gain big political ends: What would he do if the bombing did not work—if it didn't stop the Serbian military forces or get them to the bargaining table? As the president's military advisers pointed out, limited air strikes had never been decisive in military engagements. At best, bombing might get the Serbs to accept an armistice based on where the troops were at the time—an armistice largely embodied in the Vance-Owen Plan. Such a settlement would amount to accepting the ethnic cleansing and Serbian possession of almost 70 percent of Bosnia, which administration officials considered morally unacceptable. On the other hand, air strikes and ending the embargo might raise the hopes of the Bosnians and encourage them to seek a military rather than a negotiated settlement. In that event, the Serbian army might cross into Bosnia and widen the war. Every alternative for dealing with the problem carried large minuses and few pluses.

Still, having boxed himself into a position of having to do something about Bosnia, the president decided on "lift and strike" after almost two months of agonizing meetings. Despite objections from the military and pessimistic intelligence reports, lift and strike would at least allow the United States to take the moral high ground without putting its military forces in harm's way. When Christopher unveiled the plan to the European allies, they were aghast, viewing the proposal as throwing gasoline on a fire. Lift and strike, they feared, would put their own peacekeeping forces already on the ground in Bosnia at risk and might lead to a wider war by provoking the entry of regular Serbian troops from Serbia. They also doubted that Croatia would allow military weapons and supplies to transit its territory, which was the only conduit for weapons to reach landlocked Bosnia. If the United States insisted on presenting a lift and strike proposal to the Security Council over their objections, the Allies noted that the Russians would surely veto the plan because of their opposition to any retaliation against the Serbs.

The president's first effort to employ military force in the cause of right and justice fizzled out—and, perhaps, happily so. None of the requisites for the success of coercive diplomacy lay in the president's favor. Since the United States had no tangible security interests in the conflict, the balance of saliencies lay with the Serbs whose capacity to fight and endure pain would, undoubtedly, prove greater than that of the American people. In any game of escalation, the United States would, most likely, be the first to stand still or back down. Second, the administration could muster no support for military action either at home or abroad. The American public might acquiesce in a few bombing missions, but they would never support use of ground troops in combat.

In three short months, the Clinton administration had traveled back to the passive policies of the Bush administration. In part, the administration's retreat also stemmed from its own changing perception of the situation in Bosnia. After reading Robert Kaplan's *Balkan Ghosts*, the president began talking about the conflict as a civil war among ethnic, religious, and communal factions rather than the kind of plate glass aggression that Harry Truman faced in Korea. Shortly after his return from Europe, Christopher characterized the Bosnian conflict not as a violation of the United Nations Charter but as "a problem from hell," a "morass" of ancient hatreds with "atrocities on all sides." "At heart," the secretary told a congressional committee, "this is a European problem."[33]

Stage 2. Pinpricks for Peace: Bombing to Deter Serbian Encroachments on UN Safe Havens (Summer 1993–Summer 1995). After the Allies rejected lift and strike, they fell behind a French proposal to create "safe havens" around six besieged Bosnian cities. Secured by UN Protection Forces (UNPROFOR), the havens would provide security and relief to the increasing number of Muslim refugees from both the war and the ethnic cleansing. The Serbs would be warned to pull their forces a safe distance from the havens and to cease immediately any armed attack against them. If they violated the zones, NATO forces would engage in retaliatory air strikes.

According to the French, establishing the safe havens provided an alternative to standing aside while the warring parties engaged in a genocidal war or employing the massive military force that would be required to defeat the Serbs and impose a settlement. Reluctantly, the United States acquiesced in the French proposal but with the caveat that no American troops would be placed on the ground as long as hostilities continued. As the President put it, "We don't want our people in there basically in a shooting gallery."[34]

Because the havens were located in Serb territory, they quickly became places of misery. Aid convoys were denied passage for months at a time in some areas. When they were allowed to transit, supplies were routinely commandeered and pilfered, and "charges" for road repairs were not common. As one observer put it, "The sight of UN Convoys being intimidated by a lone Serb gunman convey (sic) a sense of the impotence of the international community and increases the scorn with which many in the former Yugoslavia treat the UN."[35] Airports and roads were often closed because of shelling or sniper fire. Many of the havens were frequently without water, electricity, fuel, food, medical supplies, and even salt. In one of the havens, sixty-five thousand people received their food and other supplies by air drops alone. Sporadic shelling of the enclaves and sniping made life traumatic for everyone inside.

Within a matter of months, the Serbs presented their first real test of the safe haven plan by besieging Sarajevo. The siege was so withering and the isolation of the city so complete that many feared the haven would never last the winter for lack of food and fuel, even if the Serbs did not take the city militarily. Appalled at what he saw on television, President Clinton asked his advisers to review what could be done to relieve the city *including the use of ground troops*. The lowest number of ground troops that the president's military advisers would tolerate for the mission was twenty-five thousand, although their preference was for a much higher number of seventy-five thousand. The mission of these forces would be to keep the road and airways open for humanitarian convoys traveling to and from Sarajevo. But even twenty-five thou-

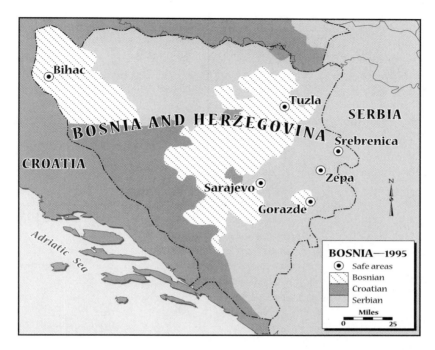

Map 3.2. UN "Safe Havens" in Bosnia

In the spring of 1994, the United Nations created six "safe havens" that were to provide security for Muslim refugees and victims of ethnic cleansing. Because the havens were located within Serb territory, supply convoys were frequently refused passage, were delayed, or their supplies were pilfered. For example, in 1994 Gorazde did without UN supplies for almost eight months. In addition, because the havens were supplied with an inadequate number of peacekeepers who were inadequately armed, the military balance lay with the Serbs, whose constant shelling and sniping made life unbearable. After Serbian forces overran Srebrenica and Zepa in the summer of 1995, NATO engaged in heavy bombing raids, which led to the Dayton peace settlement.

sand appeared too high to sell to Congress, and the use of ground troops was dropped.

The advisers then moved toward a threefold plan:

1. threatening the Serbs with air strikes unless they pulled their forces and weapons away from the havens and stopped seeking to "strangle" the city by preventing or impeding the flow of aid;
2. getting the United States actively involved in seeking a diplomatic settlement;

3. as part of that diplomacy, telling the Muslims that while America would help them to get the best settlement possible, the time had arrived for settlement.

If the Allies balked at this approach, they would be told that, unlike Lift and Strike, America would act alone if necessary.

Having decided on a plan of action, administration officials began working through the labyrinth of allied and UN diplomacy. On August 2, NATO agreed to make immediate *preparations* for stronger measures "if the strangulation of Sarajevo and the other areas continues." However, the boldness of the plan was quickly and significantly watered down. At the insistence of the British and the French, the idea of using force to get the parties to the conference table was dropped. In addition, the two allies also insisted that the United Nations as well as NATO should be required to give consent before any air strikes could take place. Within a week, UN Secretary General Boutros Boutros-Ghali claimed that only he had the authority to order NATO air strikes.

Once the proposal was in the United Nations' hands, it was watered down further. No strikes would be launched for past violations. If shelling took place in the future, air strikes could be undertaken only against the particular weapons engaged in the violations if, in fact, they could be located in the hilly and often cloud-covered terrain. Thus, the Serbs could not be hit where they might really be hurt, at weapons and ammunitions depots or command-and-control centers.

Despite all of these debilitating modifications, frequent threats by the president and other officials during the negotiating process got the Serbs to back down enough to put the question of air strikes in limbo. Eleven days after the NATO resolution, Serb forces evacuated their two most threatening positions overlooking Sarajevo, which, incidentally, were also the two Serb positions most threatened by possible NATO air strikes. Then, they allowed supplies and aid to dribble into the besieged city—not enough to make a big difference but enough to allow those reluctant to engage in air strikes to claim that strangulation was not occurring. Finally, the Serbs agreed to join a new round of peace talks. Although the talks went nowhere, the Serbian participation also helped to forestall the use of force by NATO.

While this first effort at coercive diplomacy was effective, it revealed how limited those effects can sometimes be. The shelling and sniping never really stopped completely nor did the harassment and delay of convoys. The Serbs were able to forestall the punishment merely by complying with the conditions in a very half-hearted way—allowing some supplies to enter, but not an abundance of them; by pulling back some weapons emplacements but not all of them; by denying official responsibility for shelling that did occur later. At best, the multilateral effort at coercive diplomacy merely deterred the Serbs from shelling the safe havens blatantly and persuaded them to allow enough aid to enter the city so that those in the Security Council who favored inaction could claim that strangulation was not taking place.

In the ensuing months, Serbian forces steadily pushed the Allies' restrictions to their limits by harassing peacekeepers and relief workers and increasing the tempo of shelling and sniping. When a shell hit Sarajevo's busy Markale marketplace, killing sixty-eight people and wounding many others on February 4, 1994, the Clinton administration's tolerance for Serbian behavior ended. After much prodding by the United States, NATO gave the Serbs a ten-day deadline to put their artillery under UN custody or move them out of range. The Serbs' response was merely to stop the shelling. As the deadline approached and the Serb weapons remained in place, it took a public threat by President Clinton in a Saturday radio address, which he delivered on television, to get the Serbs to comply.

However, the Serbs merely moved their weapons to Gorazde and began shelling that safe haven, killing sixty-seven people in the first ten days alone. When the Security Council authorized air strikes to protect the UN protection forces rather than the people in the havens, Secretary General Boutros-Ghali demanded that the Serbs pull back their forces from the beleaguered city. When they refused, NATO planes struck the Serbian artillery positions. Although President Clinton's original idea was to hit the Serbs hard, the NATO attack was a pitiful display of power. With a hundred planes ready for action in Italy and on aircraft carriers in the Adriatic, NATO sent only three planes on its first mission: The first two dropped a total of six bombs, two of which failed to explode. The third plane, a British Sea Harrier plane, was lost at sea after it attempted to bomb a Serbian tank. In addition, a French reconnaissance plane, was damaged by Serbian fire.

Rather than scaring and deterring the Serbs, the NATO military strikes merely enraged them. The Serbs responded by shelling the city so savagely that seven of the UN's military observers fled. Within days, Serb tanks entered the city, and when they did, it was too late for air strikes—NATO's bombs would fall on the very people the UN peacekeepers had been sent to protect. The Serbs reduced the safe haven to a small Muslim enclave that was virtually defenseless. Only after a public threat from President Clinton that broader and heavier air strikes were in the making did the Serbs stop the slaughter and pull their tanks out of the haven.

The kitten was out of the bag. Before the Gorazde raids, the Serbs had reason to fear the NATO forces, for they did not know what

President Clinton would do if they pushed his patience too far. In Gorazde, the NATO/UN coalition showed its mettle. As in Vietnam, NATO's restraint and use of minimal force for minimal ends signified neither restraint nor magnanimity but fear, timidity, and an unwillingness to pay any significant price to maintain the integrity of the havens.

For almost eighteen months thereafter, the shelling, the harassment, and the blocking of UN relief shipments continued unabated. While horrible things were happening in Bosnia, NATO and the United Nations dithered. Like the Emperor Nero, the governments of NATO fiddled while Rome was burning, and, like Nero, those governments knew both that Rome was burning and that they were fiddling. But they just could not agree on what to do. The Clinton administration would not negotiate an agreement favorable to the Serbs, and the Europeans would not get tough. Meanwhile, Muslim women, children, and the elderly lived out hungry, huddled, and miserable lives in what had become de facto prisoner of war camps paid for by "the international community."

The Serbs expressed their utter contempt for UN forces and relief workers in the meanest and pettiest ways imaginable, even refusing to allow mail to get through to the peacekeepers in Srebrenica. Whenever Serbian actions occasionally pushed the tolerance of the UN/NATO countries to the breaking point, a few more pinprick bombs would be dropped. At first, the Serbs responded to these attacks with some desultory compliance; then, after NATO planes bombed two ammunition dumps at Pale in May 1995, Serb forces took 380 UN hostages and offered to release them only if NATO agreed to no further air strikes. Once the United Nations agreed, the safe havens and the peacekeepers were completely at the mercy of the Serbs, who stopped virtually any movement of UN relief supplies through their territories.

By July 1995, the situation was completely intolerable. Sarajevo was without gas, electricity, or running water. The Serbs were shelling the city continuously, and traffic into the city by air or road had stopped for months. At the end of the month, the Serbs took Srebrenica, expelled forty-two thousand Muslims, and killed thousands of young men. Then, they moved onto Zepa, which lay ten miles south of Srebrenica. When UN peacekeepers rejected an ultimatum to stand aside, the Serbian forces fired on the peacekeepers and moved into the city.

The safe haven idea was bankrupt, and the credibility, if not the honor, of NATO and the United Nations was going if it was not gone. As the chairman of the Senate Armed Services Committee put it, "UNPROFOR cannot deliver humanitarian supplies to the enclaves, enforce a Sarajevo exclusion zone, protect the UN protected areas, or even protect its own troops."[36] After the hostage taking and the elimination of two safe areas, even British and French officials began talking about honor.

Stage 3. Bombing for Peace: Operation Deliberate Force (Late August and September 1995). In the end, it took massive air strikes, the threat of more strikes, and the carrot of a peace settlement favorable to the Serbs that ended three long years of ghastly war.

When Srebrenica and Zepa fell, the Clinton administration decided on a threefold plan to terminate the fighting, and they leaned on the Allies to go along:

1. After the next Serb provocation, massive bombing raids would be directed against significant Serb assets. "Nomore pinpricks," quipped Secretary of State Christopher. The bombing campaign would be graduated and escalat-ing, hitting Serb air defenses and artillery around Gorazde, and then moving on to broader targets in Serb-held territory.

2. The carrot of a diplomatic settlement generally favorable to the Serbs would be combined with the threat of further strikes against Serb assets.

3. UNPROFOR forces were to be moved to more secure areas over the summer months to make the bombing raids more palatable to the reluctant Europeans, and a British and French Rapid Reaction force would be beefed up to relieve and rescue any UN forces besieged in retaliation for the stronger raids. In addition, NATO withdrew the UN secretary general's veto over the use of air power.

Given the Serbs' utter contempt for the United Nations, it did not take long for NATO to find a provocation to put its new plan in operation. On August 28, the Serbs shelled a marketplace in Sarajevo, killing forty-three people and wounding eighty others. NATO had its provocation. Two days later, four days of bombing began. After taking out the Serbs' air defense network, NATO's planes attacked Serb positions in the exclusion zone around Sarajevo as well as targets around Gorazde and Tuzla. The planes also bombed command and control centers, ammunition depots and factories, and surface-to-air missile sites throughout Serb held territory. In all, 750 strike missions were flown against fifty-six targets.

While the raids were not as devastating as NATO planners had hoped, the Serbs agreed to begin negotiating at Geneva on the basis of an American plan that would give them 49 percent of Bosnia. On the ground, they sat still in the evident hope that Russian protests and their acceptance of peace talks would pressure a halt to the bombing. But the Clinton administration was undaunted. Under

American pressure, NATO threatened to resume its bombing unless the Serbs moved their weapons out of the exclusion zone, ended their attacks on the remaining three safe areas, and restored water and electricity to Sarajevo. When the Serbs refused to comply, a second round of bombing pounded Serb positions. When a third round was threatened, the Bosnian Serbs finally relented under pressure from Serbian leader Milosevic.

Operation Deliberate Force was successful for a variety of reasons. The threat of massive strikes against significant Serbian military assets had become a really usable military instrument of diplomacy because the military balance of forces was changing where it really mattered—on the ground. Over the previous six months, a beefed-up Croatian army, trained by retired U.S. military officers, had thrown Serbian forces out of Croatian territory they had held since 1992. In addition, weapons supplied by Islamic states enabled the Muslims to join Croatian forces in retaking areas held by Serb forces within central Bosnia. By mid-summer 1995, the Serbian controlled part of Bosnia had been reduced from 70 percent to 55 percent.[37] With the growing strength of the Croatian and Muslim military forces, the destruction of Serbian military assets could turn the ground war against the Serbs.

Second, after three years of shelling, harassing, killing, pillaging, and broken promises, Serbian credibility was bankrupt. For more than two years, the international community had "given peace a chance," and all they had to show for it was the starvation and shelling of the innocent, genocidal ethnic cleansing, harassment of humanitarian aid workers, and the humiliation of UN peacekeepers—some of whom had been taken hostage while others were chained to Serb weapons that might be targets for NATO air strikes. By the time NATO struck, the use of powerful air strikes had almost universal support within the United States and the NATO countries.

Third, NATO's stick was also combined with the Clinton administration's carrot, a peace plan that gave the Serbs what they had been fighting for—an ethnically cleansed Serbian Republic in Bosnia that would have its own army as well as the prospect for uniting in some unspecified way with Serbia. Ironically, the carrot that the Clinton administration offered to the Serbs was more favorable to them than the Vance-Owen Plan, which it had excoriated as a Balkan Munich in the spring of 1993. Given the changing configuration of military power on the ground in Bosnia, the Clinton administration's diplomatic carrot was a significant inducement to the Serbs.

Operation Deliberate Force was perhaps the last straw rather than the decisive straw in getting the Serbs to the conference. Even before the bombs began to fall, the Serbs had agreed to allow Slobodan Milosevic negotiate a peaceful settlement of the conflict on their behalf. What the bombing and the threat of more bombing probably did was to formally get the Serbs to bargain seriously.

An Autopsy on the Bosnian Crisis: Some Lessons about the Uses of Force

1. *Interests Are Defined by the Amount of Resources a Nation's Leaders Are Willing to Expend to Secure Them.* If a nation's leaders and its people are unwilling to bear the costs of engaging an army on the field of battle, this probably indicates that they have no vital interests involved in the conflict. People may not like the sacrifices and the costs of war, but they will bear them if they believe their vital interests are at risk. In the international arena, talk is cheap. No matter how much political leaders may chatter about vision, ideals, and moral conceptions, they will seldom make sacrifices to secure those values unless tangible national interests are threatened as well—and even then, they may not act. Values may drive the rhetoric of foreign policy, but interests drive the substance of policy.

Since the end of the Cold War, most international conflicts have challenged America's "moral sensibilities" rather than its material or security interests. When such conflicts arise, *doing nothing appears morally intolerable, half measures will not do much good, and risking lives and treasure in the cause of right will seldom gain domestic or international support.* While such cases present unenviable choices, they also have a long history. Over the previous 150 years, leaders and publics in democracies have frequently "seen things out there" that they did not like or that they considered morally unacceptable—the Russian repression of liberal revolutions in Hungary in 1849 and again in 1956, the Japanese invasion of Manchuria, the Italian invasion of Ethiopia, the communization of East European countries after World War II, China's invasion of Tibet in 1959, and ethnic cleansing in Bosnia in 1993. In each of these cases, the balance of interests lay overwhelmingly with the "perpetrator" of the wrong, rather than with the morally outraged and disinterested observer. That none of the morally outraged nations was willing to right the wrong that outraged them on the field of battle is understandable.

While moral posturing might seem harmless or gratuitous, such is not the case. By turning issues of power and interest into moral issues, nations invariably get themselves into boxes that make it difficult or almost impossible to settle conflicts diplomatically. While seemingly immoral, the British and

French position in regard to Bosnia did have a sense of moral dignity to it. If no one was really going to help the Muslims, was it not more moral, and more honest, to try to get the best settlement one could rather than to allow the violence to continue? Was this position less moral than a position that raised hopes but, when the chips were down, never delivered on the promise of living up to moral principles so easily proclaimed? Would not an early acceptance of the Vance-Owen Plan have been better than the years of bloodshed that followed?

2. *Force as a Last Resort Is Not Always the Best Resort.* The Bosnian case also calls into question the commonly reiterated belief that "force should always be used as a last resort." The Clinton administration had a good chance of bringing peace, if not justice, to Bosnia in the spring and summer of 1993. Had the administration thrown its weight behind the Vance-Owen Plan and threatened withering air strikes if the Serbs did not stop fighting, a peace settlement might have come two years earlier. While the Serbs would have fought to the end to avoid being placed under a Croat-Muslim majority government, they probably would have accepted a peace treaty that gave them a great deal of autonomy. In the end, the force employed as a last resort in August 1995 gained no more justice than equivalent doses of force, *or perhaps even the mere threat of force,* might have gained two and a half years earlier. What moral purpose was served by waiting?

Secretary of State Christopher's characterization of the Dayton Accords as a triumph for the principle of multiethnicity is, of course, a fiction. The Dayton Accords reflect the territorial results decided on the field of battle, just as the Vance-Owen and Vance-Stoltenberg Plans did. Although the accords contain provisions for rounding up and trying indicted war criminals, fulfillment of those provisions has remained largely a dead issue. Of seventy-five indicted war criminals, only thirteen were brought into custody by 2000, and two of the most notorious ones, Radovan Karadzic and Ratko Mladic, remained in power behind the scenes.[38]

Of the 1.5 million refugees, 900,000 were still refugees four and a half years after peace, and only 120,000 minority refugees had returned to their homes. Nor were the Serbs alone in violating the refugee provisions of the Dayton Accords. Days before receiving a $13 million loan for economic development, Croatian president Franjo Tudjman claimed that 200,000 Serbian refugees would never return to their homes in Croatia and that "Nobody in the world can force us."[39] Similarly, Alija Izetbegovic, the leader of Bosnia's

Muslims and one of its three-person presidency, disappointed many of his former backers in the West when he vowed publicly that Muslim refugees would not be evicted from properties they had taken over from non-Muslims—no matter what Bosnia's courts decreed. "We cannot undo the ethnic cleansing," a senior UN official soberly observed.[40]

After Dayton, Bosnia became not a multiethnic democracy but three monolithic ministates—a Serb-dominated Republika Srpska, a Muslim Bosnian enclave, and a heavily Croat zone. After four and a half years of peace, unemployment was at about 40 percent in the Bosnian-Croat Federation and 50 percent in the republic of Srpska. Prospects for economic revival were dim, and the days of foreign aid and international attention were running out for Bosnia. According to Peter Ford of *The Christian Science Monitor*, "Most of the goals of Dayton set remain unfulfilled, officials acknowledge, and some of the most important ones may never be reached. . . . The absence of war is the only clear success that the peace has so far bequeathed."[41] That force was used in the last resort is of little consolation to those who lost their lives, their loved ones, their property, and their dignity in the years of warfare and ethnic cleansing that followed the failure of the Vance-Owen Plan or its successor, the Vance-Stoltenberg Plan. What, in fact, was gained by waiting more than two years before using force as a last resort?

3. *Wars Are Won on the Ground.* No country has ever won a war by dropping a few bombs here and there, and no country ever will. Once another army has begun fighting and taking military objectives, only forces on the ground can stop them or roll them back. To be sure, air power can make the difference between victory and defeat by supporting ground operations, interdicting the flow of supplies, and reducing the enemy's economy to rubble. But by itself, the contribution air power makes to victory is rarely decisive. During the last eleven months of World War II, the Allies had complete command of the air over Germany, and their daily bombing raids wreaked havoc and devastation on civilians. Yet, up to the very end of the war, German forces received enough weapons and supplies to fight fiercely.

During the Korean War, air power was absolutely crucial, because without it UN troops would have been pushed into the sea two times—once by the invading North Korean troops in the summer of 1950 and then by Chinese and North Korean troops the following year. In both cases, close air support of ground forces and the interdiction of enemy supplies and troops made the difference between survival and defeat.

On the other hand, air strikes alone could never have prevented a victory by the North Koreans in the summer of 1950.

In fact, the Korean War is particularly instructive for assessing what air power can and cannot do, because the Allies were able to employ their air forces under the best of conditions. Within a matter of weeks, allied air forces had cleared the skies and were conducting nearly a thousand air strikes a day by the end of 1950. In the summer of 1951, allied air forces initiated "Operation Strangle," a systematic and concentrated campaign to cut off the North Korean front lines from supplies in the rear. Night after night and day after day, three-quarters of all land-based and air craft carrier flights bombed away massively. Still, one year later, several thousand tons of supplies were still reaching Chinese and North Korean forces daily and enabling them to fight tenaciously.

The mission's failure stemmed from the simple fact that a Chinese division required only 50 tons of supplies per day against the 610 tons required by an American division. Massive efforts by enemy repair crews would quickly undo enough of the damage to allow sufficient supplies to get to the front. While the bombing might have prevented the North Korean and Chinese forces from launching a major offensive, victory for the allied forces still required strong ground forces that could hold the line.

Once the armistice negotiations began, the joint chiefs decided to use air power as an instrument of coercive diplomacy. Since almost all the marginal economic targets had been destroyed in North Korea, Operation Pressure Pump opened raids to targets in formerly restricted areas close to the Soviet borders, where the North Koreans had built numerous industrial plants in complete safety. In one day alone, 1,403 sorties blasted Pyongyang, and the target list, according to air force historians, "read like a guide to public offices in Pyongyang with such points of interest as the Ministry of Rail Transportation, the Munitions Bureau, Radio Pyongyang, plus many factories, warehouses, and troop billets."[42] Attacks on four hydroelectric power plants in June 1952 were so effective that, "For the rest of the war," notes one scholar, "the lights never really went on again in North Korea."[43]

By the end of 1952, every major industrial target in North Korea lay in ruins. Pyongyang and most other cities were reduced to rubble, causing hundreds of thousands of civilian casualties. When the communist forces still refused to alter their position that all prisoners of war had to be sent home whether they wanted to return home or not, the Allies suspended negotiations indefinitely, and relentlessly continued the pressure bombing. When negotiations reopened in the spring of 1953, the joint chiefs decided to put even more pressure on the communists by targeting dikes that were necessary to secure North Korea's harvests. When the dams were hit, water flooded croplands and cities, creating great civilian damage and destroying valuable crops, which outraged public opinion in allied countries. The communist negotiators, remained unmoved and their forces managed to fight fiercely, even initiating offensives right up to the signing of the armistice.

The experience was similar but even more frustrating in the Vietnam War. After President Johnson's desultory bombing campaign in the spring of 1965, the joint chiefs tried to pressure the North Vietnamese by interdicting the flow of supplies into South Vietnam. From the summer of 1965 until the winter of 1966–1967, 93 percent of the air effort was dedicated to a Vietnam equivalent of "Operation Strangle." While 70 percent of North Vietnam's petroleum, oil, and lubricant facilities were destroyed, the results were disappointing because the 245,000 Vietcong guerrillas derived most of their support from the local population and weapons captured from the South Vietnamese. The guerrilla forces required only about fifteen tons of supplies a day from the North or roughly ten ounces for each guerrilla.

When the interdiction campaign failed, the joint chiefs turned to "Operation Sharp Knock," the Vietnam equivalent of "Operation Pressure Pump." In a few days, all of the industrial and transportation targets around Hanoi, Haiphong, and the former safety zone around the Chinese border were destroyed—all to no avail. In the joint chiefs' inventory of fixed targets, there were only twenty-seven industrial assets to bomb—nineteen power plants and eight manufacturing plants. Taking out these economic assets had little military or economic significance. The $370 million worth of damage done by all of the bombing from 1965 to 1968 was easily negated by $600 million in economic assistance and a billion dollars in military assistance from its allies. The loss of North Vietnam's nineteen power plants was made up by two thousand portable generators it received from communist bloc nations. With nothing of military or economic value left to bomb, President Johnson scaled back the bombing of North Vietnam, and, after the election of 1968, ended it altogether.

On the other hand, the utility of air power was demonstrated after most American ground troops had been withdrawn under President Nixon's Vietnamization Program, and the North Vietnamese decided to seek a military victory through a conventional invasion of South Vietnam in the spring of 1972. When Hanoi's fourteen divisions consisting of 120,000 regular troops spearheaded by six hundred tanks and artillery pieces began decimating South Vietnamese forces, American air attacks saved the day by stopping and helping to turn back the offensive. Air power succeeded in this instance because it had a tactical military role to play—it reduced by 70 to 80 percent the flow of fuel and ammunition that North Vietnam's tanks, artillery, and ground forces needed to succeed. Without fuel and ammunition, North Vietnam's offensive ground to a halt. Still, the best that air power could do was help forestall a North Vietnamese victory. When the North Vietnamese launched another massive invasion in 1974, the time had come to honor America's pledge to provide air power in the event of a North Korean invasion. However, by then, Richard Nixon had left office in disgrace and when Congress reneged, South Vietnam fell in a conventional military battle.[44]

4. *There Is No Free Lunch.* "Feel-good bombing" will not win wars or turn back determined armed forces on the ground. As retired Marine General Bernard E. Trainor noted in an essay that appeared in the *New York Times* right after NATO's pinprick bombing near Gorazde, the use of air strikes with the intention of bringing opponents to their senses by inflicting pain is "a pipe dream": "Since the advent of air power, bombing alone only stiffened the resolve of a resolute enemy. No political objective has ever been achieved by air power alone."[45]

For those who really wanted to "do the right thing" in Bosnia, there were, of course, experts who could and did tell them how to do it. At the very outset of the crisis, former NATO supreme commander general estimated that just to open the supply road from Croatia to Sarajevo and to keep it open would require "something like 70,000 troops or more."[46] At about the same time, retired Lieutenant General William Odom claimed in a *Wall Street Journal* essay, "It would take a fairly large force, perhaps 300,000 troops, and they would have to remain there for years, if not decades." Odom continued, "Air strikes have never brought down a regime, caused an army to surrender, or ended a civil war." "Invade, Don't Bomb" was the title of his essay.[47] Several years later, former secretary of state and supreme allied commander of NATO Alexander Haig told the Senate Armed Services Committee that, "A NATO force of 100,000, give or take, could dominate the situation, break the back of the Serb resistance, and deal out justice to war criminals."[48] In November 1994, President

Clinton's own secretary of defense bluntly admitted what securing moral rectitude in Bosnia would require and then quickly added that doing the right thing was not worth the cost: ". . . it would take hundreds of thousands of troops and probably significant casualties to impose the outcome we want, peace. That's a level of blood and treasure that is not commensurate with our national interests. Therefore, we're not about to enter that war as a combatant."[49]

No one should ever contemplate the resort to force lightly: *To be effective, force must hurt and hurt badly, and one can expect to get hurt badly in return.* When it comes to warfare, the Gulf War was the exception, not the rule—at least for the allied side, which came out virtually unscathed. The devastation wreaked on Iraqi soldiers and civilians alike was terrible. However, in most wars, the costs of victory for the winner are frequently not much less than the costs for the loser as any Russian who lived through World War II or any Vietnamese who lived through almost thirty years of guerrilla and conventional warfare will affirm.

5. *In Any Contest of Wills, the Balance of Interests Is Usually a Better Predictor of Outcomes Than the Balance of Absolute Military Power.* In most international conflicts, the party to whom an issue is more important will prevail, unless the other party has overwhelming military power at its disposal. Great Powers frequently lose small wars because the "stakes" in a conflict may be much higher to the "objectively weaker" party than to the "objectively stronger party."[50] Consequently, when the going gets tough, countries with the lesser stakes will bail out, as when the French pulled out of Indochina and Algeria, the United States bailed out of Vietnam, and the Soviets extricated themselves from Afghanistan, but in every case, only after great costs.

Coercive diplomacy frequently fails because the requisites for its success do not lie with the nations attempting to coerce; in fact, if they did, the coercing party would probably not be engaging in coercive diplomacy—deterrence would have silently worked, preventing the target country from doing what it was doing in the first place.

Much of President Clinton's frustration in the realm of foreign policy stemmed from the simple fact that the interests of his adversaries have been more important to them than the president's ideals and visions were to him. In Somalia, Aidid's 2,000 supporters could never have defeated a UN force of 21,800. But, his forces could harass UN troops and make them pay in casualties, and as the casualties imposed by his forces increased, the steadfastness of the UN coalition quickly evaporated. After losing fifteen servicemen, President Clinton decided to withdraw, and others who served in the UN contingent were quick to follow. In the Bosnian conflict, in the repeated haggles with Saddam Hussein over UNSCOM weapons inspectors, and in regard to complaints about China's human rights policies, similar imbalances of interests brought the Clinton administration back to the policies of George Bush.

6. *Finally, Never Forget: There Is Much That No Amount of Military Force Can Do.* Military forces can frequently deter and fight successfully when deterrence is breached. But beyond these traditional military functions—in those gray areas between war and peace—military force is often of limited utility And, there are many problems for which military force is useless or irrelevant.

During the Cold War, containment might have deterred the Soviets from using military force to change the territorial status quo, but it could not prevent them from increasing the size of their military forces, modernizing them, or even developing nuclear weapons. When revisionist or dissatisfied states do threatening things, such as developing nuclear weapons on their side of the line, there may be little that status quo powers can do, especially if they are reluctant to initiate the use of military force.

Military weapons are also of little utility in stopping the spread of influence by revisionist states. The big difference between Stalin and his successor Nikita Khrushchev was that Stalin was interested in expanding Soviet control over territory while Khrushchev sought to expand Soviet influence throughout the world. Through a diplomacy of foreign aid, friendship treaties, military assistance programs, support for the neutrality and the anticolonial struggles of nonaligned nations, the Soviet leader posed political challenges for which the West's military weapons were irrelevant and inappropriate.

Force can make people bow, but it cannot change people's minds. Soviet troops and tanks could make people in Eastern Europe submit to communism, but they could not implant the legitimacy of communism in their minds and hearts. When those tanks and troops were withdrawn and the people of Eastern Europe were given the freedom "to have it their way," as Mikhail Gorbachev's foreign minister put it, communist regimes came tumbling down within a matter of months.

Perhaps no president has experienced the painful limits of military force more than President Clinton. No amount of military force could get the warring factions in Somalia to put their differences aside and create a stable government. In Haiti, the threat of military force could persuade a ruthless military junta to step down, but neither American and UN military forces nor civilian aid workers, for that matter, could create a stable democracy and a sound economy. As American forces were withdrawing from Haiti, the country had been without a government for two years: "All the king's horses and all the king's men could not put Humpty Dumpty together again."

In Kosovo, NATO air power was able to coerce Yugoslav forces into withdrawing from the largely Muslim province, but military force could not get the Albanian and Serbian populations to live in multicultural harmony. Ironically, NATO forces wound up doing what Serbian forces had been doing before America's bombing—defending Kosovo Serbians from Kosovo Albanians. As frustrating as these failures may be, one should not be surprised at them. Almost fifty years after the civil rights legislation of the 1960s, the integration of blacks and whites into a color-blind society is still a long way off.

Only a *diplomacy* that works to assuage underlying sources of conflict and enmity can lead nations from hostility and tension to tolerance and, perhaps later, amity and friendship. In the first volume of his history of the Second World War, Winston Churchill argued that the long-term prospects for peace in Europe lay not in the punitive peace treaties at the end of World War I nor in the armed strength of the victorious status quo powers. Peace in Europe, he claimed, would come only after the eventual elimination of hostility between Frenchmen and Germans:

> To me, the aim of ending the thousand-year strife between France and Germany seemed a supreme object. If we could only weave Gaul and Teuton so closely together economically, socially, and morally as to prevent the occasion of new quarrels, and make old antagonisms die in the realisation of mutual prosperity and interdependence, Europe would rise again. *It seemed to me that the supreme interest of the British people in Europe lay in the assuagement of the Franco-German feud, and that they had no other interests comparable or contrary to that.*[51]

One need only consider the state of Europe today to see the wisdom of Churchill's assessment.

Knowing what military force can and cannot do and understanding the limits of military force are essential for a sound diplomacy. Going to war is always easy; staying in if the going gets rough is never easy, especially for democracies; ending a war without a victory is never easy, but getting out is better than staying stuck in an unwinnable war of attrition.

Whenever the penchant to employ military force arises, policymakers should read and reread the following passages from a column written by Carl Rowan at the very outset of the crisis in Bosnia. In response to former British Prime Minister Margaret Thatcher's call for the use of NATO forces to bomb military targets in Serbia and the supply lines of Serb forces in Bosnia, Rowan had the following response:

> We are seeing now, as we learned painfully in Vietnam, and after foolish celebrations over "Desert Storm," that there are stark limitations in the use of military power in the world—limitations of politics, racial passion, ethnic hatreds, and human wills that are more passionate than smart bombs. . . .
>
> Let us face the reality that the world has no "great power" capable of curbing the cruelties that one people impose upon another. The U.S. is not a superpower in terms of having the riches with which to erase economic woes in the Soviet Union, mass starvation in Somalia, terrible deprivation among Muslim prisoners in "Yugoslavia" or the Kurds in Iraq, and still solve its troubles at home
>
> Because no country can impose order, or peace, or ward off starvation or murder, we are still dependent on the diplomacy that has silenced some of the passions of would-be-warriors from the beginning of time.[52]

Summary of Salient Points

Be wary of the itch to use military force; those who give in to it frequently rue the day they did so

1. War often unleashes consequences quite contrary to the expectations of those who initiate it.
2. Wars are usually not lost because national leaders fail to calculate but because they miscalculate. Overconfidence, pride, and hubris lead decision makers to overestimate their own capacities and underestimate the will, tenacity, and power of their victim and their victim's allies.
3. When a nation's military strategy envisages only peace or total war, it may find itself with two unenviable choices when less than total challenges arise: total war or acquiescence.
4. Limited war capabilities enable a status quo power to avoid the choice between total war and surrender, but limited wars are costly and unpopular.
5. States seeking to keep the peace against limited challenges must create regional and local structures of deterrence.
6. When deterrence fails but neither limited war nor giving in seems satisfactory, states frequently resort to coercive diplomacy.
7. While limited wars and limited uses of force are often inconclusive and unproductive, the conditions for decisive uses of force frequently do not exist.

8. Interests are defined by the amount of resources a nation's leaders are willing to expend to secure them.

9. In any contest of wills, the balance of interests is usually a better predictor of outcomes than the balance of absolute military power.

10. Force as a last resort is not always the best resort.

11. Military power alone cannot stop the spread of influence by revisionist states; it cannot make people change their minds; it cannot create stable governments; it cannot get people to live in multicultural harmony.

12. Knowing what military force can and cannot do is essential for a sound diplomacy. Going to war is always easy; staying in if the going gets rough is never easy, especially for democracies; ending a war without a victory is always difficult, but getting out is better than staying stuck in an unwinnable war of attrition.

Notes

1. The quotations in these first two paragraphs were taken from the War and Peace section of Daniel B. Baker, *Power Quotes* (Washington, DC: Visible Ink, 1992), 316–44.
2. Eliot Cohen, "Churchill and Coalition Strategy in World War II," in *Grand Strategy in War and Peace,* ed. Paul Kennedy (New Haven: Yale University Press, 1991), 66.
3. Serge N. Goncharo et al., *Uncertain Partners: Stalin, Mao, and the Korean War* (Stanford, CA: Stanford University Press, 1993), 155.
4. David McCullough, *Truman* (New York: Simon and Schuster, 1992), 787.
5. Louis Halle, *The Cold War as History* (London: Chatto and Windus, 1967), 206.
6. "World Policy and Bipartisanship: An Interview with Senator Tom Connally," *U.S. News and World Report,* May 5, 1950, reprinted in *FRUS, 1950* (Washington, DC) VII: 65–66.
7. "Memorandum of Conversation by the Chargé," ibid., 77.
8. Alonzo L. Hamby, *Man of the People: A Life of Harry S. Truman* (New York: Oxford University Press, 1995), 534.
9. Matthew B. Ridgway, *The Korean War* (Garden City, NY: Doubleday, 1967), 11.
10. Harry S. Truman, *Years of Trial and Hope* (New York: New American Library, 1956), 378–79.
11. Glenn Paige, *The Korean Decision [June 24–30, 1950]* (New York: The Free Press, 1968), 128. Paige provides a highly detailed, invaluable, almost hour-by-hour discussion of the unfolding of the Korean crisis during its first week.
12. Ibid., 164.
13. Ibid., 173.
14. Dean Acheson, *The Korean War* (New York: W. Norton, 1971), 20 [italics added].
15. Paige, *The Korean Decision,* 181.
16. Hamby, *Man of the People,* 534.
17. Ridgway, *The Korean War,* 245.
18. This discussion and the quotations in this section are taken from Goncharov, *Uncertain Partners,* 136–46.
19. These quotations were taken from the War and Peace section of Baker, *Power Quotes,* 316–44.
20. Ibid., 144.
21. Ibid., 208.
22. Henry Kissinger, "Military Policy and Defense of the 'Grey Areas,'" *Foreign Affairs* 33, no. 3 (April 1955), 420.
23. Louis J. Halle, *The Elements of World Order: Essays on International Politics* (Lanham, MD: University Press of America, 1996), 105.

24. This is in Adam Ulam, *The Rivals: America and Russia Since World War II* (New York: Viking Press, 1971), 140, but worded a little differently.

25. Ibid., 138.

26. All of the quotations in this paragraph are taken from Robert A. Pape, "Coercive Air Power in the Vietnam War," *International Security* 15, no. 2 (Fall 1990), 114.

27. Robert E. Osgood, *Limited War Revisited* (Boulder, CO: Westview Press, 1979), 43–44.

28. Baker, *Power Quotes*, 341.

29. The quotations from Clausewitz are taken from Harry G. Summers, *The New World Strategy: A Military Policy for America's Future* (New York: Simon and Schuster, 1995), 30 and 232.

30. Ibid., 341.

31. Elaine Sciolino, "The Foreign Policy Race: Madeleine Albright's Audition," *New York Times Magazine*, September 22, 1996, 67.

32. Elizabeth Drew, *On the Edge: The Clinton Presidency* (New York: Simon and Schuster, 1994), 147.

33. Ibid., 162.

34. For this and other quotations presenting the president's changing views on the Bosnian conflict see: Hanna Rosen, "I did the best I could," *The New Republic*, August 7, 1995, 14.

35. *A Global Agenda: Issues before the 48th General Assembly* (New York: Council on Foreign Relations, 1993), 26.

36. U.S. Senate, Committee on Armed Services, *Situation in Bosnia*. Hearings held on June 7, 8, 14, and 15, September 29, October 17, November 28, and December 6, 1995. (Washington, DC: U.S. Government Printing Office, 1996), 67. Hereafter cited as *Situation in Bosnia*, Hearings.

37. This figure was reported in "The Balkans: Near Peace and Quiet," *Time*, September 25, 1995, 42.

38. See, for example, Craig Whitney, "Bosnia Is Peaceful Now But Will It Stay That Way," *New York Times*, November 17, 1999, A6.

39. Susan Ellingwood, "The Dayton Game: A Casualty of Peace," *The New Republic*, July 14 and 21, 1997, 16–17.

40. Peter Ford, "Bosnia Four Years Later: Few Gains," *The Christian Science Monitor*, February 28, 2000, 7.

41. Ibid., 1.

42. Robert Futrell, *The United States Air Force in Korea, 1950–1953* (New York: Duell, Sloan, and Pearce, 1961), 489.

43. Peter R. Faber, "Power Plants: UN Air Attacks On," in *The Korean War: An Encyclopedia*, ed. Stanley Sandler (New York: Garland Publishing, 1995), 269.

44. This section draws heavily on Pape's "Coercive Air Power in the Vietnam War." Professor Pape's comprehensive study of the utility of air power should be read by anyone interested in this subject: *Bombing to Win: Air Power and Coercion in War* (Ithaca, NY: Cornell University Press, 1996).

45. Bernard E. Trainor, "Gorazde Cease-Fire Is Irrelevant," *New York Times*, April 27, 1994, A17.

46. "No military quick fix," *USA Today*, August 10, 1992, 7.

47. William Odom, "Invade, Don't Bomb," *Wall Street Journal*, February 18, 1994, A12.

48. *Situation in Bosnia*, Hearings, 64.

49. Ibid., 105.

50. Andrew Mack, "Why Big States Lose Small Wars," *World Politics* 27, no. 2 (January 1975).

51. Winston Churchill, *The Second World War: The Gathering Storm, volume 1* (Boston: Houghton Mifflin, 1961), 26.

52. "Being the World's 'Superpower' Cop Isn't Fun," *Liberal Opinion Week*, August 24, 1992, 20.

CHAPTER FOUR

Maintaining Peace
Is the Job of the
Status Quo Powers

. . . good will, unilateral disarmament, the avoidance of alliances, teaching and preaching of the evils of war by those states who, generally satisfied with the world, seek to preserve peace, are of no avail.

What seems to work best, even though imperfectly, is the possession by those states who wish to preserve the peace of the preponderant power and of the will to accept the burdens and responsibilities required to achieve that purpose. They must understand that no international situation is permanent, that part of their responsibility is to accept, and sometimes even assist changes, some of which they will not like, guiding their achievement through peaceful channels, but always prepared to resist with force, if necessary, changes made by threats or violence that threaten the general peace.

—Donald Kagan, *On the Origins of War and the Preservation of Peace*, 1995

Since revisionism is the driving force in international politics, dealing with revisionism lies at the heart of the problem of war and peace. If revisionist powers meet no resistance, they will be limited only by their own ambitions. If they are to be thwarted, only status quo powers will thwart them. The problem for leaders of status quo powers lies in recognizing the relationship between the policies and strategies of revisionist powers and their own broader interests in maintaining an environment conducive to their security and well-being.

National Defense, National Security, and World Peace

Strategic thinking begins with an understanding of the distinction among three fundamental concepts: national defense, national security, and world peace. All too often, people think about foreign policy largely in terms of national defense. For example, many opponents of the war in Vietnam were not opposed to fighting for their country. What they opposed was fighting for a country four thousand miles away that appeared to have no relation at all to America's national security. What many critics favored, whether knowingly or not, was a noninterventionist or isolationist foreign policy. On one fundamental point, such critics were on the mark: The United States possessed, on its own, adequate resources to build a military defense system that would deter any potential revisionist power from ever thinking of attacking American soil.

In the age of nuclear weapons, America's physical security is more assured than ever before. As Professor Robert Tucker noted almost thirty years ago:

> ... many people still have considerable difficulty in coming to terms with the changed structure of the American security position. . . . A Soviet Union in control of Western Europe would be no less vulnerable to destruction by American strategic power than it is today. Nor would America be more vulnerable to destruction by the Soviet Union than it is today. The point cannot be made too often that to the extent security is equated with physical security, conventional balance of power calculations have become irrelevant—or very nearly so— for the great nuclear states.[1]

The difficulty with an isolationist foreign policy is that it cedes to others the power to determine the terms on which America will operate in the world—where we would trade, what the terms of access would be, and what the political makeup and affiliations of the states surrounding us would be. Isolationism might secure our physical survival, but it could not guarantee the quality of our lives and insure easy access to the world abroad.

As noted in Chapter 2, America enjoyed the luxury of an isolationist foreign policy in the nineteenth century only because American and British foreign policy interests coincided. When those interests did not coincide, as we saw in Chapter 1, America found its neutral rights violated, its sailors impressed, and its ports vulnerable to British occupation, and it had to accept Jay's humiliating treaty. According to the historian Robert Leckie: "America was free [of 'the broils of Europe'] because Waterloo had conferred upon Britain an immense, world-wide prestige and had ushered in the *Pax Britannica*, that relatively peaceful century during which Britain 'controlled extra-European events and localized European wars.'"[2]

With the decline of British naval power America's luxury of splendid isolation was at risk. To continue to travel the seas unmolested while perfecting its union at home, the United States would have to develop its own military resources and, perhaps, find allies to maintain those conditions on which its security had been based. As Walter Lippmann noted, "The United States did not [enter World War I] because it wished to found a League of Nations; it went to war to preserve American security":

> . . . if Germany won, the United States would have to face a new and aggressively expanding German empire which had made Britain, France, and Russia its vassals, and Japan its ally. . . . In such a position the defense of the Western hemisphere would require immense armaments over and above those needed in the Pacific, and America would have to live in a perpetual state of high and alert military preparedness.[3]
>
> [Yet], it had not been demonstrated to [the American people] how much the defense of the hemisphere depended upon having friendly and strong partners in the British Isles, in the French ports on the Atlantic, at Gibraltar and Casablanca and Dakar, or how much the defense of the Philippines depended upon French Indo-China, and upon British Hong Kong, Malaya, and Burma, and upon the attitude and strength of Russia and upon China in Eastern Asia.[4]

If status quo nations are to exist in a secure and orderly world and have a significant say over what that world is to be like, they must confront revisionist powers far from home, and all too frequently in areas that seem of little intrinsic importance. Yet, doing so is very difficult for democracies whose people are reluctant to send their sons to die for far-off places like Manchuria, Czechoslovakia, Korea, Vietnam, and Kuwait. In 1939, a young John F. Kennedy clearly articulated this problem in the senior thesis he wrote at Harvard University: "Like England, we have general commitments that we may not be able to fill. For example, we have warned the Japanese to stay out of Dutch East Netherlands, yet, if they seized it, would the cry, 'Are the Dutch East Indies worth a war,' go up strangely similar to the old cry in England at the time of Munich, 'Are the Sudeten Germans worth a war?'"[5]

For democracies, the easiest course of action when revisionist powers begin making demands is to minimize or rationalize. The reason for this penchant is simple: When revisionists begin their quests, the territorial security of the status quo powers is seldom at stake. In the early phases of revisionism, challenges usually involve threats to positionality, status, prestige, or credibility—values that are conjectural, nebulous, and, therefore, highly debatable.

The role of such intangible values is illustrated well in the transcript of a stormy conference in 1976 that Secretary of State Henry Kissinger held with some of his aides. At that time, the Soviets had just flown thousands of Cuban troops into Angola and insured victory for the pro-Soviet faction in that country's postindependence civil war. What mattered to Kissinger was not so much the outcome of a civil war in Angola but the precedent that the Soviet and Cuban intervention might create.

For the first time in the Cold War, the Soviets and their Cuban clients had intervened militarily far from their traditional spheres of influence and into an area that held vital resources for the West.

According to Kissinger:

> *Our concern in Angola is not the economic wealth or a naval base. It has to do with the USSR operating 8,000 from home when all of the surrounding states are asking us for help. This will affect the Europeans, the Soviets, and the Chinese.*
>
> *. . . The president says to the Chinese that we're going to stand firm in Angola and two weeks later we get out. I go to a NATO meeting and meanwhile the Department leaks that we are worried about a naval base or says it is an exaggeration or aberration of Kissinger's. I don't care about the oil or the base but I do care about the African reaction when they see the Soviets pull it off and we don't do anything. If the Europeans then say to themselves if they can't hold Luanda [the capital of Angola], how can they defend Europe? The Chinese will say we're a country that was run out of Indochina for 50,000 men and is now being run out of Angola for less than $50 million.*[6]

Kissinger's views on Angola were hotly debated at the time, and they are still controversial. But, *debates about national security are not debates about defending our borders; they are debates about defending the borders of others.* They are also debates about how different kinds of changes in those borders affect our status, our credibility, and our influence. This broader conception of national security was well articulated by George Kennan in a talk he gave to the National Defense Committee of the United States Chamber of Commerce in 1947:

> *We must remember that the first line of American defense might be many thousands of miles from American shores. We already hold a number of outlying bases which it is essential for us to staff and it might be necessary for us on very short notice to seize and hold other . . . outlying island bases on other continents, if only for the purpose of denying the use of them to others during the period required for further military preparations. But here, again, . . . the greatest value of our forces lies in their quality as a deterrent. If we do not maintain such forces there will always be an incentive to unruly people elsewhere to seize isolated and limited objectives on the theory that we would be able to do nothing about it at the moment and that they could count on making the seizures with impunity and talking about it afterward.*[7]

In addition to the distinction between national defense and national security in a broader sense, one must also distinguish between national security and world order or world peace. While security for most status quo nations requires more than national defense, it also always requires less than a world of peace and harmony. *Peace is divisible, and some conflicts matter and others do not.* For status quo powers, the task is one of distinguishing between revisionism that might jeopardize their security and revisionism that will not, a distinction that is easily recognizable in two recent examples: America's decision to go to war against Saddam Hussein and its decision to "give peace a chance" in Bosnia.

The conquest of Kuwait clearly threatened the one vital resource on which all of the industrialized countries depend for their livelihood and their comfort. While some people rallied around the slogan, "no blood for oil," it is easy to see why President Bush decided to go to war. Oil is air conditioning; it means not having to take mass or public transit; it means not having to carpool to work; it means keeping thermostats as high as we want in winter; and it means having gas-guzzling vehicles to carpool children to Little League games or to transport the kids and their electronic gear off to college in some semblance of comfort. In Bosnia, no material American interests were at stake, and Americans were unwilling to spill the blood of their sons and daughters for the abstract principles of peace and world order alone—especially when nearby European powers were reluctant to do much beyond helping to alleviate the suffering of the victims. In fact, in the case of Bosnia, it is not clear which side was really the aggressor or revisionist—the Croats and Muslims living in Bosnia who sought independence from Serbia or the Serbs in Bosnia who did not want to live in an independent Bosnia and sought union with Serbia. What did occur was an extremely bloody ethnic and civil conflict.

The difficulty for status quo powers lies in knowing which areas are vital to their security defined broadly and which are not. Such questions are very difficult to answer, and no matter what set of answers a given group of decision makers might decide on, they will face opposition at both the strategic and tactical levels. Yet, the only alternative to addressing these questions is a retreat into continental isolationism or a quest for world hegemony, neither of which is acceptable to most Americans.

Interests, Commitments, Solvency, and Vigilance

Because no nation can police the entire global status quo, each Great Power must have a conception of those vital interests on which the survival of its people depends. Once these vital interests are identified, the nation must begin making commitments and preparing to secure those interests by creating and positioning military forces that will deter potential revisionists or defeat them if deterrence fails. Finally, policymakers must continually reexamine these interests, commitments, and military forces in light of changing challenges, technology, and conditions.

The process can be presented simply:

Interests—>Commitments—>Military Preparedness—>Vigilant Monitoring

When commitments are not supported with adequate military power, a nation's foreign policy is *insolvent.* According to Walter Lippmann:

> *. . . a foreign policy consists in bringing into balance, with a comfortable surplus of power in reserve, the nation's commitments and the nation's power. The constant preoccupation of the true statesman is to achieve and maintain this balance. Having determined the foreign commitments which are vitally necessary to his people, he will never rest until he has mustered the force to cover them. In assaying ideals, interests, and ambitions which are to be asserted abroad, his measure of their validity will be the force he can muster at home combined with the support he can find abroad among other nations which have similar ideals, interests, and ambitions.*
>
> *. . . For nations, as for individuals, the level may vary at which a solvent balance is struck. . . . But whether he is conducting the affairs of Germany, which has dynamic ambitions, or the affairs of Switzerland which seeks only to hold what it already has, or of the United States, [the statesman] must still bring his ends and means into balance. If he does not, he will follow a course that leads to disaster.*[8]

Although this advice may sound simple, it never is:

- States often err in assessing what is required for their security by either under-committing or over-committing themselves.
- They may fail to provide the military forces necessary to deter challenges, let alone defend their commitments should deterrence fail.
- They may fail to be vigilant enough to notice rising challengers or insolvencies that might require a cutting back of commitments.

Still, these simple concepts have been used effectively by successful diplomats, and the larger interests of states do appear to be relatively enduring. America's commitment to the Monroe Doctrine was reaffirmed in the nation's opposition to Louis Napoleon's attempt to implant a European monarchy in Mexico, the dollar diplomacy of the 1890s, the nation's reaction to the Zimmermann telegram in 1917, which offered a German alliance with Mexico if America went to war with Germany, the Cuban missile crisis of 1962, and Ronald Reagan's efforts to oust the Marxist Sandinista regime in Nicaragua.

Britain's traditional security interests as a status quo power required the maintenance of a balance of power among the European continental powers and its control of vital choke points and sea-lanes on which the security of its empire depended. In regard to Europe, Britain allied with coalitions seeking to contain revisionist powers seeking hegemony. With stability on the continent, Britain was free to develop and expand its vast empire. However, by the end of the nineteenth century, four rising powers raised potential threats to Britain's solvency. The burgeoning industrial power of a united Germany raised questions about Britain's ability to maintain peace in Europe by throwing its weight on the side of the weaker powers. In addition, the growing fleets of Germany, Russia, Japan, and America all represented potential challenges on the seas.

In the early 1900s, Britain could deal with these rising challengers in one or more of three ways—spending more of its own resources on naval forces so that it could unilaterally keep its commitments, gaining allies among states that had similar interests and would share some of the burdens of defense and deterrence, or cutting back on its commitments. In 1902, Britain allied with Japan to balance an expanding Russia in the Pacific. By allying with Japan, Britain could move more of its fleet into the Atlantic where it faced a growing naval challenge from Kaiser Wilhelm's Germany. Meanwhile, the rise of American naval power at the turn of the century actually complemented British power because both countries had a common interest in open seas and free access to foreign markets. Through the second Hay-Pauncefote Treaty of 1901, Britain ceded defense of the Panama Canal to the United States, and thereby devolved security for British shipping and maritime interests in the Western Hemisphere on to the United States.

Elements of Strategic Thinking: Containment and Conciliation

Leaders of revisionist states also have to establish hierarchies of interests and objectives. No matter what their ambitions and dreams might be, they, too, live in an anarchical international system. Like all other states, revisionist states must maintain and attend to their territorial integrity, their economic base, and their domestic needs and priorities. And they, too, have limited resources. As Barry Buzan has noted, "The logic of this bottom line is clear and compelling, . . . even the most rabid revisionist state cannot pursue larger objectives if it cannot secure its home base."[9] In sum, revisionist states face the same problems of solvency as status quo powers. During the interwar period, Manchuria was a vital and almost non-negotiable interest for Japan while the price in lives and treasure that it would be willing to pay for the Dutch East Indies was lower, and the price it would be willing to pay to take the Philippines or the Hawaiian Islands was lower still. However, if they met no resistance in their quest to expand, why would they stop?

Similar hierarchies existed for the Soviet Union, whose revisionism was also spurred by defensive and promotional motivations. Consider carefully, for example, the dual motivations that lay behind the following set of priorities ascribed to Soviet decision makers in a National Security Council study of 1955:

A. The security of the regime and of the USSR.
B. Maintaining the Soviet hold on the European satellites, and keeping China within the communist bloc.
C. Elimination of U.S. influence from Eurasia, and the isolation of the United States.

D. Expansion of Soviet communist power throughout Eurasia.

E. Elimination of the United States as a competing power center.

F. The spread of communism throughout the world.[10]

Such hierarchies of interests provide the key to leaders of status quo powers seeking to maintain the peace. Two simple assumptions provide the basis for devising strategies of peace:

Assumption 1: The more revisionist states have satisfied their basic security needs, the less willing they will be to pay for further increments of territory, power, influence, and status.

Assumption 2: The more costly and risky the pursuit of lesser objectives appear to be, the less likely that revisionist powers will pursue them.

In devising strategies for peace, status quo powers must always respect the basic security or defensive needs of a revisionist power while at the same time indicating a willingness to engage in various degrees of resistance if that power moves beyond those needs and begins to intrude on the security interests of others. As noted in the last chapter, the ability to deter does not necessarily require an ability to prevail in combat— the status quo powers must merely be able to threaten costs that are high enough to make the costs of using force by the revisionist power higher than any potential gains. Of course, revisionist leaders vary in the prices they would be willing to pay for various objects. What might deter a Stalin, for example, might not deter a Hitler. Consequently, *status quo strategies must always be tailor-made.*

Based on these assumptions, the core ingredients of a successful strategy for maintaining the peace requires three things of a status quo power:

1. knowing what its own vital interests are and creating the commitments and military forces, either alone or with allies, to secure those interests;
2. appreciating the security needs of revisionist powers while simultaneously creating structures of power that will deter them from moving beyond their security perimeters and threatening the security needs of other members of the oligarchy;
3. working to create a distribution of power, status, and territory that is considered legitimate or acceptable by all the members of the oligarchy.

Reality, of course, is never as simple as precepts imply. Knowing what one's own vital interests are is difficult enough. Knowing what a revisionist's vital interests are can be more difficult since revisionist leaders frequently justify their demands or actions by wrapping them up in rhetoric about defensive needs, past grievances, "abnormalities," or noble sounding principles. In addition, leaders of revisionist states frequently present their demands and actions as limited, "once and done" affairs that will not really affect the overall balance among the Great Powers in any significant way.

Leaders of status quo powers have a lot of figuring to do when faced with demands for change. Are they dealing with a revisionism driven largely by defensive or incremental motivations, or are they confronting a revisionism that is seeking to change the status quo in fundamental ways? Revisionism that is defensively driven or incremental should be met with policies of *compromise* or *conciliation* that are also accompanied with clear statements about limits and the positioning of military forces to make those statements believable. Revisionism that appears to have little defensive rationale behind it or appears likely to threaten power relations in fundamental ways should be met with polices of firmness and containment based on deterrence.

Knowing exactly what type of revisionism one is dealing with provides the greatest challenge that foreign policymakers face. Revisionists seldom present their real intentions in a clear, unvarnished manner; in fact, they, themselves, may not even know what their ultimate goals may be, for their appetite may increase with the eating. Status quo powers face what Hans Morgenthau has termed "the problem of detection" when confronted with demands for change.[11] According to Morgenthau, leaders of status quo powers must ask whether a revisionist power is seeking to overthrow the existing distribution of power or is merely seeking adjustments within the status quo. "The answer to that question," Morgenthau asserts, "has determined the fate of nations, and the wrong answer has often meant deadly peril or actual destruction; for upon the correctness of that answer depends the success of the foreign policy derived from it."[12]

But even if successful, containment alone can only attain an *armed truce or cold peace*. The long-term goal of any strategy for peace must be to transform the revisionist power into a satisfied state. What status quo powers must work toward is an international system in which all of the members of the oligarchy know that their basic security needs are met and realize that their security resides in respecting the security interests of the other powers. To create that transformation, power alone is not enough. Strategies are needed to induce revisionist powers to shed, or at least limit, their revisionism. As Henry Kissinger noted in his *Diplomacy:* "Power is too difficult to assess . . . to permit treating it as a reliable guide to international order. Equilibrium works best if it is buttressed by an agreement on common values. The balance of power inhibits the capacity to overthrow the international order; an agreement on shared values inhibits the desire to overthrow the international order. . . . An international order which is not considered just will be challenged sooner or later."[13]

The problem of attaining genuine peace is two-sided: it involves creating structures of power that will deter the use of force and seeking to conciliate the grievances of revisionist states in ways that do not reduce the security of the other Great Powers. However, we know much more about how to deter than we do about how to create conditions that lead to legitimacy. As Gordon Craig and Alexander George note in their *Force and Statecraft: Diplomatic Problems of Our Time,* when it comes to strategies for integrating revisionist states, "There is, in fact, no systematic, comparative study of this historical experience that would provide today's policymakers with conceptual and generic knowledge of this phenomenon."[14]

Still, there are a few rules of thumb. Legitimacy exists when there is a mutual acceptance of the overall territorial status quo by the Great Powers and mutual agreement on the norms and rules of international decision making. Obtaining such a consensus with a revolutionary or hegemony-seeking power is, obviously, an impossibility precisely because such powers are, in fact, seeking to alter existing norms, rules, laws, and distributions of power—both internationally and domestically—in fundamental ways.

All that status quo powers can do in such cases it to wait for time and the deterrent structures of power to force on elites of the revisionist power a significant degree of what George Kennan called "moderation and circumspection"—moderation and circumspection that in time would lead to "a mellowing" of the revisionist power.

During this period of "cold peace," status quo powers must also make their own defensive aims absolutely clear, and they must always keep the door open for a more normal relationship. It was, in fact, especially important for the United States to make clear its willingness to live in peace with even a *communist* Soviet Union that respected the territorial integrity, rights, and security of other countries and carried out its international agreements. *Only because Mikhail Gorbachev could be sure about the defensive nature of our policies could he undertake to wind down the Cold War without fear for the Soviet Union's security.*

Conflicts with revisionist powers are never conflicts with the people of those powers or the forms of government under which they live. As the members of the Coalition against Napoleon told the people of France, they were waging war neither against the French people or the French Revolution but against the expansionist foreign policies of France. Similarly, the United States is not opposed to a government in Iran based on Islamic fundamentalism; what it opposes is that regime's efforts to spread Islamic fundamentalism to other states through subversion, terrorism, and military aid to fundamentalist allies.

While the greatest mistake of status quo powers lies in not seeing what threatens their interests until it is too late, other notable pitfalls can stem from perceiving conflicts with revisionist powers in ideological terms and dismissing the idea of any possibilities for coexistence, rapprochement, and even progress toward a legitimate international order. In this regard, President Nixon's opening to China is especially noteworthy. Despite his reputation as a cold warrior, Nixon understood clearly that our conflicts with China stemmed not from its having a communist regime, but from its foreign policies—its expansionist ambitions and its support for wars of liberation in the developing world. Once those policies were placed in limbo, Nixon decided that it was time to reduce America's enemies among the Great Powers from two to one. Although decades of conflict, tensions, distrust, and even fighting against each other in Korea were obstacles standing in the way of reconciliation, the relaxation of tensions and the building of a partnership between the two nations occurred with striking rapidity. A similar change occurred in American-Soviet relations after Mikhail Gorbachev began to chart his "new course" in foreign policy.

While Frederick the Great was right when he said that a diplomacy without force is like a symphony orchestra without instruments, a diplomacy based on force alone will always be inadequate, especially in the age of nuclear weapons. If deterrence fails, the consequences could be catastrophic. But nuclear weapons aside, the problems nations face have always been as much political as military. Consider, for example, the interesting observation made by A. J. P. Taylor about British attempts to contain Russian expansion into the Ottoman Empire during the nineteenth century: "The Western powers could not alone inflict on Russia a decisive and lasting defeat; nor, even were she defeated, could they devise terms which would ensure against a renewal of expansion."[15]

During the Cold War, the United States faced a similar situation: the West could never win the Cold War through a decisive military victory, for that would mean a nuclear war, which would be suicidal for both parties. At the same time, victories in this limited war or that civil war would never really be decisive either. A victory in one area such as Korea, for example, would not ensure against a renewal of efforts to expand the Soviet sphere of influence later, as in Vietnam, Africa, or Central America. Still, until the revisionist power stops its course of revisionism, status quo powers have no alternative but to continue with policies of containment, deterrence, and coercive diplomacy.

Once the Soviet Union gained nuclear weapons, it became increasingly clear that both sides had an interest in alleviating tensions and creating ground rules for their competition, if only to avoid nuclear war. President Nixon's policy of détente complemented our containment policies by seeking to restrain Soviet behavior through the incentives of greater trade, investment, and cooperative undertakings. Greater interaction, Nixon believed, might lead to more normal relations and over time, perhaps, a winding down of Soviet revisionism. President Clinton's efforts to normalize relations with North Korea and Libya reflect more recent examples of strategies designed to move beyond the cold peace of containment and deterrence. In all such instances, timing and situational factors are crucial. Nixon's détente policies were highly controversial at the time, and their merits and effects are still being debated by historians, just as Clinton's overtures to North Korea and Libya are debated today. But in the end, genuine peace can come about only when status quo powers and revisionist powers become reconciled.

Two Perennial Problems Facing Status Quo Powers: Defending Undesirable Regimes and Fighting Limited Wars in the "Gray Areas"

DEFENDING UNDESIRABLE REGIMES. During the Cold War, many Americans were extremely uneasy about the nation's many alliances with authoritarian and repressive regimes, which frequently ruled over people mired in poverty. While President Truman acknowledged that the government of Greece "was not perfect" in his 1947 address to the Congress requesting aid for Greece and Turkey, many other Americans were appalled at the "right-wing dictatorship" that the United States was going to support under the guise of defending democracy. By the mid-1960s, in fact, "the free world" that America led contained notorious dictatorships in Latin America, the Middle East, and Asia, and in the last decade of the Cold War, the United States was supporting right-wing juntas in El Salvador and Guatemala whose human rights records were atrocious.

The president who first sought to address this problem systematically was Jimmy Carter, who had made human rights the center of his 1976 presidential campaign bid. In an address to the graduating class at Notre Dame in May 1977, President Carter outlined his administration's new directions in foreign policy. "Being confident of our own future," he told the assembled graduates, "we are now free of that inordinate fear of communism which once led us to embrace any dictator who joined us in that fear." Rather than containing communism by supporting traditional dictatorships, the Carter administration would now promote democracy by proclaiming American principles, waging an international war on poverty, and serving as an example for others to follow. "Words are action," Carter emphasized, and through words, he hoped "to persuade the Soviet Union that one country cannot impose its system of society upon another, either through direct military intervention or through the use of a client state's force, as was the case with Cuban intervention in Angola."[16]

True to his word, President Carter emplaced economic sanctions against authoritarian allies and refused to come to the aid of dictatorships that were besieged by "revolutionary forces" fighting for "freedom." Thus, Somoza fell to Marxist guerrillas in Nicaragua, and the autocratic shah of Iran fell to an infinitely more repressive theocratic dictatorship of the Ayatollah Khomeini. Carter's inactivity when old allies were under siege was purposeful. Rather than support dictators who violated human rights, Carter preferred to see them fall.

For Leonid Brezhnev and Fidel Castro, President Carter's diplomacy based on "words," "moral suasion," and "cooperation" could mean only one thing: America would no longer resist their efforts to increase the number of "progressive regimes" around the world by providing military aid to pro-Soviet guerrilla forces or intervening with Cuban troops in less-developed countries. As Carter pursued a foreign policy that was "designed to serve mankind," the Soviets and their allies used military force to secure friendly Marxist regimes in Angola, Mozambique, Ethiopia, Nicaragua, Southern Yemen, and Grenada, and they were working with the Cubans and Nicaraguan Sandinistas to overthrow the government of El Salvador.

After the fall of the shah and the taking of American hostages, Carter began to have doubts about the efficacy of words and the power of example. When the Soviets invaded Afghanistan in December 1979, the president told Frank Reynolds of ABC news: "My opinion of the Russians has changed more drastically in the last week than even the previous two and a half years before that. It is only now dawning upon the world the magnitude of the actions that the Soviets undertook in invading Afghanistan. . . . the action of the Soviets has made a more dramatic change in my opinion of what the Soviets' ultimate goals are than anything they've done in the previous time I've been in office."[17]

Suddenly, actions began to replace words as the basis for American diplomacy. Carter withdrew the SALT II Treaty from the Senate. He embargoed grain sales to the Soviet Union. He boycotted the 1980 Moscow Olympics. He authorized the CIA to provide assistance to the Mujaheddin resistance forces in Afghanistan. He initiated one of the largest military buildups in history. He increased assistance to El Salvador, a notoriously repressive dictatorship that was besieged by revolutionaries trained and aided by Nicaragua and Cuba, and he announced that the United States would use any means, including nuclear weapons, to prevent the oil fields in the Middle East from falling into Soviet hands.

In commenting critically on Carter's policy of speaking up for human rights and refusing to aid traditional dictators, former President Nixon made the following remarks in his book *The Real War*, which was written in 1980:

> . . . when a key country like Iran is involved, we must never forget that our choice is usually not between the man in power who is our friend and somebody better, but rather between him and someone far worse.

We must not set higher standards of conduct for our friends than for our enemies.

We must not insist on forcing American-style democracy on nations with different backgrounds and different problems. They must move in their own way at their own pace towards the goals that we in the West have taken hundreds of years to achieve.

. . . Exerting more pressure on friendly regimes that provide some rights and do not threaten their neighbors than we exert on hostile regimes that provide no rights and do threaten their neighbors is not only hypocritical, it is stupid. Alliances are arrangements of convenience. Allies do not have to love one another or even admire one another; it is enough that they need one another. Being in an alliance neither obliges nor entitles us to deliver condescending lectures in political morality to our partners.

. . . The United States has been taking a beating all over the world because the deck has been stacked: neutral or Western-oriented nations have been open hunting grounds for the Soviets and their proxies, while communist countries have been privileged sanctuaries; and the Russians have been giving their clients guns, while we have been giving ours lectures on human rights.[18]

But, do Nixon's comments mean that the United States should have supported any dictator under siege? Of course not—not any more than Carter's professions of support for democracy led him to renounce support for all dictatorships. Despite his opposition to dictatorships and violations of human rights, Carter had no qualms of conscience about befriending what was clearly the most repressive regime of his era, the People's Republic of China, a regime that, despite its repressive and totalitarian nature, Carter considered "a key force for global peace."[19]

Decision makers must work with the world as they find it, and societies are not tinker toys whereby traditional dictatorships can be turned into stable democracies by merely pulling one structure apart and shaping the tinkers into another one. Such cannot happen and never will. The real issue is not so much democracy but viability—whether a regime is stable and has the loyalty of its people. South Korea was a dictatorship in 1950, but its people did not rise up in support of the invading North Korean forces as Kim Il Sung expected. In South Vietnam, on the other hand, getting a regime that could secure the loyalty of the South Vietnamese people and getting them to resist efforts by guerrillas to communize the country was a major difficulty facing three American presidents.

Answers to questions of whom to support, when, where, and to what extent will always depend on circumstance and probable consequences. At the outset of the Cold War, the United States had to decide whether to support the traditional and semiauthoritarian regimes in Iran, Turkey, and Greece or watch them be bullied and pulled into Stalin's totalitarian sphere of influence. When the tide turned in these three countries, Secretary of State Acheson spoke to this question in an address to members of The Advertising Council in February 1950. The following excerpt from his remarks is well worth several careful readings:

> We must be prepared to meet whenever possible all thrusts of the Soviet Union. It will not always be possible to anticipate where these thrusts will take place, and we will not always be able to deal with them with equal effectiveness.
>
> In the case of Greece and Turkey we were able to meet them effectively because the Greeks and the Turks were determined to maintain their independence. There were a lot of Greeks and Turks [who] did not like their government. There were a lot that did. But they were united in a common belief that they preferred it to any form of government that might be imposed on them from the outside. The Greeks were able with our assistance, to meet military force with military force. The Turks have successfully resisted the powerful pressure brought against them. It should be borne in mind that in this case we are not dealing with threats to Greece and Turkey alone. The thrust that the Soviet Union was making in this case was directed at domination of the entire Near East and, then, at all of Europe.
>
> It has been suggested by some people that the Greek and Turkish Governments were not our kind of democracy and therefore we should not have given aid to them. Of course, they do not have exactly the same kind of institutions that we do. But we are not dealing here with the kind of situation where we can go from one country to another with a piece of litmus paper and see whether everything is true blue, whether political, economic, and social climate is exactly, in all its details, the kind we would like to have either for them or for us. The only question that we should ask is whether they are determined to protect their independence against communist aggression, and if they are, we should recognize our basic unity with them on this point.[20]

Finally, there is the question of prospects for the future. Imperfect countries today may evolve into creditable regimes over time, a point well made by Max Hastings in *The Korean War:* "In Korea, as in Vietnam, the democracies supported the cause of a flawed society. Yet they were fighting against opponents representing an even harsher tyranny. Who can doubt that if Hanoi had been defeated, South Vietnam would enjoy today the same prosperity as South Korea, and its people at least a greater measure of freedom today than they can look for under communism."[21]

DEALING WITH THE GRAY AREAS. A more serious problem with a strategy of containment is the following dilemma:

On the one hand, if a major status quo power announces that it will seek to contain a revisionist power everywhere, a so-called "perimeter" policy, it immediately runs into Lippmann's problem of insolvency. No nation has the resources to defend every regime sitting next to a revisionist Great Power, nor do its interests require that it intervene everywhere.

On the other hand, if the nation announces that it will defend only vital areas, a so-called "strong point" policy,[22] it may quickly find itself with "the Acheson problem." If a status quo power indicates that certain areas fall outside its defense perimeter, as Acheson did in January 1950, the revisionist power may think it has been given a green light to invade. In that event, the status quo power winds up fighting a war of inadvertence—a war it might not have had to fight if it had announced a perimeter strategy in the first place.

If the United States made a mistake during the Cold War, it was in thinking that it had to support every regime that came under siege in the noncommunist world. In effect, America's strategic thinking was like that of a chess player whose strategy had as its central principle: never cede any pawn under any circumstance. Such, for example, was implied in the ringing refrain in John F. Kennedy's inaugural address that the United States would "pay any price, bear any burden, meet any hardship, support any friend, oppose any foe to assure the survival and success of liberty."

In fact, the United States never followed the strategy heralded in Kennedy's refrain. *Circumstances, resources,* and *prospects for success* always played a significant role in determining the responses of American decision makers to moves by communist powers. In the late 1940s, the Truman administration decided to de-commit when it concluded that no amount of American aid would enable the nationalist regime of Chiang Kai-shek to defeat Mao Zedong's communist forces. Several years later, President Eisenhower chose to fold rather than raise the ante by using air strikes to relieve battered French garrisons entrapped at Dien Bien Phu during France's Indochina war. When Chinese forces crushed a rebellion in Tibet five years later, President Eisenhower again did nothing because Tibet mattered little in a strategic sense, and the United States had no usable military instruments that could have made a difference at any reasonable cost. In 1961, an American-supported anticommunist government in Laos was clearly losing a civil war against communist and neutralist forces. After hearing what the joint chiefs said it would take to turn the tide, President Kennedy opted for a face-saving agreement that "neutralized" Laos and allowed him to withdraw gracefully.

Obviously, "gray area" countries should possess well-armed, deterrent forces, but once deterrence fails, hard calculations have to be on the basis of the following criteria:

- The precise objective of any military operations and the potential obstacles to obtaining those objectives.
- The resources it would take to secure those objectives under different conditions.

- The extent to which military operations might draw down resources needed to secure other commitments.
- The viability of the regime under attack. The strength of its will and capacity to resist.
- The impact of action inaction on the nation's credibility and prestige.
- The circumstances under which the situation arises.

The Pattern Is More Important than the Particulars.

What really matters is not so much the fate of one or more pawns, but the overall pattern and scorecard. What matters is that status quo powers pursue a strategy of resisting in areas where resistance will work, imposing costs on the other side even when resistance fails, rolling back some of the revisionist's gains, and seeking to divide the opponent's coalition.

No other president understood these points better than Ronald Reagan. Many of his critics have pointed out the Cold Warrior president's inconsistency in invading Marxist Grenada but not Marxist Nicaragua. Yet Reagan's "inconsistency" reflected simple prudence. Taking Granada was an easy win that sent a clear message: The United States would take advantage of opportunities wherever the Soviet side was vulnerable. An American invasion in Nicaragua would have created a great political uproar in the United States and abroad, and it might have entrapped American troops in a Vietnam-like quagmire. Instead of invading, Reagan supported the Contra forces, which bled the Sandinista regime economically and taxed it politically. In addition, he also sought to impose costs on the Soviet side by supporting anticommunist guerrilla forces in Angola and Afghanistan. His goal was simple: he wanted the Soviets to know that *they were dealing with a competitor and not a passive defender* who merely stood around waiting for the Soviets to make their next move.

Coalitions May Not Be as Fearsome as They Might Seem.

Coalitions of like-minded powers, whether status quo or revisionist, are always more fragile than many people might think. Interests of coalition partners are seldom identical, and nations do not like to take risks or make sacrifices to secure the interests of other powers, no matter how close their ideological affinities may be.

We have already seen that Stalin was unwilling to risk war with the United States to liberate North Korea or Taiwan. Earlier, Stalin's reluctance to support Yugoslavia in its dispute with the Western powers over Trieste led Marshal Tito to rethink his relationship with Moscow. Similarly, Stalin's insistence that the revolutionary effort in Greece be "folded up" after the Truman Doctrine was announced led Tito to believe that in a crunch he might have to face the West alone. To cite one final Cold War example, Soviet Premier Nikita Khrushchev was frequently at odds with Mao Zedong over the issue of Taiwan, which the Chinese leader wanted to invade.

In the interwar period, the solidarity of the fascist powers was always more bravado than reality. When Britain and France declared war on Germany after the invasion of Poland, Italy remained neutral. Only Hitler's lightning victories in 1941 and the fall of France led Mussolini to get into the act for fear of losing a share of the spoils that a German victory might yield. When Hitler invaded Russia, Japan did not lift a finger to help the Germans. In fact, fascist Japan and Bolshevik Russia were neutral until the very end of the Pacific War. Only when victory was certain did Stalin decide to enter the war, and even then, only after being promised territorial gains by FDR at Yalta. Meanwhile, General Franco did everything he could to keep Spain neutral during the war despite the generous Italian and German military assistance that made his victory in the civil war with loyalist forces possible.

As a general rule, the larger an ideological bloc becomes the more it will tend to fragment through schisms based on the conflicting interests of its members. For example, by the end of the 1970s, the Soviet Union was the only country in the world surrounded by hostile communist powers. Communist China had become its avowed enemy. Communist Yugoslavia was armed by the West. Communist Albania had left the Soviet bloc and was allied with Communist China. Communist Romania had slipped into a policy of neutralism. Communist Poland was on the verge of dissolution by the anticommunist forces of solidarity. Czechoslovakia and Hungary were seeking as much independence and autonomy as they could get away with.

As Harvard professor Adam Ulam noted years ago, the expansion of communism was never in the national interest of the Soviet Union. Every time a country was added to the bloc, the responsibilities of the Soviet Union increased—new allies meant more expenditures for aid and increased risks and obligation to provide security for the new pawn. In the late 1970s and early 1980s, Rand Corporation economist Charles Wolf estimated that client states were costing the Soviet Union close to 5 percent of its GNP.[23]

During the Cold War, American policymakers tended to overestimate the power of ideology in international politics and underestimate the power of both nationalism and national interests. Yet, conflicting nationalisms and national interests were at the root of the Sino-Soviet split that was decisive in leading to an end of the Cold War. President Nixon's opening to China and the American-Chinese rapprochement overwhelmingly trumped any Soviet gains from the communization of Vietnam, Cambodia, and Laos—and the West's gain was attained by the stroke of a pen.

Circumstances and Contexts Always Matter.

When the North Koreans invaded South Korea in 1950, Europe and Japan were still struggling to get on their feet economically, Czechoslovakia had been communized recently through a conspiratorial coup, China had just fallen, and the Soviets had broken America's atomic monopoly. The context was one of fear and trepidation among America's closest allies, and American acquiescence in a successful North Korean invasion might well have created the impression of an unstoppable colossus that would have demoralized America's European allies and, perhaps, turned them to neutralism.

When America began its involvement in Vietnam in the late 1950s and early 1960s, power still appeared fluid. Nikita Khrushchev had precipitated a major crisis over Berlin and threatened NATO allies with nuclear strikes. In the Third World, the gregarious Soviet premier was promoting "sacred wars of national liberation" to tie the resource rich, newly independent countries to the Soviet bloc. In Fidel Castro, both Khrushchev and Kennedy saw a dedicated revolutionary whose charismatic power might turn Latin America into a continent of revolutionary, anti-American regimes. On his trip to America in 1959, the ebullient Soviet leader bluntly asserted, "We will bury you." In the context of the early 1960s, the conflicts in Laos and Vietnam were seen as part of a menacing Soviet offensive.

Within a few years, however, the context had changed considerably. By the mid-1960s, Europe and Japan were politically stable and their economies were booming. The Soviets had backed down in Berlin, and their retreat in the Cuban missile crisis revealed how inadequate Soviet nuclear forces were in comparison to America's. Meanwhile, Khrushchev's "wars of liberation" campaign turned out to be a flop almost everywhere—guerrillas supported by Fidel Castro were defeated in Venezuela and made no inroads elsewhere. Soviet sponsored leftists in the Congo were similarly defeated, and most postcolonial nations decided on a path of nonalignment on cold war issues.

Only in Vietnam were communist forces doing well, having the same advantage that they had against the French. Vietnam was the only area in the former colonial world where a communist movement was able to capture the forces of anticolonialism and nationalism. The strongest weapon that the communist forces had in Vietnam was not their military strength but their legitimacy as liberators from French colonialism. While the loss of Vietnam would be regrettable, the stakes in the conflict, both geopolitically and psychologically, were a lot less in the mid-1960s than they were just a few years earlier. At the same time, the ability to prevail was much more difficult because South Vietnam was less viable than South Korea had been and the guerrilla tactics of the enemy made it difficult to bring American military assets to bear on the situation.

On the other hand, there is no free lunch in life, and even with a fairly solvent containment policy, the time may come when points must be defended with military force. In the age of nuclear weapons, total war is unthinkable, and a policy of isolationism would allow others to set the terms under which we live. While every point on the map is not of equal strategic importance and every point need not be defended under any circumstances, there is a basic truth to former Secretary of State Dean Rusk's quip that, "If you don't pay attention to the periphery, you will find out that your back yard has become the periphery."

Still, limited wars are America's Achilles' heel no matter how impeccable their logic may be: limited casualties resulting from limited wars in far-off places may well prevent massive casualties in total wars. Yet, it goes greatly against the American grain to have its young men die for less than total or noble causes. All democracies treasure their youth, and they hesitate to sacrifice them in lands far from their soil.

The problem of limited wars in "gray areas" is inherent in any strategy for dealing with revisionism and maintaining the peace. While there is no simple formula for dealing with this problem, a few simple precepts should always be borne in mind:

> For really vital points, put your own troops in harms' way and arm them well.
> For points on the periphery, provide generous arms and military and economic assistance.

When it became clear that the American people would tolerate "no more Vietnams," President Richard Nixon did not simply cut bait with allies in the gray areas. Instead, he pledged that the United States would still supply and train local troops, and, if allies were still subjected to aggression, the United States would use its tremendous air and fire power to impose horrendous costs on communist efforts to change the status quo by military force. Nixon's purpose was not to impose the costs, but to deter attempts at violent change in the first place through his threat to impose costs.

Work to restrain revisionist ambitions by stressing the costly consequences that forceful efforts to change the status quo might entail. Creating peace, according to Henry Kissinger, has as much to do with seeking to restrain ambitions as it does with efforts at deterrence. Containment seeks to maintain peace by threatening potential costs to efforts at expansion; a diplomacy that seeks to restrain ambitions emphasizes the benefits that restraint might gain. For example, during the late 1970s, many people worried that the death of the aging Marshal Tito might tempt the Soviets to invade Yugoslavia and put a client government in power as the marshal's successor. Thus, the question arose as to whether the United States should fight or stand by in the event of a Soviet invasion. To fight, of course, risked at best another Korea and at worst escalation to a European or global nuclear war. However, to stand by and do nothing might weaken the cohesion of NATO and seriously split the alliance.

The solution to this dilemma lay not so much in Yugoslavia as elsewhere. If the Soviets did intend to invade Yugoslavia, the United States still had options other than making noble-sounding but futile speeches in the United Nations. Even before such action took place, the United States could have clearly spelled out the possible consequences by directing a series of questions to Soviet decision makers: How, in the event of an invasion, could the United States convince the West Germans that they should continue to forgo nuclear arms and rely on the word of the United States? How could the United States resist German demands for access to nuclear weapons to deter a similar fate for themselves? Even if the United States refused such a German request, would the Germans acquiesce and not seek to obtain weapons on their own? And if they did, would a nuclear-armed Germany be in any country's interest, let alone worth the restoration of Yugoslavia to its former status as a Russian satellite? What *diplomacy* might have stressed to the Soviets were the larger incentives they had for allowing Yugoslavia to continue as the nonaligned and nonthreatening state it has been for more than twenty-five years.

A similar situation exists today in regard to China. A frequent question in the late 1990s was whether America should go to war if China used military force to regain Taiwan. When the question is asked that directly, the answer is almost forgone—Americans would never go to war with China over Taiwan. What the United States could do is to ensure, through the placement of its forces, that the Chinese would entail significant costs and risks in undertaking a military operation. Then, through diplomacy, the United States could seek to restrain the Chinese in regard to Taiwan by trying to have the situation "fudged" or put off.

During the Cold War, China's fear of the Soviet Union led it to place the issue of Taiwan in limbo because it did not want to alienate the United States, which it needed to balance the Soviets and to gain assistance in modernizing its economy. Once the Cold War ended, so did China's fear of Russia, and, increasingly, China's success as a modernizing nation has provided it with alternatives to America for investment and trade opportunities. China now needs to be less solicitous of American views about Taiwan. Still, the United States is not without leverage in getting China to see that the risks and potential costs of a military operation against Taiwan may have far larger and more enduring costs for China than a policy of patient waiting.

Status quo powers should support countries that prefer neutrality, and, if possible, insure that neutrals have the arms they need to deter any power seeking to undo that neutrality. Americans disliked many positions that nonaligned leaders took during the Cold War—their opposition to America's nuclear testing, their insistence that communist China be admitted to the United Nations, their continual carping about Portuguese colonialism and apartheid in Africa, and their demands for a new international economic order that would transfer wealth from rich countries to poor countries. Still, genuinely neutral countries were always an asset rather than a liability for the United States because such countries remained sources of power independent of the Soviet bloc. As President Eisenhower noted to his brother, Edgar, in 1956:

> For a long time, I have held that it is a very grave error to ask some of these nations to announce themselves as being on our side. . . . Such a statement on the part of a weak nation like Burma, or even India, would at once make them our all-out ally, and we would have the impossible task of helping them arm for defense.
>
> Moreover, if a country would declare itself our military ally, then any attack made upon it by Communist groups would be viewed in most areas of the world as a more or less logical consequence. Since so much of the world thinks of the existing ideological struggle as a power struggle, the reaction to the kind of incident I talk about would be, "Well, they asked for it."
>
> On the other hand, if the Soviets attacked an avowed neutral, world opinion would be outraged.[24]

All Strategies for Peace Must Be Tailor Made

All of the benchmarks presented above will always be only a starting point for thinking strategically about foreign policy. As I tell my students, no one will ever come up with a checklist that will provide ready answers whenever a new foreign policy issue arises. While there are great continuities in history, novel contexts and situations always make decision making difficult.

However, one thing is certain: *If status quo powers refuse to make the commitments necessary to secure their vital interests or if they fail to provide resources adequate to secure those commitments, their security and their lives will be hostage to the pleasure and sufferance of others.* Well intentioned, "peaceful foreign policies" or self-abnegating gestures seldom restrain or quench the appetites of revisionist powers as Donald Kagan notes in the quotation opening this chapter. In his now classic study of Metternich's diplomacy Henry Kissinger wrote the following on the very first page: "Whenever peace—conceived as the avoidance of war—had been the primary objective of a power or a group of powers, the international system has been at the mercy of the most ruthless member of the international community."[25]

But so much for theory. The following two notable case studies were selected to illustrate the theoretical principles presented in this chapter: Neville Chamberlain's efforts to create a peace with Nazi Germany and Harry Truman's effort to build a relationship with Russia after World War II.

CASE STUDY
Conciliation without Containment: Neville Chamberlain Deals with the German Problem[26]

By the time Hitler came to power, most members of the British elite firmly believed that German complaints about the Versailles settlement were completely justified and demanded rectification. The problem in such situations, however, is figuring out how to rectify the injustices without looking weak or whetting the appetite of the aggrieved party. In addition, rectification requires those who benefit from those "injustices" to give up peacefully what they then possess, and as Henry Kissinger has noted, "No nation agrees to re-draw its borders—especially to its own disadvantage—unless there is an overwhelming necessity to do so."[27]

In the case of Versailles, the Czechs would have had to yield the Sudetenland and Poland would have had to accept changes in Germany's favor in the areas of Danzig and the Polish corridor. Given the obvious opposition to such proposals from France, Poland, and Czechoslovakia and, given the fact that inertia is always a strong force in politics, British leaders did nothing until Hitler began initiating changes through unilateral faits accompli.

As noted in Chapter 1, when Hitler revealed in March 1935 that Germany already possessed an air force and would build an army of five hundred thousand men, Italy, France, and Britain responded with mere paper protests that warned against future "unilateral actions" to change the status quo in Europe. When the German dictator challenged this warning one year later by marching his troops into the demilitarized Rhineland, the British response was one of acquiescence, if not tacit approval. Yet, with this one stroke, *taken from a position of overwhelming military weakness,* Hitler negated the military structure undergirding the Versailles settlement. With Germany now able to fortify its war-making industrial heartland against attack, only one question remained: would the territorial provisions of Versailles be revised on the basis of some consensual European settlement or on the basis of unilateral German dictates?

Such was the situation when Neville Chamberlain became prime minister of Britain in March of 1937. Although in his seventies, Chamberlain was an energetic, if not driven, worker who put in long days that would tire men half his age. He was cultured, highly intelligent, articulate, self-confident almost to the point of arrogance, firmly grounded in his convictions, and a skilled and formidable debater in parliament. He ran his government in an authoritarian manner and made no bones about the fact that he would be in charge of foreign policy. The image of Chamberlain as a tired and doddering old man who was completely out of his league in dealing with Hitler belongs in the realm of historical mythology.

By the time Chamberlain took office, the idea of a settlement with Germany had become increasingly central to British diplomacy. Britain and France would offer generous colonial and economic concessions in return for Germany's acceptance of minor changes in the Versailles treaty regarding central Europe.[28] The objective was to reintegrate Germany into Europe as a coequal, satisfied Great Power that then would stabilize central Europe and stand as a bulwark against Bolshevism. While Germany might not gain all it wanted from such a settlement, her gains would greatly exceed the costs of a long war that would probably yield not much more.

Chamberlain played a major role in shaping this approach when he served as chancellor of the Exchequer in the previous Baldwin government. On becoming prime minister, Chamberlain deeply believed that his own personal power would get Hitler to see reason. "If only we could sit down at a table with the Germans and run through their complaints and claims with a pencil," he told Soviet ambassador Maxim Maiskey, "this would greatly relieve tension."[29] While reaching out to Germany, Chamberlain allowed Britain's relationship with France to cool to underscore Britain's independence and to avoid stirring up any fears of encirclement in German minds. However, Chamberlain never believed in peace at any price. As the case of Czechoslovakia makes clear, Chamberlain was willing to go to war if Germany tried to settle by military force issues that could be settled peacefully by reasonable men.

Chamberlain's first opportunity for an overture to Hitler came in November 1937 when Lord Edward Halifax, a noted British huntsman, received an invitation from Hermann Goering to attend an international hunting expedition in Berlin. After meeting with Goering and other high officials, Halifax had to travel to Berchtesgaden to talk with Hitler, who did not attend the exposition because of his opposition to killing animals. There, Halifax was sobered by the extent of Hitler's demands and his passionate ranting and raving about his critics in the British Parliament and press. Still, Halifax made it clear to Hitler that the Chamberlain government would not oppose changes in central Europe as long as they were made peacefully. While Hitler read Halifax's message as a sign of British irresolution, Chamberlain saw the visit as "a great success" because it achieved its object: "creating an atmosphere in which it is possible to discuss with Germany the practical questions involved in a European settlement."[30]

Several months later, Hitler had his infamous meeting with Austrian chancellor Schuschnigg at Berchtesgaden. Having submitted to Hitler's demands that the Nazi Party be legalized and that a leading Austrian Nazi-sympathizer, Seyss-Inquart, be appointed minister of the interior, Schuschnigg quickly saw the handwriting on the wall as Nazi demonstrations and riots broke out all across Austria. To forestall a German invasion undertaken under the pretext of a necessity to restore order, Schuschnigg proposed a plebiscite on the question of Anschluss for Wednesday, March 9, 1938. Hitler's response was immediate: Schuschnigg had three hours to call off the plebiscite and resign; otherwise, his country would face a withering German invasion. "We are yielding to force," Schuschnigg told the Austrian people in his resignation speech one hour after Hitler's deadline had passed.[31]

Hitler's conquest of Austria was not the kind of peaceful change that Chamberlain had in mind. When Halifax heard the news, he placed his face into his hands and exclaimed, "Horrible, horrible." When the Foreign Office lodged an official protest, the Germans replied that Austria was no business of Britain. Two days after the invasion, Chamberlain told the House of Commons that, as a member of the League of Nations, Austria and the other countries of Eastern Europe were of interest to Britain and that Hitler's means of incorporating Austria was a shock to all who were working for peace. What Chamberlain objected to was not the change in Austria's status, but the unilateral and bullying way in which it was done.

The Anschluss engulfed Hitler's next victim with German military power on three sides. Although Goering had assured the Czechs that, "on his word of honor," Germany had no designs on Czech territory, Hitler quickly began planning Operation Green, an invasion of Czechoslovakia that would be legitimated by "a period of diplomatic discussions which would gradually lead to a crisis and war." After a manufactured incident, such as "the murder of the German Minister in the course of an anti-German demonstration," German military forces would engage in a lightning strike.[32]

While military plans and forces were being readied, the political campaign got under way. The techniques were the same as in Austria. German SS agents worked with the Sudeten Germans in manufacturing incidents and "provocations," which were followed by demonstrations, agitation, riots, and the publication of grievances and demands. Hitler instructed the Sudeten leader, Conrad Henlein, to make demands that the Czechs could never accept. In this way, the onus for the continuing crisis would lie with the Czech government, and the ensuing unrest would legitimate German military intervention in defense of self-determination for an oppressed minority.

Czechoslovakia was also on Chamberlain's mind. Ten days after the Austrian conquest, Chamberlain told the House of Commons that:

> *his government's most urgent duty [was] how best to restore this shaken confidence, how to maintain the rule of law in international affairs, how to seek peaceful solutions to questions that continue to cause anxiety. Of these the one which is necessarily most present to many minds is that which concerns Czechoslovakia and the German minority in that country; and it is probable that a solution of this question, if it could be achieved, would go far to re-establish a sense of stability over an area much wider than the immediately concerned. . . .*
>
> *. . . So far as Czechoslovakia is concerned, it seems to His Majesty's Government that now is the time when all the resources of diplomacy should be enlisted in the cause of peace.*[33]

By late summer 1938, Hitler's manufactured crisis was in full swing. Infiltrated SS troops were provoking crises, incidents, and riots. Property was being destroyed and refugees were storming into Germany. In September, the Czech government accepted all of Henlein's "unacceptable demands" but one—that it defer to Germany in matters of foreign policy, an outrageous demand to be part of a proposal for internal reform. The response of the Sudetens? They broke off negotiations. On September 12, Hitler delivered a fiery speech at a Nuremberg rally in which he called for self-determination and claimed that, while the Arabs in Palestine were defenseless and abandoned, the Sudeten Germans were not. Germany would take care of her own, Hitler told his partisans, and he issued the following ominous warning: "I hope that foreign statesmen will be convinced that these are not mere words."

On the day after Hitler's fiery speech, Chamberlain decided to take the daring gamble of flying off to Germany to resolve the crisis personally with Hitler. His strategy was to pressure the Czechs to meet Hitler's demands in return for a British guarantee to defend the remainder of Czechoslovakia. At the same time, he would give a stern warning to Hitler: If Germany initiated military force over the Sudeten issue and Czechoslovakia and France resisted, Britain would declare war on Germany.

The first meeting occurred in Hitler's lair at Berchtesgaden on September 15. While both men talked about the importance of good Anglo-German relations, Hitler was unyielding: "The return to the Reich of 3 million Germans in Czechoslovakia he would make possible at all costs. He would face any war, and even the risk of a world war, for this. Here the limit had been reached where the rest of the world might do as it liked, he would not yield a single step."[34]

Taking at face value Hitler's repeated claim that Germany had no other territorial demands beyond the Sudetenland, Chamberlain bluntly responded: "It ought to be possible for the Fuehrer and himself to prevent a world war on account of these 3 million Sudeten Germans."

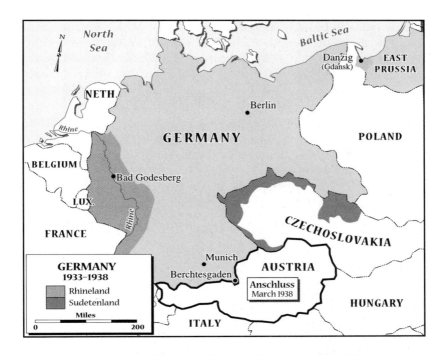

Map 4.1. Neville Chamberlain Faces Adolph Hitler

After Adolph Hitler announced Germany's rearmament and occupied the demilitarized Rhineland (see Chapter 1, p. 15), British elites decided to rectify the Versailles treaty. After Hitler united Austria with Germany through threats and intimidation, Neville Chamberlain made three trips to Germany to settle the Sudetenland question peacefully—first in Hitler's lair at Berchtesgaden, next to Bad Godesberg, and last to Munich—which led to the infamous Munich agreement. After having proclaimed that the Sudetenland was his last territorial demand, Hitler quickly insisted on rectification of the Polish "corridor," which split Germany in two, and the restoration of Gdansk to Germany. When Poland refused, Hitler unleashed his "blitzkrieg," which led Britain and France to declare war on Germany.

However, when Chamberlain tried to get into the details of resolving the problem, Hitler replied that "all these discussions were of a purely theoretical nature, since the march of events was continuing at a rapid pace." The issue, Hitler told Chamberlain, was "knowing whether Britain was now prepared to assent to the detachment of the Sudeten German districts on the basis of national self-determination, and in this connection he (the Fuehrer) was obliged to observe that this right of self-determination had not just been invented by him in 1938 specially for the Czechoslovak question but that it had been brought into being in 1918 in order to create a moral basis for the changes made under the Treaty of Versailles." For conversations to continue, Hitler repeated, "the British Prime Minister must first of all state whether he could accept this basis or not, namely, the secession of the Sudeten German region by the virtue of self-determination." Chamberlain replied that, although he personally accepted self-determination as a principle for settlement, he would have to return to Britain to get the assent of his government and the other parties.

Six days later, Chamberlain returned to Germany. In their meeting at Godesberg, Chamberlain reported that the British, French, and Czech governments were all willing to support the principle of self-determination. After Chamberlain presented their procedures for implementing the principle, Hitler responded that the prime minister's proposals, "could not be maintained." It was his duty, he said, to ensure that the territorial claims being made by the Poles and Hungarians for parts of Czechoslovakia be settled as well.

Chamberlain was stunned: "He had got exactly what the Fuehrer wanted and without the expenditure of a drop of German blood."[35] Moreover, he had taken "his political life into his hands," by gaining the assent of all three governments. "When he first traveled to Germany he had been cheered; on this trip," he told Hitler, "people booed and claimed he was 'selling the Czechs, yielding to dictators, capitulating,' etc."

"Why were the proposals he had made not been regarded as acceptable?" Chamberlain asked. His hope, he said, "was to show the world that the orderly operation of treaty revision could be achieved by peaceful means." When the prime minister asked if he had any proposal to make, Hitler replied that, "A frontier line must be drawn at once—he did not hold with commissions, committees, etc., he declared parenthetically—from which the Czechs must withdraw the army, police, and all State organs; this area would be at once occupied by Germany."

Hitler's foreign minister Joachim von Ribbentrop then produced a memorandum that demanded the Czechs begin evacuating the Sudeten areas on September 26, less then two days ahead, and complete the withdrawal by September 28. Once the areas were in German hands, a commission would arrange plebiscites in mixed areas by November 25. After much discussion, Hitler announced that the memorandum represented his last word, although he would agree to delay the invasion date to October 1 to give Chamberlain time to return to Britain and confer with his colleagues and allies.

When the Czechs rejected the memorandum, Chamberlain wrote to Hitler that if German troops entered the Sudetenland, he felt sure that the Czech government would resist and implied that war would follow. On the same day, Hitler gave a speech at the Berlin Sportpalast in which he berated the Czech government and claimed that his demand for the Sudetenland was "the last territorial claim which I have to make in Europe, but it is the claim from which I will not recede and which, God willing, I will make good." At the end of his address, Hitler delivered a clear ultimatum: "My patience is now at an end! I have made Mr. Beneš an offer which is nothing but the carrying into effect what he has already promised. The decision now lies in his hands: Peace or War."

In response, Chamberlain expressed his incredulity "that the people of Europe who do not want war with one another should be plunged into a bloody struggle over a question on which agreement has already been largely obtained." Later that evening Lord Halifax authorized the following warning: "[if] a German attack is made on Czechoslovakia, the immediate result will be that France will be bound to come to her assistance, and Great Britain and Russia will certainly stand by France."[36]

With Europe verging to war "over a timetable," as Chamberlain put it, the prime minister sent his close personal adviser, Horace Wilson, to Berlin for one last effort to get a negotiated settlement. After listening to a letter from Chamberlain and further remarks from Wilson, Hitler agreed to one final meeting but only on the conditions that the Czech government accepted the Godesberg memorandum and that the meeting terminate in two days; otherwise, the invasion would take place on October 1. When Hitler later said, "I will smash the Czechs," Wilson reiterated Chamberlain's message that if Hitler invaded Czechoslovakia and France became involved, Britain would stand behind France." When Hitler heard the translation, he responded by saying, "I don't care a bit. I am prepared for every eventuality."

Despite these harsh words, Hitler put off his mobilization until 2:00 P.M. on September 29 to allow representatives of the four Great Powers to meet at Munich. When they assembled, Mussolini quickly tabled a set of proposals that he passed off as his own but had been written by the Germans. The proposal contained everything Hitler demanded at Godesberg. This time, however, France and Britain agreed that the Czechs, who were excluded from the deliberations, would not be allowed to reject the decision. The agreement also contained provisions for the settlement of Polish and Hungarian claims against Czechoslovakia. In return for yielding, the Czechs would receive a British and French guarantee of their new boundaries. German and Italian guarantees would also follow once the Hungarian and Polish claims had been resolved.

Believing Hitler's assertion that the Sudetenland was his last territorial demand in Europe, Chamberlain was confident that he had attained peace in Europe. The next morning he met with Hitler alone and presented for his signature an Anglo-German Declaration. This declaration was, in fact, the paper that Chamberlain waved when he returned to England and proclaimed that he had obtained "peace in our time." The central passages of the document read as follows:

> We regard the agreement signed last night and the Anglo-German Naval Agreement as symbolic of the desire of our two peoples never to go to war again.
>
> We are resolved that the method of consultation shall be the method adopted to deal with any other questions that may concern our two countries, and we are determined to continue our efforts to remove possible sources of difference and thus to contribute to assure the peace of Europe.[37]

Chamberlain's hopes, however, were quickly dashed. Six months later, Hitler took the rest of Czechoslovakia. With all of Czechoslovakia gone, Poland was engulfed militarily, and Hitler's plans for seizing Danzig and Memel were already being laid.[38] Foolishly, the Poles believed that Hitler would spare them because of their role as cynical accomplices in the dismemberment of Czechoslovakia. However, their illusions were shattered less than one month after Munich when German foreign minister von Ribbentrop demanded Danzig and an East-West corridor.

During the Polish crisis, it became apparent that Chamberlain's behavior at Munich reflected neither weakness nor fecklessness but a desire to be fair and conciliatory. As the crisis began to build during the spring of 1939, Chamberlain remarked that, "Herr Hitler's attitude made it impossible to continue to negotiate on the old basis." He told his cabinet that, "No reliance could be placed on any assurance given by the Nazi leaders," and he announced publicly that the British government would resist "any further act of aggression on the part of Germany."[39] Chamberlain placed no pressure on the Poles to yield, and in April he pledged that if Hitler attacked Poland, Britain would come to her aid. One month later, he gave guarantees to Romania, Greece, and Turkey as well. To put further pressure on Hitler, Chamberlain even opened negotiations with Stalin to threaten Germany with a two-front war. But none of this diplomacy had any deterrent effect. When German troops stormed into Poland on September 1, 1939, a unified but unenthusiastic Britain went to war.

Neville Chamberlain sought to give Hitler a choice between the peaceful satisfaction of genuine German grievances and war. But he never really examined or tested the core assumption of his diplomacy—that Hitler was a limited revisionist who could be satisfied by undoing the worst of Versailles and welcoming him into the ranks of the oligarchy. Because of this assumption, Chamberlain had no qualms whatsoever about revising Versailles as long as it was done peacefully and with the assent of all the Great Powers.

One of the ironies of Chamberlain's diplomacy is that he wound up doing Hitler's work for him. Instead of Hitler having to apply pressure on the Czechs, it was Chamberlain who did the pressuring. In retrospect, Chamberlain's behavior does look like one delivering up to Hitler an object of prey. But a search for justice, not fear or cowardice, guided Chamberlain. His goal was to rectify long-standing injustices to Germany and the German people.

A more serious problem was Chamberlain's failure to integrate diplomatic and military strategies. While Chamberlain was for rearmament, his rearmament plans were limited to defending the British Isles and the empire. What he and many others in his generation failed to realize was that if Britain created military forces that could help to defend others, it would be less likely to have to defend itself, and to the extent that Britain only had forces to defend itself, the more likely it would find itself in a war defending itself. Chamberlain's efforts at conciliation were never matched with a military strategy that would place allied forces in harm's way if Germany trespassed beyond the limits of reasonable conciliation. This failure stemmed, in part, from the failure of British decision makers to see the significance of Eastern Europe to their security. While many British leaders readily proclaimed that Britain's defense lay on the Rhine River, they failed to see that there was more to securing that line of defense than merely agreeing to defend France in the event of a German invasion.

To deter and contain Hitler—to induce him to restrict his revisionism to rectifying Versailles—Chamberlain needed to build a structure of military power that would pose significant costs if Germany moved beyond clearly drawn lines. At a minimum, such a strategy would provide Germany's potential victims with greater capabilities to resist. It might even have included placing British troops in harm's way. Through such actions, potential victims would gain the courage to resist, and Hitler would have known that he could not expect the luxury of cheap and easy conquests.

To compound Germany's difficulties, the French might have reconfigured their defensive forces to allow strikes into Germany's industrial heartland if Hitler moved into Eastern Europe. Even after the Rhineland was in German hands, reconfigured French forces could still have threatened German industrial assets in ways that would have made military moves into the East risky. All of these moves could have been done without bringing in the Russians.

No one will ever know whether such acts would have contained Hitler. However, while most Germans did not like the situation in the Sudetenland, few were willing to go to war, especially world war, for the Sudeten Germans. If British and French troops had joined Czech forces in the Sudetenland fortifications, if Britain and France had warned that they would fight a limited war, and if they had placed their support behind the Czech's Fourth Plan, which offered the Sudetens three autonomous districts, Chamberlain might have combined power and legitimacy in ways that would have shoved Hitler into a corner and isolated him, even within the German government. After all, it was precisely Chamberlain's threat of a general war after the Godesberg meeting that led Hitler's generals and top Nazi aids to persuade him to go to Munich.

Hitler may have wanted a war, but he was not the only German who mattered. Had he sought to take Germany into a suicidal war, he might well have found that his marching orders were not followed. Even by themselves, the Czech fortifications would have made the success of Operation Green a costly one (as German generals realized when they took over the installations), and a fair settlement offer would have placed Hitler in the position of going to war over a proposal that essentially guaranteed the Sudetens everything they had demanded. To be sure, a diplomatic strategy that combined local military power with legitimacy might have attained only an "armed truce," but, certainly, armed truce was preferable to costly military losses on the installment plan or a general war. After all, the Cold War was an armed truce was until well into the 1960s.

Unfortunately, Chamberlain thought only in terms of general war or nothing, and since Britain was not prepared for total war, appeasement was all the more necessary, despite its counterproductive nature. In fact, Chamberlain gave little thought to the military impact of Hitler's smaller victories, although each one made the next conquest all the more easy, and each success made stopping him all the more difficult. In addition to adding eight new divisions to the Reichswehr, Hitler's capture of Austria made Czechoslovakia much more vulnerable than it was before. By acquiring Vienna, Hitler also gained control of crucial rail lines throughout southeastern Europe that could negate the effect of a naval blockade in the event of general war.

According to historian Williamson Murray, the conquest of Czechoslovakia made a crucial difference in Germany's ability to wage general war. In addition to the armament complexes at Skoda and Bruen, Germany gained 1,502 aircraft, 469 tanks, 500 antiaircraft guns, 43,000 machine guns, a million rifles, a billion rounds of ammunition, and 3 million rounds of artillery ammunition. All told, enough weapons to equip thirty German divisions. While thirty divisions were not directly added to the Wehrmacht, the conquest of Czechoslovakia gave Germany a surfeit of weapons that could be bartered or sold abroad to earn foreign exchange or used to fill out reserve units.

By April 1939, an average of twenty-three trains per day carried ammunition and weapons from Czechoslovakia to Germany.[40]

Chamberlain's diplomacy illustrates well the distinction between national defense and national security. What is necessary to fight and win a total war and what is necessary to prevent such a war in the first place are separate questions, each requiring a different politicomilitary strategy. Minimizing the chances of having to fight a total war involves making it extremely difficult for a revisionist power to get into a position from which it can risk such a war, and that is done by making every little victory as costly, draining, and difficult as possible.

Even after Czechoslovakia, Chamberlain failed to understand this distinction. While he gave solemn guarantees to Poland, Romania, Greece, and Turkey, he provided no military assistance to any of these countries. In fact, these essentially paper pledges only helped to confirm Hitler's assumption that Chamberlain would not act. Poland, like Czechoslovakia, he remarked to an associate, would be "served up to me by her friends."[41] On the eve of the invasion of Poland, members of the German high command raised concerns about what Britain and France might do in response. Hitler's response was curt and biting: "Our opponents are little worms. I saw them at Munich."

Obviously, the diplomacy of Mussolini and Hitler also failed because of their entrapment in wars of miscalculation, which they lost. But the significant question to ask about them is not why they failed, but why they got as far as they did in the first place. To answer that question, we find ourselves back with the status quo powers: Why did *they* fail to act in time?

CASE STUDY
Containment with the Prospect of Conciliation: Harry Truman Confronts Joseph Stalin

As World War II drew to a close, Soviet leader Joseph Stalin annexed the Baltic States of Estonia, Latvia, and Lithuania, all of Poland east of the Curzon line, and the Romanian provinces of Bessarabia and Bukovina. In Poland, Romania, Hungary, and Bulgaria, national communists were installing totalitarian governments under the protection of Soviet armed forces. In Yugoslavia, Tito's communist forces had triumphed over the royalist, Çhetnik forces, while in Greece, resistance forces were armed, powerful, popular, and heavily communist. Only in Czechoslovakia did it appear the people would choose their own form of government.

By midsummer 1945, American and Soviet leaders were deadlocked on almost every postwar issue—from the governments in

Eastern Europe to reparations from a defeated Germany. As Soviet tyranny replaced Nazi tyranny wherever Stalin's troops marched, the Truman administration quickly lost any hope for a new world order based on a harmonious relationship between the United States and the Soviet Union.

But what could be done? Given the power vacuum in Europe, isolationism appeared untenable because the Soviets could march to the shores of Brittany in a matter of weeks if American forces left the continent. Going to war with the Soviet Union over Eastern Europe was also unthinkable. Russia's prestige was at its apex in America, and the war-weary American people insisted on "bringing the boys back home." At the same time, a negotiated settlement that recognized the Soviet-imposed regimes in Eastern Europe would make a mockery of every principle that the United States stood for. Yet, as the Truman administration quickly found out in the spring of 1945, moralistic homilies, "tough talk," and economic diplomacy did nothing to make Stalin accede to American principles in Eastern Europe.

What did the Soviets want, and why did they want it? What were America's interests, and how could they be secured? These questions preoccupied decision makers during the winter of 1945–1946. Then, when Stalin sought territorial concessions and greater Soviet influence in Turkey and Iran, the time for thinking was over: Harry Truman had to decide whether to stand by and acquiesce in further Soviet aggrandizement or support governments under siege in resisting Soviet encroachments.

In June 1945, the Turkish ambassador in Moscow paid a courtesy call on Foreign Minister Molotov before returning home for a visit. Out of the blue, the Soviet foreign minister said that if Turkey wanted a new friendship treaty with the Soviet Union, it would have to cede the Turkish districts of Kars, Ardahan, and Artvin to the Soviet Union,[42] "lease" strategic bases to the Soviets on Turkish soil for joint defense of the Straits; and agree to a revision of the Montreaux Convention that would, in effect, leave the Soviets in control of the vital waterway.

The Turkish ambassador rejected Molotov's demands on the spot, and two days later the Turkish government formally rejected them. The Turks knew well that no country harboring Soviet troops and bases on its soil remained independent for long and Soviet control of the Straits would realize the czarist dream of a commanding position in the eastern Mediterranean. In terms of the territories, these had been taken from Turkey in 1878 and were returned by Stalin, himself, when he was commissar for nationalities and the new Bolshevik government renounced all imperialist, czarist treaties in 1921! Like clockwork, the Soviets responded to the rejection with a Hitler-like campaign of diplomatic pressure, vilification of Turkey in the Soviet and satellite press, and ominous troop maneuvers. The government of Turkey was unyielding, however, claiming that it would fight alone if necessary.

When a year of pressure and intimidation failed to make Turkey yield, the Soviets sent notes to the United States, Britain, and Turkey proposing a "new regime" for the Straits. Presumably, they hoped that Britain and the United States would pressure Turkey into yielding. But Truman was not Chamberlain. In fact, during the previous year's "war of nerves," when ominous Soviet troop movements led to fears of an invasion of Turkey, Truman sent the U.S. battleship *Missouri* into the east Mediterranean. The ostensible mission of the *Missouri* was to return the ashes of the Turkish ambassador who had died in Washington during the war. Its real mission was to demonstrate American support for Turkey.

This time, Truman immediately joined the British in a joint display of naval force by dispatching the new super aircraft carrier *Franklin D. Roosevelt* along with two cruisers and three destroyers off to the eastern Mediterranean. Then, the secretaries of state, war, and army met to discuss what could be done to support the Turks "regardless of the consequences." After a series of meetings, the secretaries and the chiefs of staff met with the president, who listened to Under Secretary of State Dean Acheson present their proposals.

The Russian effort, Acheson said, was a desire to control and dominate Turkey, which, in turn, would be followed by the communist domination of Greece. The consequent loss of Greece and Turkey would then give the Soviets an opportunity to dominate the Middle East and the sea-lanes in the Mediterranean. The secretary proposed that the president approve a memorandum, which concluded with the following passages:

> . . . it is always extremely difficult to persuade the Soviet Union, once formally committed on a subject, to retreat. Experience has shown such a retreat cannot be brought about by skillful argument or appeal to reason. The only thing which will deter the Russians will be the conviction that the United States is prepared, if necessary, to meet aggression by force of arms. There is a strong possibility that if the Soviet Union is given clearly and unequivocally to understand that the United States will firmly and with determination support Turkey in case Turkey is made the object of Soviet measures threatening the independence, sovereignty, or territorial interests of Turkey, the Soviet Union will pause and will not push the matter further.
>
> In our judgment the best hope of preserving peace is that the conviction should be carried to the USSR, Turkey, and all other powers that in case the United Nations is unsuccessful in stopping Soviet aggression, the United States would not hesitate to join other nations in meeting red aggression by the force of American arms.[43]

When President Truman quickly registered his approval, Army Chief of Staff General Dwight Eisenhower feared that the president's alacrity belied an unawareness of the grave consequences that might follow from his decision. Thus, he asked the president if Acheson could go over the facts again. According to Joseph Jones, when the acting secretary finished his second presentation:

> the President opened a convenient desk drawer and drew out a large map of the eastern Mediterranean, the Middle East, and Central and South Asia. It was made in sections, covered for protection with transparent plastic, the sections held together with black tape permitting them to be folded and opened readily. The whole map was well worn and had the air of long and frequent handling. Unfolding the map, Truman proceeded to give a ten- to fifteen-minute dissertation on the historical importance and present-day strategic significance of the area, which at least one person present described later as "masterful." Concluding, he turned good-humoredly to Eisenhower and asked whether he was satisfied now that the situation was understood. Eisenhower joined in the general laughter and admitted that he was.[44]

Acheson told the press two days later that the situation was serious and the United States would stand firmly behind Turkey. Two days after that, the United States, Britain, and France presented the Soviet government with formal notes rejecting the request for exclusive control of the Straits by the Black Sea countries and Soviet bases on Turkish soil. The Russians then tried again with a second note. When the three powers remained unyielding and Turkey refused to enter into any bilateral conversations with the Soviets, the issue slowly died.

In Iran, the situation was more difficult because Soviets troops were occupying the northern third of the country under a temporary wartime agreement that allowed British and Soviet forces to occupy Iran until six months after the end of the war. Although Foreign Secretary Molotov had agreed that Soviet forces would be withdrawn by March 2, 1946, the Soviets armed and organized rebel forces who declared a Democratic Republic in the province of Azerbaijan in December 1945. When Iranian forces sought to enter the province to restore order, Soviet troops stood in their way and declared that any advance into the area would be treated as an attack on the Soviet Union itself.

When the beleaguered Iranians turned to the United States, Secretary of State Byrnes told them to take their case to the United Nations, and they did. At the very first meeting of the UN Security Council, Iran argued that the Soviets were violating the 1942 agreement by not allowing Iranian troops to enter their northern provinces. With America standing behind the Iranians and the glare of publicity focused on the Soviets, Stalin made a deal, which was announced on March 24, three weeks after the troop withdrawal date of March 2. Soviet troops would leave, but the Iranians had to grant autonomy for the budding satellite regime in Azerbaijan and grant an oil concession to the Soviets in northern Iran.

The departure of Soviet forces still left the problem of dealing with Azerbaijan, which refused, with Soviet support, to allow troops of the central government to enter its province. At first, Prime Minister Qavam thought he could bring the province back by being conciliatory to both the rebel leaders and the Soviets; in fact, his behavior became so conciliatory that American officials feared he was moving into the Soviet camp.

By August 1946, the prime minister decided that his conciliatory approach combined with the protracted and inconclusive negotiations with the Azerbaijanis were merely giving the Soviets time to create a satellite regime, as more and more Russian army officers were spotted in civilian clothing or in uniforms of the provincial armed forces. Evidently having learned from Henlein, the leaders of the rebellious province would always raise new demands whenever the central government agreed to their earlier ones. Adding to his alarm was Qavam's conclusion that the members of the communist Tudeh Party, whom he had taken into his cabinet on the assumption that they were "patriotic Iranians," were "clearly directed by the Soviet embassy."[45]

Unless he acted forcefully and quickly, Qavam feared that Iran would go the way of Poland, Bulgaria, and Romania. However, if he gave his troops orders to force their way into the rebellious province, the Soviets might respond with a counter-invasion. If that happened and a Russian veto paralyzed the United Nations, Qavam feared he might become the Hailie Selassie of the 1940s while Iran suffered the fate of Ethiopia and the United Nations joined the League on the scrap heap of history. Crucial to his planning was finding out what the United States was prepared to do if the Soviets invaded Iran and their veto rendered the UN inoperable.

When Qavam raised his concerns at the American embassy, Ambassador George V. Allen replied that if the Iranians pleaded their case "strongly and unreservedly before the Security Council," the United States would not "sit idly by" if a veto paralyzed the United Nations in the event of "flagrant support by the USSR for [a] separatist movement in Iran."[46] Assured by these comments, Qavam decided to present Iran's case before the United Nations personally. While he was preparing his address, the Soviet ambassador summoned him to a meeting where he was told to call for elections to a new parliament, which, presumably, would ratify the Soviet-Iranian oil agreement. The prime minister immediately saw the handwriting on the wall. Since the elections in Azerbaijan would be rigged, a large bloc of parliamentarians from that area

Map 4.2. Soviet Threats to Turkey and Iran

In 1945, the Soviets demanded naval bases in Turkey for the joint defense of the straits plus the return of Kars and Aradhan, tiny territories that Turkey lost to Czarist Russia in 1878 and were freely returned by the Soviet Union in 1921. In Iran, Soviet troops that were occupying one-third of the country did not leave within six months after the war's end as they had agreed. In addition the Soviets supported a rump "democratic republic" in northern Iran and refused to allow Iranian troops to enter the territory. Stalin's actions poisoned relations with Turkey, frightened Iran, and alarmed the United States, which gave support to both countries. America's containment policy had its origins in these two crises.

could join with Tudeh Party members from the rest of Iran in dominating the Majlis and, thereby, turn Iran into a Soviet satellite. To forestall that possibility, Qavam replied that he would send the central government's armed forces into Azerbaijan "to assure that the election procedures are duly fulfilled."

When the Soviet ambassador warned that, "the sending of Iran troops into Azerbaijan was considered by the Soviet [government as] undesirable because it would create difficulties within Azerbaijan and on the Soviet-Iran frontier," Qavam immediately met with the U.S. ambassador again and asked what the "American government's reaction would be to his government's notifying the UN Security Council of the Soviet ambassador's statement." The ambassador forwarded Qavam's request to Washington, and the response from Acting Secretary Acheson was blunt and quick: "You can assure Qavam that this Government will give its unqualified support to Iran or any other power the integrity and independence of which may be threatened by external forces, provided that the power shows courage and determination to maintain its own independence and freedom of action and provided it is willing to make its position clear to the world." To support these words, Acheson pledged immediate and long-term defensive military assistance as well as loans for economic development.

Even with these pledges of firm military support, the Iranians were fearful of the Soviet response. Still, Qavam steeled up his courage. He informed the Security Council of the Soviet ambassador's warning, and then sent his troops marching toward Azerbaijan.[47] Even before the troops arrived, the leaders of the "Democratic Republic" fled, and when the government's forces entered Tabriz, the population welcomed them with cheers. When the U.S. consul drove through the streets of Tabriz in his flag-bedecked limousine, people "cheered, applauded, and shouted, 'long live America.'"[48] In fact, as Ambassador Allen reported, "local people themselves overthrew the regime."[49] That the democratic republic had so little support came as a surprise to Qavam, the shah, the Americans, and, perhaps not least, the Russians. After five long and frightening years, Iran had regained its sovereignty.

The crises in Iran and Turkey set the Truman administration on a path of resistance, deterrence, and containment that would mark American foreign policy until the very end of the Cold War. While the decisions regarding Iran and Turkey were of an ad hoc nature, the occasion for articulating an overarching foreign policy strategy was quick to follow. In February 1947, the British government informed the United States that it could no longer afford to support the embattled governments of Greece and Turkey. Unless the United States stepped in, the British note informed the Americans, Greece would, undoubtedly, fall to communist guerrilla forces and Turkey would be unable to modernize and maintain the large army that its security against Russian pressure required.

Less than a month later, President Truman stood before the Congress and asked them to support a plan of economic and military assistance to Greece and Turkey. "I believe that it must be the policy of the United States to support free people who are resisting attempted subjugation by outside minorities or by outside pressures," he told the legislators, who responded by passing the legislation by overwhelming margins. In June, Secretary of State Marshall used his Harvard commencement address to propose a program of massive economic assistance to the war-torn nations of Europe. By helping Europeans to rebuild their economies, the internal danger of communism would recede. One year later, the creation of NATO signified the willingness of the United States to go to war if the Soviets crossed the postwar European fault lines with military forces. When the Soviets broke America's atomic monopoly, the Truman administration decided to place American troops on the ground in Europe to enhance the credibility of its NATO commitment.

While none of these decisions was uncontroversial, Truman's diplomacy is instructive in a number of ways. First, it wisely reflected an understanding of the difference between national defense in a narrow sense and national security in a wider sense. With the collapse of Britain's ability to maintain the balance of power in Europe and the Near East, Truman was well aware that if America did not take up Britain's role, vital areas would be ceded to the pleasure of the Soviet Union. He also wisely saw that American support for local governments willing to resist Soviet pressure would probably threaten costs high enough to deter the Soviets. With more than half a million Turks in arms, American military assistance would help to insure that Turkey would not be an easy prey for even the victorious Soviet army.

Second, the president's containment policy clearly differentiated areas of major and lesser importance. While the loss of the Baltics and Eastern Europe was tragic, it did not significantly threaten the rest of Europe or the global balance of power. To be sure, the United States never publicly "wrote off Eastern Europe," but by the end of the 1940s and early 1950s, both sides had accepted a spheres-of-influence policy in Europe. Meanwhile, with Marshall Plan aid, America's European allies began to realize economic prosperity and political confidence.

Third, Truman's policy never threatened any of the Soviet Union's significant security interests. By ceding Eastern Europe, the Truman administration bowed to both the realities of Soviet power and those roots of Soviet revisionism that lay in genuine security fears. Truman never talked about victory or rollback. While the United States was willing to recognize and respect Soviet security needs and interests, it merely expected no less from them. Truman drew a line around those areas where the Soviets clearly had no security-based need to expand. His goal was to create "cushions of distance," as Secretary of War Patterson put it—"cushions of distance" between the new Soviet empire and areas of vital importance to the United States.

In hindsight, we know that Truman's actions had their intended effect. On encountering resistance and a possible military conflict with the United States, Stalin made no bones about his having to stop. After the United States began military and economic aid to Greece, Stalin decided to take no risks for the Greek communists. In a meeting with the Yugoslav leader Milovan Djilas in 1949, Stalin bluntly barked: "The revolution in Greece must be folded up: [The

Greek communists] have no prospect of success at all. What do you think, that Great Britain and the United States—the United States, the most powerful state in the world—will permit you to break their line of communication in the Mediterranean Sea! Nonsense. And we have no navy. The uprising in Greece must be stopped, and as quickly as possible."[50]

Stalin's comments reveal an important lesson for status quo powers. After he made the decision to back Turkey, President Truman told his advisers that the United States might as well find out then rather than five or ten years later whether the Soviets were bent on world conquest. But Stalin did not want war. What he wanted was Soviet hegemony in Turkey, Greece, and Iran, a point well made by Winston Churchill in his "Iron Curtain" speech at Westminster College in February 1946:

> I do not believe that Soviet Russia desires war. What they desire is the fruits of war and the indefinite expansion of their power and their doctrines.
>
> . . . there is nothing they admire so much as strength, and there is nothing for which they have less respect than for military weakness.
>
> If the Western democracies stand together in strict adherence to the principles of the United Nations Charter, their influence for furthering these principles will be immense and no one is likely to molest them.[51]

While containment was, at best, an armed truce, such was preferable to any of its proposed alternatives at the time—war, preventive nuclear war, isolation, or an ostrich-like internationalism that ignored or even welcomed Soviet expansion as a progressive force in the world. Containment gave Europeans hope and kept them and other nations free without threatening or jeopardizing the Soviet Union's own essential security needs. Containment provided peace, and it bought time—time for people to reflect, time for new leaders to arise, time for old issues to cool and for new ones to arise, and time for people to get on with their lives. At the height of the Cold War, Secretary of State Acheson expressed this point extremely well in an address before the UN General Assembly in September 1950:

> The Soviet leaders are realists, in some respects at least. As we succeed in building the necessary economic and defensive military strength, it will become clear to them that the non-Soviet world will neither collapse nor be dismembered piece-meal. Some modification in their aggressive policies may follow, if they recognize that the best interests of the Soviet Union require a cooperative relationship with the outside world.
>
> Time may have its effect. It is but thirty-three years since the overthrow of the Czarist regime in Russia. This is a short time in history. Like many other social and political movements before it, the Soviet revolution may change. In so doing, it may rid itself of the policies which now prevent the Soviet Union from living as a good neighbor with the rest of the world.

We have no assurance that this will take place. But as the United Nations strengthens its collective security system, the possibilities of this change in Soviet policy will increase. If this does not occur, the increase in our defensive strength shall be the means of ensuring our survival and protecting the essential values of our societies.

But our hope is that a strong collective security system will make genuine negotiation possible, and that this will in turn lead to a cooperative peace.[52]

Finally, this case study underscores the importance of legitimacy in conflicts among nations. The Soviet position in both conflicts was weak legally and preposterous substantively. In Iran, the Soviets were clearly violating their legal commitments to refrain in any way whatsoever from violating the territorial integrity and sovereignty of Iran and to withdraw their troops within six months after hostilities ended. In Turkey, the Soviets had no legal right to change the regime in the Straits without the consent of other powers to the Montreaux Convention, and as a sovereign power, Turkey had the legal and moral right to refuse the Soviets request for bases. In regard to Ardahan, Kars, and Artvin the Soviets had no legal right to regain territory that had been freely conceded to Turkey without that government's consent to give it back.

Unlike Hitler, Stalin did not make it easy for anyone who sought to excuse the Soviet behavior in Iran. After spending several days listening to Stalin and Molotov reiterate their positions on the Iranian situation in December 1945, Secretary of State Jimmy Byrnes found their arguments incredible:

The more I thought about Generalissimo Stalin's excuse for retaining troops in Iran, the less confidence I had in the Soviet position. It was absurd to claim, as he had, that the Red Army of 30,000 well-trained and fully equipped troops must stop the poorly trained and inadequately equipped Iranian force of 1,500 from marching toward Azerbaijan on the public highway because it feared a disturbance would be created. His statement that he feared saboteurs from little Iran would come over into the Soviet Union and set fire to the Baku oil fields seemed an equally poor excuse for maintaining a large army inside the borders of Iran.[53]

When Iran presented the facts of their case before the United Nations, the weakness of the Soviet case became readily apparent, and the Soviets undoubtedly realized the wisdom of Stalin's position at Yalta that the veto power of the Big Five should apply to items that could be placed on the agenda for discussion.

In regard to Turkey, Stalin's arguments were equally unpersuasive. On the one hand, Stalin insisted that Soviet bases in Turkey and joint defense of the Straits were necessary because Turkey was too weak to defend the waterway on its own. A few minutes later, he would argue that Russia had to share in the control of the waterway because Turkey could unilaterally close the Straits. "It is impossible to accept a situation in which Turkey had a hand on Russia's throat," Stalin told FDR and Churchill at Yalta.

While world opinion plays only a limited role in international disputes, the spotlight of publicity exposed the Soviet's flimsy case in Iran and strengthened the legitimacy of the uncompromising stand that America and Britain took against the Russian positions. Also enhancing the legitimacy of the American and British positions was the growing Soviet record in dealing with the liberated countries in Eastern Europe. For the Soviets, a "friendly government" meant a Soviet-dominated government and, wherever the Red Army was in occupation, Hitler-like repression was rampant against all but Soviet sycophants. In this vein, the memorandum that Truman approved for dealing with the Soviet note on the Straits in August 1946 stated that "It is our experience that when the Soviet Union obtains predominance in an area, American and, in fact, all Western influences and contacts are gradually eliminated from the area."[54]

The Soviet position was also made difficult by the fact that, if their bullying did not work, the decision to initiate the use of force would have to lie with them. Iran and Turkey were not like Eastern Europe, where the Red Army was in complete control. If the Iranians and Turks did not yield to threats and intimidation, Stalin would have to decide whether what he sought was worth the risks that the use of military force would involve—a war with Turkey, guerrilla war in Iran, and who knew what kind of response from the United States.

Still, Stalin was in a strong military position. As Dean Acheson noted in his memoirs, the Soviets always mounted their demands where their military position was stronger than that of the Allies. By itself, the Iranian government could not withstand a Soviet invasion. Even with American pledges of support, it was not clear what the United States could do militarily if the Soviets invaded. But the use of blatant military force against either country would not have been cost free, and what the real costs might be was uncertain, if not unknowable, to the Soviet dictator.

A Comparative Postmortem

Of the two central decision makers in these cases, Neville Chamberlain had the more difficult problem because Hitler's demands rang with convincing legitimacy—the Versailles settlement was not a fairly negotiated settlement but a "diktat" explicitly designed to keep Germany down; in drafting the treaty, self-determination for Germany had been violated, most notably in regard to the Sudeten Germans and the prohibition of a union between Austria and Germany; France had rejected "equality" of arms with Germany at the League Disarmament Conference; and Poland was not about to solve the "corridor" problem through peaceful negotiations. Stalin's demands, on the other hand, had flimsy, if any, legitimacy behind them and his bullying of Turkey was akin to the tactics of Hitler and Mussolini. Unlike Truman, Chamberlain was also constrained simply by a lack of military forces to station in Eastern Europe that could buttress his appeasement policies with credible deterrent forces that might reign in Hitler.

In both cases, however, genuine conciliation and the construction of a legitimate international order with the likes of Hitler and Stalin was beyond the realm of possibility. In revolutionary eras—when Great Powers seek hegemony or pursue revolutionary foreign policies aimed at transforming the domestic political, economic, and social structures of other states—containment, deterrence, and "a cold peace" are the best one can hope for.

Legitimacy can come about only after the revolutionary ardor or the zeal for hegemony begins to dry out through a natural deflation (what George Kennan termed "mellowing") of revolutionary exuberance, frustration caused by failed efforts (as in Korea), the risks and costs that might be entailed if structures of containment are tested, and the dubious worth of the gains that are attained by expansion. Once these forces come into play and new decision makers come to power, status quo powers can begin to reach out and seek a modus vivendi or more normal relations, even if only in limited areas like trade and travel at first. America's opening to China began with a Chinese invitation for an American team to join a ping pong match. Similarly, American normalization with states like Iran, Libya, and even Iraq will begin gingerly, incrementally, and most likely while the revisionist state keeps much of its revolutionary rhetoric intact.

Both Chamberlain and Truman had two choices and only two—secure the existing balance of power or go to war in the future to restore it. Truman did the former, while Chamberlain wound up with the latter. Converting Stalin to Wilsonian internationalism was not an option, as George Kennan made clear in his cables from the U.S. embassy in Moscow during the winter of 1966. It would take forty years for a Wilsonian internationalist by the name of Mikhail Gorbachev to take power in the Kremlin, and what led to his ascent was all of the factors mentioned above:

- a long-standing wall of deterrent power that made any hegmonic expansion too risky to undertake;
- a coalition of status quo powers whose intentions were recognized by the Soviets, themselves, as undeniably defensive;
- problematic gains (What had the Soviet Union gained from the communization of Cuba?) and significant losses after forty years of struggle (China);

- an increasingly costly string of dependent client states such as Cuba, Angola, and Ethiopia;
- an increasing preoccupation with internal economic and social problems that were reaching crisis proportions; and
- an agenda of possible ventures that held only risks, costs, and problematic gains for Soviet security (the losing venture in Afghanistan and conflicts with the United States over Nicaragua and El Salvador, for example).

The end of the Cold War came about not because of good intentions or wishful thinking. America won the Cold War because of three things: "a long term, patient but firm and vigilant containment of Russian expansive tendencies,"[55] the clarity of its solely defensive purposes, and its willingness to extend the hand of friendship to even a communist Russia that was willing to accept the territorial status quo, respect the rights of other states, and abide by its international agreements.

Summary of Salient Points

Maintaining peace is the job of the status quo powers

1. If status quo nations are to exist in a secure and orderly world and have a significant say over what that world is to be like, they must confront revisionist powers far from home, and all too frequently, in areas that seem of little intrinsic importance. Debates about national security will always be debates about the borders of others.
2. Peace is divisible; some conflicts matter, others do not.
3. Solvency—a bringing into balance of interests, commitments, and military forces—is the hallmark of a sound foreign policy.
4. Revisionists states also have hierarchies of interests, limited resources, and domestic needs and priorities.
   a. The more revisionist states have satisfied their basic security needs, the less willing they will be to take risks and bear the costs of further increments of territory, power, influence, and status.
   b. The more costly and risky the pursuit of lesser objectives might be, the less likely revisionist powers will be to pursue them.
5. In devising strategies for peace, status quo powers must respect the core security or defensive needs of a revisionist power.
6. Deterrence alone can only bring an armed truce or cold peace; real peace requires efforts to transform revisionist powers into satisfied states and construct a "legitimate international political system."

7. Two perennial and perhaps unresolvable problems facing status quo powers involve defending "undesirable regimes" and fighting limited wars in "gray areas."

8. While all strategies for peace must be tailor-made, a few rules of thumb should always be borne in mind.

   a. The pattern of response is more important than particulars.

   b. Coalitions may not be as fearsome as they seem.

   c. Circumstances and contexts always matter.

   d. For really vital points, put your own troops in harm's way and arm them well.

   e. For points on the periphery, provide generous arms and military and economic assistance.

   f. Work to restrain revisionist ambitions by stressing the costly consequences that forceful efforts to change the status quo might entail.

   g. Neutral countries can be as useful as allies in certain cases.

Notes

1. Robert Tucker, *A New Isolationism: Threat or Promise* (New York: Universe Books, 1972), 120 (emphasis supplied).
2. Robert Leckie, *The Wars of America, volume 1* (New York: Bantam Books, 1969), 315.
3. Walter Lippmann, *U.S. Foreign Policy: Shield of the Republic* (Boston: Little, Brown, 1943), 37, 34–35.
4. Ibid., 38–39.
5. John F. Kennedy, *Why England Slept* (New York: Wilfred Funk, 1940), xxiv.
6. Secret/Sensitive Memorandum of Conversation, December 18, 1975, printed in *The Nation*, October 29, 1990, 492–93 [emphasis is mine].
7. George Kennan, *Memoirs 1925–1950* (Boston: Little, Brown, 1967), 311–12.
8. Lippmann, *U.S. Foreign Policy*, 9–10.
9. Barry Buzan, *People, States, and Fear: The National Security Problem in International Relations* (Chapel Hill: The University of North Carolina Press, 1983), 177.
10. Quoted in John Lewis Gaddis, *Strategies of Containment* (New York: Oxford University Press, 1992), 142. The quotation from President Eisenhower that appears below is taken from the same place.
11. Hans Morgenthau, *Politics Among Nations* (New York: Alfred A. Knopf, 1985), 82.
12. Ibid., 82–85.
13. Henry Kissinger, *Diplomacy* (New York: Simon and Schuster, 1994), 79.
14. New York: Oxford University Press, 1995, 155.
15. A. J. P. Taylor, *From Napoleon to the Second International: Essays on Nineteenth-Century Europe* (New York: Penguin, 1993), 222.
16. Jimmy Carter, "Power for Humane Purposes," reprinted in Stanley J. Michalak, Jr., *Competing Conceptions of American Foreign Policy: Worldviews in Conflict* (New York: HarperCollins, 1991), 102–7.
17. Taken from Gaddis Smith, *Morality, Reason, and Power: American Diplomacy in the Carter Years* (New York: Hill and Wang, 1986) 223–24.
18. Richard Nixon, *The Real War* (New York: Warner Books, 1980), 34, 276, 278, and 298, respectively.
19. Jimmy Carter, "Power for Humane Purposes," 104.
20. "Remarks to the Advertising Council," February 16, 1950, *Department of State Bulletin*, March 20, 1950, 28. I have added paragraph breaks to ease readability of what was a very long paragraph.
21. New York: Simon and Schuster, 1987.
22. These terms are taken from John Gaddis's informative and instructive, *Strategies of Containment*, see especially, ch. 3.

23. See Charles Wolf, *The Costs of the Soviet Empire* (Santa Monica, CA: Rand, 1984).

24. Cited in Gaddis, *Strategies of Containment*, 154.

25. Henry Kissinger, *A World Restored* (Boston: Houghton Mifflin, 1957), 1.

26. This case study is based on the following sources: Winston Churchill, *The Second World War, The Gathering Storm, volume 1* (Boston: Houghton Mifflin, 1961); John Gunther, *Inside Europe* (New York: Harper and Row, 1936, 1938, 1940 editions as noted in footnotes); Neville Henderson, *Failure of a Mission: Berlin 1937–1939* (New York: G. P. Putnam's Sons, 1940); Francis L. Loewenheim, ed., *Peace or Appeasement? Hitler, Chamberlain, and the Munich Crisis* (Boston: Houghton Mifflin, 1965); Keith Middlemas, *The Strategy of Appeasement: The British Government and Germany, 1937–1939* (Chicago: Quadrangle Books, 1972); Charles Loch Mowat, *Britain Between the War, 1918–1940* (Chicago: University of Chicago Press, 1955); Williamson Murray, *The Change in the European Balance of Power* (Princeton: Princeton University Press, 1984); R. A. C. Parker, *Chamberlain and Appeasement: British Policy and the Coming of the Second World War* (New York: St. Martin's Press, 1993); R. A. C. Parker, *Europe 1919–1945* (New York: Delacorte Press, 1967); Robert Payne, *The Life and Death of Adolph Hitler* (New York: Popular Library, 1973); Norman Rich, *Hitler's War Aims* (New York: W. W. Norton, 1973); E. M. Robertson, *Hitler's Pre-War Policy and Military Plans, 1933–1939* (New York: Citadel Press, 1967); Telford Taylor, *Munich: The Price of Peace* (Garden City, NJ: Doubleday, 1979), Gerhard Weinberg, *Foreign Policy and Hitler's Germany: Starting World War II, 1937–1939* (Chicago: University of Chicago Press, 1980).

27. Kissinger, *Diplomacy*, 108.

28. See Taylor, *Munich*, 670, and Weinberg, *Foreign Policy*, 244–45.

29. Middlemas, *The Strategy of Appeasement*, 53.

30. Keith Feiling, *The Life of Neville Chamberlain* (London: Macmillan, 1947), 332.

31. Quoted in Gunther, *Inside Europe*, 103.

32. This memorandum is printed in Loewenheim, *Peace or Appeasement?*, 11–12.

33. Reproduced in ibid., 7–10.

34. A memorandum of the meeting is printed in ibid., 21–27.

35. For British notes on the Godesberg conversations, from which this and the following quotations are taken, see ibid., 29–36.

36. Ibid., 52.

37. Ibid., 69.

38. Roberston, *Hitler's Pre-War Policy and Military Plans, 1933–1939*, 159.

39. These quotations are taken from the minutes of a cabinet meeting held on March 18, 1938, which are reprinted in Taylor, *Munich*, 42–43.

40. Murray, *The Change in the European Balance of Power*, 293.

41. Robertson, *Hitler's Pre-War Policy and Military Plans, 1933–1939*, 159.

42. Three provinces located near the Russo-Turkish border in the Caucasus.

43. A full copy of the memo, which is well worth reading, can be found in *FRUS, 1946* (Washington, DC, 1969), VII: 840–43.

44. Joseph M. Jones, *The Fifteen Weeks (February 21–June 5)*, (New York: Viking Press), 63–64.

45. See the report by the vice consul at Tabriz and the cable from Ambassador Allen, Murray's successor, on June 5 and August 25 in *FRUS, 1946*, 1969, VII: 494–95 and 512–13, respectively.

46. Ibid., 511.

47. Ibid., 549.

48. Ibid., 561.

49. Ibid., 565.

50. Milovan Djilas, *Conversations With Stalin* (New York: Harcourt, Brace and World, 1962), 181–82.

51. Winston Churchill, excerpted in *The Annals of America, Volume 16, 1940–1949* (Chicago: Encyclopaedia Britannica, 1968), 365–69.

52. *Department of State Bulletin*, October 2, 1950.

53. James Byrnes, *Speaking Frankly* (New York: Harper and Brothers Publishers, 1947), 119.

54. *FRUS, 1946*, VII, 840.

55. The words are those of George Kennan taken from his "The Sources of Soviet Conduct," (1947) reprinted in Michalak, *Competing Conceptions of American Foreign Policy*, 33.

CHAPTER FIVE

There Is No Viable Alternative to Power Politics

There ought to be a rule that bold proposals for the social and political betterment of mankind be accompanied by explanations of how these ideas will be brought to reality and why, if they're so brilliant and beneficial as all that, they haven't already been implemented.
—Katha Pollitt, "Subject to Debate," *The Nation*, 1995

While philosophers and statesmen have dreamed of abolishing war ever since the ancient Greeks, both their dreams and their schemes have always been to little avail. Either their proposals have been ignored, or, when tried, they have been found wanting, as states resort to old patterns of unauthorized uses of violence and threats of force. Only by understanding the flaws in what has been tried can we gain a set of realistic expectations about the possibilities for closing the gap between the world as it is and the world as we would like it to be.

As optimists, we like to think that solutions exist "out there," new ideas that, once discovered, could usher in a new era of peace and amity among nations. The truth is: none exists. The few alternatives to military force have been well known for centuries; they have been analyzed and evaluated repeatedly; and whenever they have tried, they have failed. All alternatives to war can be subsumed under one of four headings:

1. Peaceful alternatives to war such as arbitration and mediation services, conciliation commissions, cooling-off or time-out periods, and international courts.
2. Pacts proscribing unauthorized uses of force or codes that denote proper conduct.
3. Arms control or disarmament pacts that abolish or reduce military weapons.

4. Formal structures of legitimate authority designed to deter unauthorized uses of force and punish those who violate proper modes of conduct.

The problem is not that such alternatives never work, because very frequently they do. Nations do arbitrate disputes. They do settle most conflicts through diplomatic negotiations on the basis of fairness, empathy, and the desire to be reputed as trustworthy and honorable. International organizations have been useful in helping parties to narrow their differences, allowing states to disengage gracefully from risky or untenable situations, observing truces, maintaining order, and facilitating coalitions of states seeking to resist or overturn aggression. Arms control agreements have limited weapons or forestalled their construction at times. Where these alternatives fail is in their exceptional, but significant, disuse—in those "lapses" when nations return to the use of force or threats of force to get whatever it is they may want.

Providing Peaceful Alternatives to War: Peace through Arbitration and Commissions of Conciliation

Although arbitration was common in the Greek city-state system, its vogue as an alternative to war in the European state system dates only from the end of the American Civil War. When a group of "disinterested gentlemen" successfully resolved the Alabama Claims case between the United States and Britain, the power of that example spurred a flurry of diplomatic activity. Between 1865 and 1895, 30 arbitration agreements were negotiated, followed by 50 more between 1895 and 1905, and in the decade before the outbreak of World War I, 123 more were negotiated.

Meanwhile, the First Hague Conference of 1899 produced a convention on the peaceful settlement of disputes, which contained this passage: "International arbitration has for its object the settlement of disputes between States by judges of their own choice and on the basis of respect for law. Recourse to arbitration implies an agreement to submit in good faith to the award." To assist states in arbitrating their differences, the conference created a Permanent Court of Arbitration, which was not a court, but a list of judges that states could call upon to arbitrate disputes.

While arbitration treaties often included the words "compulsory" and "obligatory," they were replete with loopholes. As Professor Frederick Schuman has noted, the treaties, "[contained] such broad qualifications and exceptions as to leave the parties almost complete liberty of action with regard to any particular controversy."[1] For example, the Anglo-French Treaty of 1903, which served as the model for many of the pre-World War I treaties, excluded disputes involving "national honor, independence, vital interests, or the interests of third parties." With wording so vague, how could any state be accused of violating its obligation to arbitrate if it trotted out one of these phrases? Even more restrictive was a clause inserted in every treaty negotiated by the United States, which required the Senate's consent to every case submitted to arbitration.

Closing such loopholes became a major preoccupation of Secretary of State William Jennings Bryan, who negotiated thirty bilateral treaties that provided for the creation of permanent *commissions of conciliation* that would hear *all disputes without exception.* However, only twenty-one of these so-called "Bryan Treaties" ever came into force,[2] and of these twenty-one, conciliation commissions were established under only ten of them. In the end, *not one dispute was ever considered under those treaties,* and the entire effort lapsed as World War I intruded and postwar secretaries of state pursued different paths to peace.[3]

Nevertheless, arbitration and mediation are useful devices in emotionally charged situations in which states want to avoid the use of force, but the involvement of honor and reputation makes resolution by traditional diplomacy difficult. Arbitration and mediation can also be a godsend when mistakes or precipitous actions create disputes that states want to "depoliticize" and settle amicably. The following two cases illustrate well the utility of arbitration as an alternative to war or traditional bilateral diplomacy.

Two Contrasting Case Studies
Woodrow Wilson Seeks to Promote Democracy in Mexico and Russian Naval Vessels Make a Mistake on the Way to Manchuria

On taking office, Woodrow Wilson found himself confronted with a new government in Mexico headed by General Victoriano Huerta. Huerta had seized power by evicting and killing the former president and vice-president and then quickly assuming the presidency under constitutional, but questionable, arrangements. From the time of Thomas Jefferson, the United States, like every other government, had generally recognized established governments diplomatically no matter how they came to power.

Wilson verged from that tradition, however, and set the nation on a new course that remains to this day—using diplomatic recognition as a sign of approval or disapproval of the government in power. Rather than recognize "a government of butchers," as Wilson put it privately, he decided to recall the American ambassador and refused to appoint another. On March 11, 1913, he turned his decision in regard to the Huerta regime into a general policy regarding the diplomatic recognition of governments in Latin America. Recognition, he announced, would be "possible only when supported at every turn by the orderly processes of just government based upon law, not upon arbitrary or irregular force."[4] That he was meddling in the internal affairs of sovereign state and engaging in a kind of pro-democracy revisionism mattered not one wit to the moralistic president.

Having decided not to recognize and traffic with immorality, Wilson hoped to force Huerta out of power by moral disapprobation. Unmoved by Wilson's ostracism, Huerta further consolidated his power in October 1913 by throwing 110 members of the Mexican chamber of deputies into prison and installing himself as an outright dictator. An enraged Wilson vowed to the British diplomat Sir William Tyrrell that "I am going to teach the South American republics to elect good men." The British, however, were unmoved by Wilson's moralism and would have no part in any effort to overthrow Huerta, whom they thought would keep foreign investments secure. Without international support, Wilson found himself in a situation that foreign policymakers of Great Powers frequently face in dealing with recalcitrant small powers: Peaceful diplomacy had failed, and the use of force would make the Great Power look like a bully and the small power look like a victim.

Looking for a pretext to take more forceful action, Wilson was given one by a fortuitous incident that occurred in April 1914. While on leave in the city of Tampico, eight American sailors mistakenly ventured into an "off-limits" area and were arrested. While local authorities quickly released the sailors and offered an official apology, the U.S. commander in the area demanded a twenty-one-gun salute. When the Mexican officials did not comply, Wilson issued an ultimatum: Salute the flag, or take the consequences.

The Huerta government then proposed arbitration, as stipulated under of the Treaty of Guadeloupe Hidalgo, signed at the end of the Mexican-American War in 1848. According to Article 21 of the treaty, all future disputes between the United States and Mexico, not settled by diplomacy, would be sent to arbitration. But arbitration would have deprived Wilson of "his duty to force Huerta [into] retirement." Instead of arbitrating, Wilson went before Congress and, by whopping majorities, gained authorization to use force—not against the people of Mexico, but the Huerta government.

The following day, Wilson learned that a German steamer was approaching Veracruz with a cargo of ammunition for the Huerta junta. With a congressional mandate in his hands, he quickly ordered Rear Admiral Frank F. Fletcher to take and occupy Veracruz, which the admiral did at the cost of nineteen Americans killed and forty-seven wounded and a cost to Mexico of two hundred killed and three hundred wounded. The issue that provoked Wilson's shelling and capture of Veracruz was neither the mistaken arrest of a few American sailors nor the purchase of German ammunition, which Huerta clearly had the right to buy. At issue was the government of General Victoriano Huerta—a government that Wilson sought to bring down by cutting off its armaments and by controlling the port's customs house, which was the government's only source of hard currency.

Instead of quickly folding at Wilson's gunboat diplomacy, Huerta dug in his heels, while his opponent who led the constitutionalist forces, General Venustiano Carranza, protested Wilson's intervention as vigorously as the dictator did. Rather than bring down Huerta, Wilson merely managed to unite the feuding Mexicans. At the same time, the president discovered that the general public did not share the congressional enthusiasm for the use of force.

Both politically and militarily, Wilson was stuck. He had 6,700 troops in Veracruz, and he was politically isolated. Realizing that he had no support for a war with Mexico either at home or abroad, Wilson accepted the mediation of Argentina, Brazil, and Chile, as did Huerta under pressure from England, France, and Germany. While the mediation effort failed to resolve the conflict, the passage of time allowed tempers to cool and attention to wane, giving Wilson an opportunity to back out quietly. In the end, Huerta fell to the power of the constitutionalist forces and went into exile three months later. However, civil war quickly returned to Mexico, and less than two years later, General Pershing and 6,000 American troops were chasing the rebel forces of Pancho Villa on Mexican soil—again to the protests of the constitutionalist government of Carranza.

The original dispute over saluting the American flag was clearly one that should have gone to arbitration under the Treaty of Guadeloupe. Wilson was clearly in violation of that treaty as well as other international laws when he refused to arbitrate, used military force to take Veracruz, and sought to bring down the Huerta government. For Wilson, settling disputes peacefully was less important than getting a government to his liking in Mexico.

Another case had a happier ending. During the Russo-Japanese War of 1904–1905, a squadron of Russian ships en route to the Far East fired on a number of British fishing trawlers in the mistaken impression that they were Japanese torpedo boats. The British government, which was allied with Japan under the Treaty of 1902, demanded an immediate explanation and reparations from Russia. Under the terms of the Convention for the Pacific Settlement of International Disputes adapted at the Hague Conference, the two parties agreed to submit the questions of fact in the dispute to a Commission of Inquiry, consisting of British, Russian, American, and French naval officers who would then choose a fifth member of the commission (they chose an Austro-Hungarian officer). In its report, the commission found the Russian squadron at fault and the Russians promptly paid an indemnity of sixty-five thousand British pounds.[5]

The different outcomes in these disputes turned on politics. The Russian government would never have ordered its naval squadron to fire on British ships of any kind, and it had no interest in provoking a conflict with Great Britain. Thus, the Russians sought to depoliticize the issue by having a group of "disinterested" and fair-minded gentlemen investigate the matter and propose terms for closing the issue. When the commission found the Russian squadron at fault and proposed terms of settlement, the czarist government did the honorable thing—they admitted that their officers had made a mistake, offered an apology, and made compensation.

In contrast, Wilson was seeking to bring down the Huerta government, and for him the issue was not whether the Tampico affair was the result of error or purpose. For the self-assured president, the mistaken arrest provided him with the pretext he needed to lay the groundwork for military action against Mexico. Although America has always been a leading force in the movement for the rule of law, arbitration treaties, and conciliation commissions, its practices have all too frequently been at variance with its principles.

Wilson's conflict with the Huerta government reveals two mistaken notions underlying proposals to use arbitration and conciliation procedures as alternatives to war: First, *all disputes between states are not resolvable in a manner that would be suitable to both parties,* and *peace is not always the highest value of states.* Wilson did not have a dispute with the government of Mexico, *he wanted that government thrown out of power.* "Zero sum" conflicts like that between Wilson and Huerta—conflicts in which one side wants everything—can never, by their very nature, be resolved by compromise. Yet, conflicts such as these lie at the core of disputes between revisionist and status quo nations. Second, while a love of peace is always easy to pronounce in the abstract, when peace stands as an abstraction against other values, peace is often the loser. Wilson was a great believer in self-determination; yet, when the Mexicans failed to determine themselves in the way he wanted, Wilson was willing to use force.

States seeking to resolve their disputes peacefully have never failed for a lack of mechanisms—skilled negotiators, arbitration panels, third-party mediators, commissions of conciliation, or courts. The problem is that some disputes are just incapable of resolution to the satisfaction of both parties, and for most states there are things "more precious than peace," to quote Wilson. As Professor Frederick Schuman has noted, "The only wars prevented by procedures of peaceful settlement are those which would never be fought, for they concern issues not directly relevant to the 'vital interests' and 'national honor' of states."[6]

The failure of efforts to seek peace through nonmilitary alternatives stems from the distinction between status quo and revisionist powers. Peace means acceptance of the status quo, and pledges outlawing war amount to freezing the map. If revisionist nations seek to change things and status quo powers refuse to arbitrate or yield peacefully, what alternative does the revisionist state have but to acquiesce or resort to military threats or military force? On the other hand, no status quo Great Power has ever forsworn the use of military force for self-defense, generously defined.

Peace through Paper: FDR's Atlantic Charter—Just Say "No" to Ripping Off Other People's Territory

Nothing is easier to achieve than consensus—on generalities. . . . When it comes to specifics, it is every man for himself.
—Thomas Sowell, January 6, 1993

If you try to set forth in a catalog what will be the exact settlement of affairs, you will find that the moment you leave the area of pious platitude you will descend into the arena of heated controversy.
—Winston Churchill cited in George Bernard Shaw,
Everybody's Political What's What, 5

In international politics, moral forces are never effective unless they are backed by power. . . .
—Martin Wight, *Power Politics*, 29

One of the enduring illusions about international relations is the belief that peace can be attained through paper—pieces of paper on which national leaders pledge never to go to war with each other, never to violate the borders of other states, or never to develop and build nuclear weapons. The Kellogg-Briand Pact, discussed in the introduction to this primer, was one such notable example of this chimerical approach to peace. An equally instructive example was FDR's Atlantic Charter, which the wartime Allies signed in the summer of 1941 and presumably would usher in a new world order in the wake of victory.

In August 1939, British prime minister Winston Churchill and President Franklin D. Roosevelt met in Placentia Bay, Newfoundland to discuss wartime cooperation and mutual assistance. At the end of the meeting, the American president tabled an eight-point joint declaration proclaiming the "common principles" that would provide a basis for organizing the postwar world. The first three read as follows:

First, their countries seek no aggrandizement, territorial or other;

Second, they desire to see no territorial changes that do not accord with the freely expressed wishes of the people concerned;

Third, they respect the right of all peoples to choose the form of government under which they will live; and they wish to see sovereign rights of self-government restored to those who have been forcibly deprived of them.[7]

Obviously, the first two of these principles posed no problem for the British government, but what about the third? Did the prime minister's signature mean that members of the British empire would be given a free choice between colonialism or independence? On returning home, Churchill made clear that the third principle applied only to those countries that had lost their sovereignty to Nazi aggression.

More problematical was the case of Soviet leader Joseph Stalin. When the Soviets signed on to the charter about a month later, they also entered a caveat: "Considering that the practical application of these principles will necessarily adapt itself to the circumstances, needs, and historic peculiarities of particular countries, the Soviet Government can state that a consistent application of these principles will secure the most energetic support on the part of the government and peoples of the Soviet Union."[8]

Three months later, the meaning of that codicil became clearer when the British foreign minister, Anthony Eden, met with Soviet leader Joseph Stalin. With German troops fighting furiously at the outskirts of Moscow, Churchill had sent Eden to Moscow to strengthen Soviet-British relations, work out an agreement on military collaboration, and establish general principles for a peace settlement with the Axis powers and postwar reconstruction.

Despite the precarious military situation facing his country, Stalin's first concern was politics—postwar politics, in fact. According to Eden, the talks began as follows:

> At my first conversation, . . . M. Stalin set out in some detail what he considered should be the postwar territorial frontiers of Europe; and in particular his ideas regarding the treatment of Germany. He proposed the restoration of Austria as an independent state, the detachment of the Rhineland from Prussia as an independent state or protectorate, and possibly the constitution of an independent state of Bavaria. He also proposed that East Prussia should be transferred to Poland and the Sudetenland returned to Czechoslovakia. He suggested that Yugoslavia should be restored and even receive additional territories from Italy, that Albania should be reconstituted as an independent state, and that Turkey should receive the Dodecanese, with possible adjustments in favor of Greece as regards islands in the Aegean important to Greece. Turkey might also receive certain districts in Bulgaria, and possibly in Northern Syria.

> *In general the occupied countries, including Czechoslovakia and Greece, should be restored to their prewar frontiers, and Mr. Stalin was prepared to support any special arrangements for securing bases et cetera, for the United Kingdom in Western European countries, e.g., France, Belgium, the Netherlands, Norway and Denmark.* As regards the special interests of the Soviet Union, Stalin desired the restoration of the position in 1941, prior to the German attack, in respect of the Baltic States [Estonia, Latvia, and Lithuania], Finland and Bessarabia. The "Curzon Line" should form the basis for the future Soviet-Polish frontier, and Rumania should give special facilities for bases et cetera, to the Soviet Union, receiving compensation from territory now occupied by Hungary. . . .
>
> . . . *In the second conversation, M. Stalin pressed for immediate recognition by His Majesty's Government of the future frontiers of the USSR, more particularly in regard to the inclusion within the USSR of the Baltic States and the restoration of the 1941 Finnish-Soviet frontier.* He made the conclusion of any Angle-Soviet [military or political] agreement dependent upon agreement on this point.[9]

These passages are important for a number of reasons. First, they reveal that while President Roosevelt was thinking about the postwar world in terms of abstract principles, Stalin was thinking about the postwar world in terms of creating a new map—a new map that would surround a dismembered and weakened Germany with strong counterweights. They also reveal that Stalin had expansionist aims, limited aims to be sure, but expansionist aims nonetheless. Fulfillment of these expansionist aims would clearly violate the charter, for the incorporation of Estonia, Latvia, and Lithuania into the Soviet Union would never "accord with the freely expressed wishes of the people concerned," as proclaimed in paragraph two. Those nations were, in fact, the first to secede from the Soviet Union when Mikhail Gorbachev presided over its dissolution.

Hitler, of course, had ceded the Baltics and eastern Poland to the Soviet Union in the infamous Stalin-Hitler Pact of August 1939, and the Soviet dictator quickly seized them. What Stalin was seeking was Britain's legitimation of his incorporation of these territories. Knowing that such might be difficult for Britain to do publicly, he suggested that the territorial cessions could be placed in a secret treaty that would not be revealed until the end of the war.

Eden responded that an agreement would be difficult because Prime Minister Churchill had stated publicly that his government would not accept territorial changes during the war. Eden also noted that, in the particular instance of the Baltics, Britain would have to be sure that the wishes of the inhabitants were taken into account.

On hearing this response, Stalin became irate and replied sharply: "Is it really necessary on this question of the Baltic States to have a Government decision [that the wishes of the Baltic peoples were taken into account]? Surely this is absolutely axiomatic. We are fighting our hardest and losing hundreds of thousands of men in the common cause with Great Britain as our ally, and I should have thought that such a question as the position of the Baltic States ought to be axiomatic and ought not to require any decision."[10]

When Eden responded by raising pledges in the Atlantic Charter, Stalin became even angrier:

> *Stalin:* I thought that the Atlantic Charter was directed against those people who were trying to establish world domination. It now looks as if the Atlantic Charter was directed against the USSR.
>
> *Eden:* No; that is certainly not so. . . .
>
> *Stalin:* Why does the restoration of our frontiers come into conflict with Atlantic Charter?
>
> *Eden:* I never said that it did.[11]

Whether or not the British should have acceded to Stalin's demands is not the issue. What is relevant is that leaders will ignore abstractions, however easily agreed to, when they conflict with their particular interests. As in the case of the Kellogg-Briand Pact, the United States and Britain could sign on to the principles of the Atlantic Charter because they were satisfied powers and had no territorial ambitions.[12] But such was not the case with the Soviets. They had lost large amounts of czarist territory after the Bolshevik revolution and would undoubtedly seek to regain that territory, as Stalin's comments to Eden indicated. After two German invasions within twenty-five years, what Russian ruler would not seek to construct a sphere of influence in Eastern Europe?

As his remarks to Eden made clear, Stalin was not going to allow paper pledges of self-abnegation to stand in the way of Russian irredentism and security in the postwar period. For him, peace would be obtained by traditional means of balance-of-power politics—territorial enlargement, the division and weakening of potential rivals (in this case Germany) spheres of influence, and the creation of a territorial settlement that would provide counterweights to future German expansion. In his approach to the postwar world, Stalin was thinking not like a communist but like the practitioners at Vienna in 1815—Castlereagh, Metternich, Talleyrand, and Alexander. Whether FDR realized it at the time or not, the Atlantic Charter contained a set of principles that, if applied, would have gone against what Stalin viewed as vital interests of the Soviet Union.

These two visions for the postwar world—FDR's Wilsonian dream of a peace based on principles and Stalin's vision of a peace based on the expansion of Soviet territory and power—would inevitably come into conflict at the end of World War II. And when these visions did clash, it was clear who would win. Like Alexander in 1815, Stalin knew he would "not have to negotiate too much" with Russian armies in possession of the Baltics, Poland, and most of central Europe. FDR's vision could only be realized as far as America's power would run.

FDR's Atlantic Charter was not a path to peace, but a path to insolvency in both a military and a political sense. While the charter might have been a great propaganda document, it was a disastrous diplomatic document because it raised hopes among the Baltic and central European peoples that the United States could only fulfill by threatening war or going to war against the Soviet Union, both of which were unthinkable. That FDR was aware of this dilemma can be seen in the following interchange, which took place in November 1944 between him and his newly confirmed ambassador to Poland, Arthur Bliss Lane. According to Lane:

> I said that in my opinion it was very important that we insist with the Soviet Government that the independence of Poland be maintained, and I added that if we were not going to be strong at a time when we had the largest Army, Navy, and Air Force in the world and at a time when the President had just received another mandate from the American people, I did not see when we were going to be strong.
>
> The President asked rather sharply and with a note of sarcasm, "Do you want me to go to war with Russia?" . . .
>
> . . . The President stated that he had entire confidence in Stalin's word, and he felt sure that he would not go back on it.[13]

At first, FDR tried to minimize Soviet violations or "fudge them over" through more platitudes such as those implanted in his Declaration on a Liberated Europe issued at the end of the Yalta Conference in February 1945. But by the time of his death, Roosevelt found himself in an exasperating position as the gap between the high principles of his Atlantic Charter and the realities of Soviet power and intentions became increasingly clear. Neither the Baltics nor even Eastern Europe represented interests that were vital enough to warrant war with the Soviet Union. Still, having pledged that the postwar order would be based on principle rather than power, the United States could not ignore Stalin's blatant violations of the charter. FDR had saddled the United States with a set of principles for which it would neither go to war to enforce nor be able to ignore when violated by Stalin.

According to the diplomatic historian Norman Graebner, the United States had a choice at the end of World War II: It could stand up for its moral principles, or it could maintain its alliance with the Soviet Union.[14] If America condemned the Soviet violations, the Soviets would most probably withdraw into a defensive isolationism and destroy America's dreams for a harmonious postwar world and an effective United Nations. If the United States sought to maintain a good working relationship with the Soviets in the postwar period, it would have to overlook these violations, something that would not be easy given both the expectations created by the charter and the brutal, totalitarian behavior of the Soviets, which was being well documented in the American and British press.

In the end, the outcome was even worse than Graebner indicated, for the United States secured neither its principles nor a working relationship with the Soviets in the postwar era. Having lost its principles and its alliance with the Soviet Union, the United States embarked on a policy of containment. Talk is cheap, and so is the proclamation of abstract principles and codes of behavior. When they are violated, however, gaps between ideals and interests become abundantly clear, and in democracies, such gaps can be disastrous if publics develop unrealistic expectations that may be unrealizable short of war.

Both during and after World War II, it was clear that neither British nor Soviet leaders would forgo what they saw as their interests. Churchill, as he quipped, did not become prime minister to preside over the dissolution of the British empire. Nor was Stalin willing to forgo what he considered legitimate territorial claims or the creation of "friendly governments" in Eastern Europe because of a paper pledge. On the other hand, it was easy for a state like the United States to forgo territorial aggrandizement because it was a territorially satisfied state.

Disarmament and Arms Control as Alternatives to Power Politics: Eradicate War by Abolishing the Instruments That Make War Possible

> *They shall beat their swords into plowshares, and their spears into pruning hooks: nations shall not lift up the sword against nation, neither shall they learn war any more.*
>
> —Isaiah 2:4

The theory underlying disarmament as an alternative to power politics lies in a simple proposition: You get rid of war by abolishing the weapons that make war possible. On a beautiful sunny morning in June 1967, Senator Joseph S. Clark articulated that theory simply and starkly in a commencement address at Franklin and Marshall College. Speaking in wake of the Seven Day War between Israel and its Arab "neighbors," the senator proposed that the United States and the Soviet Union impose disarmament on their client states in the Middle East. Thereafter, he said in an epigram that gained resounding applause from the audience, "If the Arabs and Israelis decide to go to war again, they will have to do so with 'sticks and stones,' for they will have no other weapons."

Obviously, none of the parties accepted Senator Clark's proposal if they even took notice of it. However, had the senator familiarized himself with the history of efforts to control or reduce arms, he would have been quickly sobered. The obstacles to arms control and disarmament have been genuine and formidable because the international system lacks a legitimate and powerful decision-making structure for resolving disputes between satisfied and dissatisfied powers. As British prime minister Edward Grey told the House of Commons on the eve of the Second Hague Peace Conference in 1907, "The difficulty in regard to one nation stepping out in advance of the others is this, while there is a chance that their courageous action my lead to reform, there is also a chance that it may lead to martyrdom."[15]

In fact, universal disarmament has been proposed only three times in the last 350 years, and in each case, the proposal was quickly modified or rebuffed.

1. In 1917, Woodrow Wilson proposed in one of his Fourteen Points that "armaments . . . be reduced to the lowest point consistent with domestic safety." When America's allies insisted that the president spell out exactly what this point meant, his spokesman, Colonel House, noted that "domestic safety" did not mean that nations would possess police forces only to control crime and domestic order. Each nation would also be allowed to maintain armed forces capable of protecting itself against invasion, a standard that almost ten years of disarmament deliberations in the League of Nations proved impossible of definition even in principle, let alone in implementation.

2. Ten years later, Soviet delegate Maxim Litvinov threw the League's Preparatory Commission on disarmament into a dither when he proclaimed, "The way to disarm is to disarm," and then tabled a draft treaty of sixty-three articles that would have abolished conscription, eliminated general staffs and war ministries, proscribed military appropriations even for defensive purposes, and liquidated all land, sea, and air armaments within one year. After almost six years of unbridgeable differences, Litvinov had done the near impossible—he united the bickering delegates into an overwhelming majority, which promptly dismissed his plan.

3. A quarter century later, at the United Nations Conference on Disarmament, Soviet premier Nikita Khrushchev trotted out Litvinov's plan almost verbatim when he called for the destruction of all nuclear weapons; a ban on atomic testing and the production of fissionable material; the closing of all military, naval, and air bases on the territory of other states; and a reduction of all conventional forces to 1.5 million for the United States, the Soviet Union, and communist China and

650,000 for Britain and France. All of this was to be done within two years, and to American surprise and dismay, the Soviet premier also proposed that the United Nations General Assembly set up an international authority that would undertake inspections of all states capable of producing nuclear weapons. The "ringer" in the plan, however, was the lack of an enforcement mechanism.

Three—and only three—grand proposals for universal disarmament over the course of 350 years, one quickly modified to reflect the reality that states would not forgo military forces for national defense, and two taken seriously by neither the recipients nor, most probably, the initiators of them.

Efforts to secure limited arms control agreements, as opposed to disarmament, have resulted in a few notable successes such as the Rush-Bagot Treaty of 1817, the Washington and London Naval Treaties of 1922 and 1930, the Atmospheric Test Ban Treaty of 1963, the ABM Treaty of 1972, and the SALT and START treaties of the 1970s, 1980s, and 1990s. In almost every case, however, these limited successes have been marred in one way or another. In some cases, controls have been at levels that allow states to *build up* to some agreed on limit, or the limits placed in one area of weaponry merely channeled arms spending into other areas, often leading to overall increases in both arms spending and arms.

What this discouraging record reflects are the political factors that led to the acquisition of weapons in the first place. None of the successes has ever led to a reduction of any of the political tensions that resulted in the quest for armaments in the first place; in fact, some successful agreements have been set aside when states later felt restrained by them. Finally, these successes have frequently been limited because significant parties refuse to participate in them.

The Atmospheric Test Ban Treaty of 1963, for example, really prevented no country that wanted to develop nuclear weapons from doing so. The treaty proscribed testing atomic weapons in the atmosphere, but the United States and the Soviet Union were still able to develop their atomic weapons and delivery systems by testing underground. China and France, on the other hand, refused to sign the treaty because they sought to join the nuclear club and lacked technical know-how to do so without testing in the atmosphere. Still, the agreement did secure the signatures of almost a hundred nations who had no intention at all of building nuclear weapons.

The Washington Naval Treaty of 1922 is a notable example of the *channeling* effect. Under that treaty, only battleships and battle cruisers were proscribed and for a very good reason—the naval establishments of the Great Powers had come to believe that such ships were military dinosaurs. Money forgone on such vessels, they believed, could better be diverted to smaller, more useful craft, such as cruisers, destroyers, and submarines, which were, of course, excluded from the agreement. When this "destroyer and cruiser gap" was plugged by the London Conference in 1930, Italy and France refused to go along because they had been allocated equivalent quotas.

Limited agreements, however, have not only channeled arms spending into other areas. At times, arms control treaties become acceptable only because they allow nations to increase their armaments to some upper limit. Successful agreements during the Cold War involved both channeling and building up. Although SALT I capped weapons *launchers*, namely, intercontinental ballistic missiles and submarine fired missiles, it did not cap the number of warheads that could be placed on those missiles, thus leading to the channeling effect. While SALT II sought to place limits on warheads, the treaty's sublimits in that area provided a ceiling that allowed the United States to "catch up" with the Soviets who were "ahead" in warheads on land-based missiles.

Not one weapon was scrapped as a result of the SALT agreements, nor did the treaties outlaw any weapons system sought by the military establishment of either side. Arms control agreements during the Cold War era did precisely what they were called: They controlled arms rather than reduced them. When the SALT talks began in 1972, the United States had 6,000 warheads and the Soviets had 2,000. When SALT I was signed, the United States had roughly 9,500 warheads to the Soviet Union's 5,000. Had SALT II been ratified and followed, the United States would have been allowed 14,000 warheads to the Soviet Union's 11,000.

The case for the SALT agreements was not that they reduced weapons but that they stabilized the arms competition and resulted in fewer weapons than would have existed without them. Without SALT I and II, proponents argued, the United States would have possessed between 15,000 and 21,000 warheads in 1985 as compared to 14,000 under the agreements, while the Soviets may have possessed 14,000 to 20,000, as opposed to the 11,000 allowed under the treaties.

After 40 years of arms control negotiations, the United States had the capability to inflict 369,769 Hiroshima equivalents (where 68,000 people were killed and 76,000 injured) on the Soviet Union while the Soviet Union possessed the capability to inflict 718,538 Hiroshima equivalents on the United States. Finally, the Cold War agreements did not cover conventional weapons, which increased significantly in the United States during the administration of John F. Kennedy, the last year of President Carter's administration, and the first term of the Reagan administration. Almost 20 years of conventional arms talks—the Mutual Balance Force Reduction talks between NATO and the Warsaw Pact—resulted in no agreements at all.

The most instructive aspect of the successful agreements is what they reveal about the relationship between political tensions and armaments.

When political tensions exist, the negotiation of even limited arms control agreements is extremely difficult and the parties err on the side of increases rather than reductions. When political tensions between nations go away, disarmament ceases to be a concern of states. If political tensions return, existing agreements will be scrapped. For example, the Rush-Bagot Treaty of 1817, which limited warships in the Great Lakes, was a very limited local agreement between England and the fledgling United States. Its success stemmed from one simple factor: America had given up its ambition of taking Canada. When that ambition ended, there was no need for warships in the lakes, especially since Britain had no interest in menacing the United States from that quarter. However, ending America-British rivalry on the lakes did not prevent both parties from almost going to war over the Oregon Territory in the 1840s or from having conflict over other issues during the rest of the century.

Even when agreements are faithfully followed, they can still be set aside when nations decide to pursue their goals though the use of arms. In 1934, for example, Japan gave notice, as stipulated under the London and Washington naval agreements, that it would withdraw from the obligations it had undertaken within two years. Thus, when the Japanese began their massive naval buildup in the latter half of the 1930s, they did do so with a clear legal conscience.

The Obstacles to Arms Control as an Approach to Peace

A hundred years of experience make it abundantly clear that the obstacles to arms control and disarmament are formidable, and they exist not because political leaders lack "political will," but because they reflect intractable problems. Just consider the following difficulties.

No state is obligated to engage in disarmament talks or to abide by any agreements that result from such talks unless it freely chooses to do so. In the mid-1990s, for example, the United Nations Disarmament Conference sought to hold discussions on ending the production of fissionable materials. However, the proposed conference was unable to begin formal discussions because it operated on the unanimity principle, which meant that any one country could prevent the talks from beginning or ending, a right that Israel chose to exercise. After India and Pakistan tested nuclear weapons in the atmosphere in the spring of 1998, the United States pressured Israel into allowing talks to take place, but as a price for allowing formal meetings to begin, Israel indicated that it felt it was under no obligation to sign any treaty that might result from the talks.[16]

Since the end of the First World War, democratic states have found it almost impossible to spurn arms control talks. How, in fact, can a democracy reject talking about anything at all, let alone something so important to peace as arms control and disarmament? All too frequently, however, this "obligation to parley" works to the disadvantage of democratic status quo powers while fostering the interests of revisionist powers. Merely by agreeing to participate in such talks, the democracies find themselves facing internal pressures against further arms spending in order not to "poison the atmosphere of the talks." Once discussions have begun, revisionist states frequently turn the talks into propaganda forums for delegitimizing the position of status quo powers on outstanding political issues. Not infrequently, they also try to score propaganda points by tabling arms control proposals that appear simple, drastic, and compelling, but which they know will be unacceptable because they have embed them with unacceptable conditions about verification and enforcement. When such proposals are predictably rejected, both the leaders of revisionist powers and publics within the democratic powers place the onus for "failure" on the leaders of the status quo powers. With the democracies unwilling to take "real steps for peace," why should anyone be surprised if revisionist powers continue building arms? Such are the ways that leaders of revisionist powers can gain sympathy from peace-seeking groups in democratic countries.

A decade of disarmament talks held under the auspices of the League of Nations did nothing for arms control, disarmament, or the cause of peace. In fact, their main contribution was not to peace but to war. They weakened the unity and will of the status quo powers, and they helped to legitimate the rearmament of the most dissatisfied and potentially powerful nation on the continent—Nazi Germany.

The problem of arriving at proportional ratios. Even when states genuinely desire to curtail or control arms, determining a "fair" ratio among their armaments can be a vexing one. In the Washington naval talks after World War I, the British and American negotiators managed to impose a ratio of 5 to 3 between them and the Japanese, while the French and Italians had no alternative but to accept a ratio of 1.7 to Japan's 3 and Britain and America's 5. At the second set of talks in London a decade later, the Japanese strongly protested their inferior status, and when their negotiators could secure only a 70 percent ratio in auxiliary ships, the civilian government in Japan was discredited and the militarists grew in political power. Meanwhile, France and Italy refused to sign the London treaty because the French feared that parity with Italy would lead to Italian naval hegemony in the Mediterranean, and the Italians would accept nothing less than parity with France even if they might decide not to actually match French levels. What Mussolini wanted was not disarmament or arms control but arms. As he put it after Italy withdrew from the conference: "Words are very beautiful, but rifles, machine guns, ships, and airplanes are much more beautiful."[17]

During the Cold War, President Nixon broke the logjam over the ratio issue when he agreed to negotiate a treaty that would leave the military forces of each side in a ratio of "essential equivalence"; however, "essential equivalence" would be achieved not through arms reductions but through controlled arms increases.

The problem of inspection. Satellites and listening devices have made the problem of inspection much easier than in the past; however, the prospect of cheating still remains, especially in regard to agreements that call for the abolition of all weapons. The efforts of the United Nations weapons inspectors in Iraq reveal that it is almost impossible to carry out successful territorial inspections if a recalcitrant state refuses to cooperate fully.

In the nuclear realm, the universal abolition of all weapons will probably never occur because large numbers of secretly hidden weapons could always escape the scrutiny of satellite and ground inspection teams in countries as large as the United States, India, China, and Russia—and whether the weapons are hidden away merely as a hedge against cheating by others or for more ominous purposes is irrelevant. Since no great nuclear power can risk the probability of cheating by others, the best we can expect are arms control agreements that allow the parties to possess arsenals large enough for deterrence in the event that other powers cheat or break out of the treaty.

For example, the first post–Cold War arms control agreement, START I, required each side to reduce its strategic nuclear warheads to 6,000 over seven years between 1994 and 2001. The second post–Cold War arms agreement, START II, stipulated reductions to 3,000-3,500 strategic nuclear warheads and the elimination of all land-based nuclear missiles possessing multiple warheads. As of this writing, the Russian parliament has not ratified this treaty, which was signed in 1993. However, if the treaty is ratified and further reductions are sought, the two powers will have to consider the relations of their forces to those of China, Britain, and France, as well as the probable forces of rising nuclear powers. Seeking a nuclear accord among all of the nuclear and nuclear-aspiring powers would raise a host of difficult questions. At the outset, some nations will want to keep all of their armaments, especially if they obtained them recently. Some might even refuse to attend such talks, while others might participate in order to sabotage them by talking about the need to resolve the issues that lead states to seek nuclear arms in the first place.

Once talks were under way, the difficult question of deciding on ratios would immediately arise. Should China have fewer weapons than the United States and Russia, and, if so, how many fewer? What should the ratio be between these three powers and France or Britain? Should India and Pakistan be allowed to build up, and if so, to what level? Then, "the unit of measurement" question will arise—will the agreement focus on delivery vehicles or warheads? Will certain kinds of weapons, such as land-based missiles with multiple warheads be proscribed? How would the agreements be enforced? Finally, how would the parties deal with the problem of potential nonsignatories such as North Korea or Iraq, for example? A world with controlled nuclear arms, let alone a world without nuclear weapons, is a long way off.

The problem of enforcement or sanctions in the event of noncompliance. Arms control agreements must also come to grips with the problem of enforcement, as exemplified in the case of the United Nations' experience with Iraq after the Gulf War. When Iraq called a halt to spot inspections in August 1998, a majority of the Security Council opposed using military force to enforce the agreement that Saddam Hussein had made at the end of the Gulf War. Instead, the council voted to continue the economic sanctions that had been set in place at the end of the war. Sanctions for noncompliance won out over military enforcement.

When Hussein threw out all of the inspectors at the end of October and the usual efforts at diplomacy got nowhere, the United States and Britain engaged in four days of futile bombing that did minimal damage at a cost of approximately $450 million. Since the strikes were opposed by Russia, China, and France, the badly split members of the Security Council descended into "study" and tedious negotiations among themselves. Russia and France wanted to lift the sanctions as an inducement for Hussein to accept a new "inspection regime" that would monitor rather than inspect. The United States and Britain, on the other hand, insisted on keeping the sanctions in place until a UN inspection team certified that Iraq had destroyed all of its long-range missiles and weapons of mass destruction.

The result of these deliberations? According to foreign affairs columnist Richard C. Hottelet: "Eleven months of convoluted palaver, negotiating, and drafting by the Council's five permanent members finally brought forth a mouse."[18] On December 17, 1999, a Security Council resolution abolished the UNSCOM and replaced it with a new UN Monitoring, Verification, and Inspection Commission (UNMOVIC) that had none of the powers and independence of UNSCOM. As another carrot to Iraq, the council agreed to remove all limits on Iraq's sale of oil and lift the limits on imports of humanitarian goods. When Iraq refused to accept the watered down regime, the council spent months trying to find ways of inducing Hussein to accept the inspectors. Thus, the victors were groveling before the defeated aggressor. As of this writing, in September 2000, no inspection team has been in Iraq for almost two years.

Questions of enforcement, of course, apply only to signatories, for nonsignatories are never obligated to comply with arms control agreements they reject, which, again, raises the problem of sovereignty. Nonsignatories of the Atmospheric Test Ban Treaty, namely, France, India, and China, are under no obligation to refrain from testing nuclear weapons in the atmosphere. But what would happen if *one of the signatories to the agreement* broke the ban and tested weapons in the atmosphere? What would the other signatories such as Sweden, Columbia,

Germany, or Canada do? What would the nuclear powers who complied with the ban do? The question answers itself: Enforcement involves costs and risks, and the alternative of "do nothing" or "wait and watch," always seems the prudent thing to do—at least in the short run. The UN General Assembly might pass a resolution requesting the agreement-breaking state to return to compliance with the treaty. At most, the nuclear powers signatory to the pact might resume testing if they thought it necessary to do so.

The problem of acceptable substitutes for war. While it is true that "War is seldom the result of the lack of procedures to settle differences pacifically,"[19] as Professor Schuman noted in 1933, it is also true that some disputes are resolvable only by military force. For example, because Austria's right to possess Lombardy and Venetia was perfectly legal and inalienable under the Vienna Agreements of 1815, how could Italy have ever been unified except by war? How could the United States have gained California from Mexico except by military force? How could Stalin ever have gotten the Estonians, Latvians, and Lithuanians to join the Soviet Union through peaceful persuasion alone? While states may be willing to place limits on certain categories of weapons, most will be extremely reluctant to discard the most useful instruments for securing or changing what they value most as long as the international system lacks an independent enforcement mechanism that stands above them.

The problem of states that refuse to accept the status quo. In the end, the root obstacle to arms control and disarmament lies in the split between those states who want to change existing distributions of territory, status, or influence, and those who want to keep things the way they are. As Professor Inis Claude has noted, a disarmament plan that freezes the status quo will be unacceptable to dissatisfied powers, while plans that might undermine the status quo by reversing power relationships will create fears among the status quo powers—especially if dissatisfied powers have proclaimed revisionist aims.[20] This dilemma was precisely the obstacle that prevented any agreement between France and Germany in the 1930s.

As the authors of one of the earliest textbooks in the field of international politics wrote in 1937: "Agreement in the matter of armaments is possible only when the policies of states do not clash. If their policies are in collision, no progress can be made in the adjustment of armaments without a previous accommodation in the matter of policy. With political agreement once achieved, moreover, the question of arms loses most of its importance because dangers of conflict have already been largely removed."[21]

The prescience of these words is striking. During the Cold War, disarmament negotiations led not to arms reductions but either to *gravestone agreements,* which merely marked certain areas as "off limits," such as the ABM Treaty, or *arms raising agreements,* such as SALT I and II, which always set limits higher than existing levels of armaments. Then, along came Mr. Gorbachev. When he called off the Cold War, fears about nuclear war between the superpowers evaporated, and the arms-control industry hit a slump. Once the policies of the United States and the Soviet Union ceased to be in collision all across the globe, disarmament and arms control lost their importance, "because the dangers of conflict [had] already been removed," to repeat the language of Simonds and Emeny.

Nothing more clearly underscores the political underpinnings of arms races than the fact that during the Cold War no one ever proposed nuclear arms limitation talks between the United States and Britain or between the United States and France, and for one obvious reason—the policies among these powers were "nowhere in collision!" Similarly, in the post–Cold War era, neither the United States nor China has even hinted about bilateral arms control talks, and again, the reason is the same.

While the United States and the Chinese have their differences, they do not even approach a scale that would lead to a competition in arms; however, if such a competition does arise, arms control talks would more likely exacerbate the relations between the two powers than ameliorate them, and the prospects for their leading to significant reductions in arms would be as scant as arms control talks among competing powers have always been. While arms can increase fears and suspicions among competing nations, they are never the fundamental basis for that competition. In fact, there has never been a case where arms control negotiations have ameliorated the political differences between contentious countries. As President Reagan once put it to Mr. Gorbachev, "We do not have differences because we have all these weapons; we have these weapons because of our fundamental differences. Resolve those differences, and we will have no need for our weapons."

The problem of armaments is neither a technical problem nor a problem of "political will" or good intentions; it is, instead, a political problem. End the political differences, and the technical arms control difficulties will no longer be important. Once competition ends, concern for disarmament and arms control disappears as well. One need only compare German and French relations in 1935 and 1965 or American and Russian relations in 1975 and 1995 to see the symptomatic nature of concern for arms control and disarmament.

When the Cold War ended, the interest of the American public in arms control ended as well. Fears about nuclear weapons and nuclear war evaporated, as did the public's concern about ratios, throw-weights, and inspection regimes. Few Americans, in fact, either know or care about the stipulations of the START agreements or their status in the ratification process. Within the matter of a few short years, the general public's concern about *Russia's nuclear weapons* descended to their level of concern about *Great Britain's nuclear weapons* during the Cold War era. What the public fears now is the acquisition of nuclear weapons by states like Iran, Iraq, North Korea, or, increasingly, troublesome terrorist groups.

Peace through Formal International Institutions Vested with Authority to Maintain the Peace and Resolve International Conflicts

> *No one willingly accepts the mandate of an international organization that subverts what he or she considers a vital interest.*
>
> —Ronald Steel, "After Internationalism," *World Policy Journal*, Summer 1995

The alternatives to power politics considered so far have all foundered on the problem of power—the lack of some structure of power that will make states fearful of not following international law or employing peaceful procedures in resolving their disputes. To some, this lack of an enforcement mechanism merely reflected an immutable fact of life that states had to learn to live with. Others, however, have sought to transcend this "reality" by creating formal international institutions that would spell out procedures for resolving disputes peacefully and punish those who did not abide by those procedures.

Collective Security—"Peace through Posse": Woodrow Wilson's League of Nations

The first such experiment in the twentieth century was Woodrow Wilson's League of Nations, which was designed to replace the balance of power with a *community of power* that would *enforce* the peace. However, enforcement was to be only a last resort of the League because, in the first resort, members were obligated, under Article 15, to submit all disputes to arbitration or judicial settlement. If parties failed to reach a settlement through those techniques, they were obligated to submit their disputes to the League council, which could make a full investigation and propose terms of settlement. These traditional alternatives to war, advocates believed, would allow for "delays" and "cooling off periods" that might abate the passions that could lead states to war.

In addition to efforts by the council, the League's assembly was also empowered, under Article 3, "to deal at its meetings with any matter within the sphere of action of the League or affecting the peace of the world." Through the assembly's airing of issues, disputing states would gain an opportunity to benefit from the views of disinterested bystanders or "the organized opinion of mankind." Even more, under Article 19, the Assembly could "advise the reconsideration of treaties which have become inapplicable" and "[consider] international conditions whose continuance might endanger the peace of the world." Through this "safety valve," the assembly could engage in what is today called "preventive diplomacy." Article 8, which recognized "that the maintenance of peace requires the reduction of armaments to a point consistent with national safety and the enforcement by common action of international obligations," sought to minimize the possibility that fears stemming from arms spending might spur the onset of war.

All of these inducements to peaceful settlement notwithstanding, the League would ultimately stand or fall on the effectiveness of its enforcement mechanisms—namely, the obligation of every member to come to the aid of any member whose territorial integrity and political independence were threatened by external aggression. "One for all and all for one," "every nation is its brother's keeper," "an attack on one is an attack on all,"—phrases such as these characterize well Woodrow Wilson's plan for collective security. These obligations were clearly spelled out in Articles 10 and 16 of the covenant:

> *Article 10: The Members of the League undertake to respect and preserve against external aggression the territorial integrity and existing independence of all members of the League. In case of any aggression or in case of any threat or danger of such aggression the Council shall advise upon the means by which this obligation shall be fulfilled.*
>
> *Article 16: (1) Should any Member of the League resort to war in disregard of its covenants under Articles 12, 13, or 15, it shall* ipso facto *be deemed to have committed an act of war against all other Members of the League, which hereby undertake immediately to subject it to the severance of all trade or financial relations, the prohibition of all intercourse between their nationals and the nationals of the Covenant-breaking State, and the prevention of all financial, commercial or personal intercourse between the nationals of the covenant-breaking state and the nationals of any other state, whether a Member of the League or not.*
>
> *(2) It shall be the duty of the Council in such case to recommend to the several Governments concerned what effective military, naval, or air force the Members of the League should severally contribute to the armed forces to be used to protect the covenants of the League.*

Notice the strong language in these articles: Members "undertake to respect and preserve against external aggression the territorial integrity and existing independence of all members of the League," *no matter against whom or by whom!* Any state violating its obligation to settle disputes through diplomacy, arbitration, judicial settlement, or on pronouncements by the council "shall *ipso facto* be deemed to have committed an act of war against all other Members of the League." In the event of such violations, sanctions and ostracism were to begin immediately. Unlike the Kellogg-Briand Pact, the League covenant imposed obligations on signatories to enforce its provisions.

While Wilson's League was innovative *as an institution,* the basic theory underlying it was neither new nor unexamined. Schemes almost identical to Wilson's "League to Enforce the Peace" had been floating around for centuries:

- in 1306, Pierre Dubois published his On the Recovery of the Holy Land;
- in 1638, the Duc de Sully's work, The Grand Design, appeared;
- in 1693, William Penn published his Essay Toward the Present and Future Peace of Europe;
- in 1710, John Bellers's Some Reasons for a European State appeared;
- in 1712, Abbé St. Pierre presented his essay on Perpetual Peace, which was the subject of much commentary by philosophers and statesmen alike.

The covenant of the League contains little that is not found in these ancient tracts. *All of these proposals take peace as their highest value, higher in fact than justice, and they identify the key to peace as the maintenance of the territorial status quo.* Only in minor details do these plans differ—whether voting should be weighted or proceed on a one-state, one-vote basis; whether a simple majority or unanimity should be required for decision making; whether enforcement should be undertaken by an international army or forces contributed by the member states.

Under Bellers's plan, the community would preserve for its members "[all] of the territory and all of the rights which they possess." According to St. Pierre, the member states would have "all the strength of Europe to protect them in the possession of what they shall enjoy."[22] At the same time, none of these peace pioneers was unmindful of the difficulty that "freezing" a given status quo might involve. As William Penn noted, a decision would have to be made "from what time titles shall take their beginning or how far back we may look to confirm or dispute them." St. Pierre, on the other hand, proposed basing his perpetual alliance on the Treaty of Utrecht, which was signed in 1713.

Like the League, all of these schemes obligated states to forgo the use of force in dealing with one another and to resolve their differences through diplomacy. If these pacific mechanisms failed, members were to submit their disputes to a decision-making body. Once the body made its decision, the parties would be obligated to accept it, and those choosing not to comply would be subject to sanctions. According to William Penn, if any members should "act independently or refuse to accept the verdict of the Diet, all the other sovereignties, united as one strength, shall *compel* the submission and performance of the sentence, with damages to the suffering party and charges to the sovereignties that obliged their submission [my italics]."

Like Wilson, however, none of these early theorists believed that the community would ever have to resort to the use of force. The mere threat of community power, they believed, would be enough to deter potential peace-breakers. According to Penn, no single state would have the power to dispute the will of the community, while St. Pierre confidently asserted that no state would be tempted to use force because "no conquests are possible." St. Pierre even believed that once his Union was set up, there would be "nothing important in [the] future to regulate between sovereigns except future or imminent successions to sovereignties," or disputes "of very little importance," such as "2 or 3 villages more or less" or "a few personal quarrels, some trifles about frontiers, or commerce."

None of these early schemes escaped critical scrutiny by philosophers or practitioners of diplomacy. In a letter to Voltaire, Frederick the Great noted that St. Pierre's plan was "most practicable; *for its success all that is lacking is the consent of Europe and a few similar trifles.*" Voltaire also dismissed the abbé's "impractical peace," and recommended either balance-of-power politics or peace through prayer and charity in personal relations. In 1756, Rousseau wrote a summary of St. Pierre's plan[23] as part of a project to edit and publish all of the abbé's writings. Later that year, he wrote his *Judgment sur la Paix Perpetuelle*, which focused on the problem that Frederick the Great raised: How does one get sovereign states to give up their sovereignty? As long as states were sovereign, Rousseau noted, they would look to their own interests rather than community interests. Seeing "no prospect of a federative league being formed," Rousseau dismissed Pierre's scheme as "an absurd dream."[24]

Until the formation of the League of Nations, the debate over these peace plans remained academic speculation. Once the League became a reality, people would at last find answers to the central questions that divided supporters and critics of the early plans:

- Would sovereign states resort to peaceful means of settlement such as arbitration, judicial settlement, and third-party intervention and develop a habit for their use?
- Would they be deterred from employing the use of force for fear of invoking the combined might of the international community?
- Would states live up to their pledges to expend lives and treasure in defense of other states no matter what the cost, what the issue, or the identity of the victim or aggressor?

Answers to these questions were not long in coming. As early as the drafting stage, it became apparent that Wilson's theory would be watered down. British leaders never shared Wilson's beliefs about replacing the balance of power with a community of power, for they knew very well that when the chips were down, they—the British empire—and not the Finns, Bolivians, or Bulgarians, would be the ones doing the policing. From the very beginning, British policymakers saw the League as no more than a formal gathering place for the Great Powers to meet and discuss how, if at all, to deal with international disputes and breaches of the peace.

Although Wilson tried to stick to his guns, wiggle words crept into the covenant. If you reread the sections from the covenant reprinted in this chapter, you will note that when it comes to actually enforcing the proscription against the use of force, the council merely "advises upon the means by which this obligation shall be fulfilled [Article 10]." When it comes to the anteing up of armed forces to do the fighting, the council was only empowered "to recommend [Article 16/2]," which is not the same as "require."

Then, there is the history of the institution. By the time the assembly first met, President Harding had announced that the League was dead, and the British government and Foreign Office were indifferent to the organization. The French, on the other hand, threatened to withdraw from the organization if Germany were admitted as a member. Germany and Russia viewed the League as a tool of the victorious Allies. As the first meeting of the assembly approached, only the Japanese were enthusiastic about the dawn of the organization. Its seat as a permanent member of the council placed Japan on an equal footing with the European Great Powers. So great was Japan's enthusiasm for the League that a special ship had to be chartered to carry its numerous delegation from Tokyo to Geneva.

At the first two meetings of the assembly, Canada led a campaign to tear the heart from the covenant, namely, Article 10, which obligated every member to guarantee the political independence and territorial integrity of every other member. Having failed in gutting the covenant on its first two tries, the Canadians were more successful at the fourth session of the assembly. When they tabled a resolution authorizing each member to decide for itself how it would fulfill its obligation under Article 10, the proposal gained the support of every member of the assembly but one, Iran. While Iran's lone "no" vote killed the resolution under the unanimity rule, the result of the vote was clear: In the event of a conflagration, the community fire brigade would be strictly volunteer.

Every reader of this book learned about the failures of the League as a schoolchild. Yet, during its nearly twenty years of active life, the organization made notable contributions to dampening down and helping to resolve numerous disputes.[25] However, when the great challenges came—in Manchuria, in Ethiopia, and in dealing with Hitler's revisionism—the League failed to meet the test, and the roots of these failures lay in some very questionable values and assumptions underlying the League's approach to peace.

1. *The Problem of the Status Quo.* Clearly, any league dedicated to preserving the territorial integrity and political independence of all its members is dedicated to *freezing the map.* Yet, most international conflicts

likely to involve violence usually concern efforts to revise the map. The difficulty of peaceful change lies in the simple fact that most nations are unwilling to yield territory peacefully. Yet, as new powers rise, maps inevitably change to reflect new-power realities, and, frequently, those changes take place as a result of war.

While most nations may accept or acquiesce peacefully in an existing territorial status quo, very few of those nations—large or small—would be willing to go to war to preserve every aspect of that status quo if efforts are made to change it by force. Yet, the Covenant required just that. As League historian F. S. Northedge notes, "[Woodrow Wilson's] first mistake was to make the system of universal guarantees the heart of the Covenant, a proposal which no other founding father of the League could accept, and which ultimately fell foul of the Senate."[26]

In the case of the League, freezing the map meant locking in the provisions of the postwar treaties that were anathema to many Germans, Poles, Hungarians, Russians, and Italians. Perhaps no one better expressed this relationship between the idealistic guarantees of the League and the reality of what the organization was committed to guaranteeing than the chairman of the U.S. Senate Foreign Relations Committee, William Borah. Responding to a French proposal to strengthen the League by providing it with an international army, Borah remarked: "An international police force to guarantee the security of the world . . . is a perfectly logical product of the Versailles Treaty. A Treaty which has neither honor nor justice at its foundation can, of course, be maintained and preserved by force and in no other way. The theory back of such a proposition is that, regardless of the right of peoples to grow and develop, the status quo must be maintained."[27]

From the very beginning, then, a tension existed between the utopian ambition of freezing the map and the reality that the great status quo powers would preserve only those portions of the map that they believed were vital to their own national interests—if even that.

2. *The Problem of Peaceful Change.* The founders of the League sought to overcome this problem of "freezing of the status quo" by drafting Article 19, which allowed the assembly to "advise the reconsideration . . . of treaties" that had become "inapplicable." However, the promise of this article was negated the very first and last time it was invoked. In 1920, Bolivia invoked the article in regard to a dispute it was having with Chile. Desiring a seaport in the territory of Tacna-Arica, Bolivia asked the assembly to reconsider the Treaty of Anscon by which Bolivia had ceded all claims to the territory in 1904. Chile contended that the League was incompetent to act in the matter because Chile, itself, was unwilling to reconsider the treaty and the League could not advise reconsideration against the will of one of the parties. The assembly appointed a committee of jurists, which issued a report favorable to Chile. Thereupon, Bolivia withdrew its request and refused to participate in any further

work of the League until 1929.[28] As Professor Frederick Dunn noted in his *Peaceful Change,* Article 19 "[was] a dead letter from the beginning."[29]

Map 5.1. Tacna-Arica

The first and last attempt to use Article 19, the peaceful change article of the League Covenant, occurred in regard to the tiny area surrounding two Chilean provinces of Tacna and Arica. In the grand scheme of things, Tacna and Arica may not amount to much, but in a land-locked country like Bolivia, little things can mean a lot. Given Chile's size, was its government being reasonable by refusing to grant Bolivia an outlet to the sea through territory that it had gained from Bolivia by war in the first place?

3. The Problem of Assigning Guilt. Cases of plate glass aggression might be easy to deal with, but all too often cases involving the use of force are not as clear cut. Revisionist powers are masters at creating pretexts or donning mantles of legitimacy precisely to isolate their victims and weaken the will of those seeking to defend the status quo. By so doing, they may make action difficult even when the party initiating the use of force is clear. For example, before invading Ethiopia, Mussolini waited for an incident, in this case a skirmish at Wal Wal, to provide a "defensive" smoke screen for his invasion. Japanese military leaders had their own men set off an explosion so that their intervention in Manchuria would look like a reaction. Then, as their military forces gobbled up Manchuria, Japanese diplomats in Geneva talked about peaceful settlement, maintaining law and order, and defending private investment and property—Western as well as Japanese property. Never did they mention the word "war."

4. *The Problem of Proportionality, Costs, Interests, Risks, and Benefits in Defending the Status Quo Everywhere.* The theory of enforcement underlying the covenant assumes that every member will act against violators of the proscription against the use of force without regard to its own interests, circumstances, or cost. Historical experience with both the League and the United Nations has clearly tested that assumption and found it sadly wanting. All nations are for peace and against aggression in the abstract, but none will sacrifice coin and lives to defend any victim of aggression, anywhere, and at anytime.

Only twice in the twentieth century did international organizations respond to the use of force with military counterforce. In 1950, the United Nations Security Council authorized the sending of military forces to defend South Korea, and in 1992, a coalition of United Nations forces drove Iraqi forces out of Kuwait. In both cases, the United States had strong national interests in responding militarily and would have done so unilaterally if the United Nations had not supported the operations. Although both military ventures gained the support of other nations, that support, in terms of troops, supplies, and weapons, paled in comparison to the efforts made by the United States.

Seventy-five years of experience with international organizations designed to maintain international peace and security makes it abundantly clear that the belief in a collective or communal deterrent to aggression is a chimera. As F. H. Hinsley put it, the fundamental failure of the League lay in its structure of government. The League was a confederation of states and confederations fail when it comes to *united* action, a truth the American States learned when they were organized under the Articles of Confederation.

The failure of the great status quo powers during the interwar years was not that they did not live up to the universal principles embodied in Woodrow Wilson's League of Nations. Their failure lay in not seeing their own national interests clearly and then pursuing them with wisdom and power. What Winston Churchill has termed the "unnecessary war" could have been prevented with or without a League of Nations. The United States would have been no more willing to go to war against Japan in 1931 had it been in the League than it was as a nonmember. Nor would the United States have been more willing to go to war with Mussolini over Ethiopia, or Germany over Poland, or Russia over Finland had it been a member of the League.

What we learn from Woodrow Wilson's "peace through community power" is that victims of aggression and states subjected to bullying by revisionist powers simply cannot count on "the community" to come to their aid. If peace is to be secured at all, it will be secured by the Great Powers, a lesson not lost on Wilson's internationalist successor, Franklin Delano Roosevelt.

Peace through a Concert or Condominium of Great Powers: FDR's "Four Policemen"

In speaking with Soviet foreign minister Molotov in June 1942, FDR expressed his disagreement with Winston Churchill's suggestion that the League of Nations be resurrected in the postwar period. Such a move, the president said, "would be impractical because too many nations would be involved." In place of Wilson's collective security:

> The President conceived it as the duty of the four major United Nations (Britain, U.S., USSR, and China, provided the last achieves a unified government, opposite which there was still a question mark) to act as the policemen of the world. The first step was general disarmament. But the four major nations would maintain sufficient armed forces to impose peace, together with inspection privileges which would guard against clandestine rearmament in which Germany had notoriously engaged during the pre-war years. If any nation menaced the peace, it could be blockaded and then if still recalcitrant, bombed. The President added . . . his aim was thus peace in our time. He thought that all other nations save the Big Four should be disarmed (Germany, Japan, France, Spain, Belgium, Netherlands, Scandinavia, Turkey, Rumania, Hungary, Poland, Czechoslovakia, etc.).[30]

His plan, "might be peace by dictation," the president then added, "but his hope was that it might be so administered that the peoples of the previous aggressor nations might eventually come to see that they have infinitely more to gain from permanent peace than from periodically recurrent wars."[31]

In laying out his scheme for peace, the president set forth the basic structure of power and authority of the United Nations largely as it exists to this day. Power in the United Nations resides not in the "international community" but in the "Big Five" that make up the core of the Security Council, which is responsible for the maintenance of international peace and security. The presence of nonpermanent members on the council, first seven and later ten, were added to "democratize" the council and provide some semblance of "accountability" for the Great Powers. Still, any of the Great Powers can bring the organization to a halt through its veto, but when united, the permanent members are capable of acting with great decisiveness, as they did in responding to

Iraq's aggression. The role of the larger international community in the United Nations lies in that "town meeting" of the world, the General Assembly, which merely has the power to make "recommendations" based on a two-thirds majority of states present and voting.

FDR's Four Policemen in the United Nations. As we now know, FDR's dream of peace through four disinterested policemen was still-born even before the delegates assembled at San Francisco to sign the organization's charter. One of four policemen had revisionist aims, which it was willing to pursue unilaterally and with little regard for the impression its behavior was having on its peers. The power vacuum created by the unconditional surrender and occupation of Germany provided Stalin with revisionist opportunities that he could not resist. As his troops moved deeply into central Europe, Stalin carved out a glacial sphere of influence in Eastern Europe and then just sat. When he sought to expand Soviet influence into Turkey and Iran and communist guerrillas waged war in Greece, it appeared that one of the policemen needed policing.

Very quickly, the United Nations turned into an organization that was quite different from what its framers intended. Throughout the Cold War, the world organization was less a forum for collaborative Great Power decision making than an arena in which the United States and the Soviet Union competed for the imprimatur of General Assembly resolutions in support of their positions on various international issues. The major achievements of the organization came about because of efforts of the middle and nonaligned powers to insulate trouble spots from intervention by the two superpowers—as in the case of Suez in 1956 and the Congo in the early 1960s.

A Concert of Powers in the Post–Cold War World? Since the end of the Cold War, the conditions required for collaboration among the Great Powers now exist, and the UN Security Council has been working largely as its founders intended—as a concert of the Great Powers with a series of nonpermanent members acting as a moral "check." All of the Great Powers generally accept the legitimacy of the post–Cold War territorial status quo. Collective collaboration on international disputes through the United Nations, as a first resort, has increasingly become the rule, and the imprimatur of the Security Council has become the benchmark of legitimacy for actions by states.

To be sure, none of the Great Powers has displayed any desire to vest the organization with resources that would give it an independent base of power, such as an international peace force under the direction of the secretary general or international taxes that would provide an independent source of revenue. Nor has any of the Great Powers given up its right to choose what organizational peacekeeping ventures it will or will not participate in; in fact, as President Clinton's withdrawal from the Somalian operation makes clear, the powers even feel free to withdraw from operations at their own pleasure.

However, these attitudes do not reflect a failure of the United Nations; they merely reflect the reality of any concert system in a world of sovereign states: The United Nations exists as an instrument of the Great Powers for their joint decision making. The United Nations is not an authority either above them or independent of them. Ironically, now that the United States has gained precisely the kind of world organization it sought during World War II, an American administration that came into office on a foreign policy platform of "assertive multilateralism" turned out to be most reluctant to abide by the consensual decision making this model requires. The biggest challenge facing the United Nations in the late 1990s stemmed from the Clinton administration's penchant for acting unilaterally, or through the ruse of NATO, whenever other members of the Security Council would not go along with American views on international issues—a penchant most notably exemplified in the case of Kosovo.

What Can One Reasonably Expect from the United Nations?

The comedian Jackie Gleason once introduced his band leader with the following banter, "Ladies and gentleman, Sammy Spear and his United Nations Orchestra: They're great when they get together, which is almost never." To a large extent, Gleason's mockery belies a set of unrealistic expectations about the organization. To make a fair and realistic assessment of the United Nations, one must become clear about what the organization was never intended to do and what it is unlikely to do in a world run by human beings rather than angels.

LIMITATIONS OF THE UNITED NATIONS INHERENT IN ITS CHARTER

1. *The United Nations Was Never Designed to Deal with the Greatest Threat to World Peace—Revisionism by a Major Power or a Coalition of Revisionist Powers.* As Professor Adam Ulam put it in discussing FDR's four policeman scheme, "a policeman is expected to act selflessly and on behalf of law and not to collect rewards from people on his beat."[32] However, when one or more of the cops do go "on the take," to continue with Ulam's metaphor, law and order will be restored only if those who have an interest in law and order seek to preserve it—and they will do so outside the organization—which is their legitimate right! NATO, SEATO, and the many bilateral defense pacts which the United States created to deter Soviet expansion during the Cold War were all founded and legitimated under Article 51, which allows states to provide for their individual and collective self-defense.

When conflicts occur among the Great Powers, international organizations become forums for propaganda. Competing powers will seek "to capture" the organization and use it to legitimate their positions on issues in conflict. After the Soviet Union invaded Hungary in 1956, the General Assembly, for almost a decade thereafter, routinely adopted resolutions condemning the intervention. Later, the balance of forces turned more favorably for the Soviets as the assembly burgeoned with nonaligned states from the developing world. During the 1980s, the Reagan administration's efforts to destabilize the Marxist Sandinista regime in Nicaragua through unilateral economic sanctions were routinely condemned by the General Assembly. Meanwhile, the assembly's annual resolution on Afghanistan never mentioned that Soviet troops were waging ferocious war in the country; only unnamed "foreign troops" were asked to leave.[33]

2. *The United Nations Was Never Designed to Deal with Unilateral Uses of Force by One of the Permanent Members against a Smaller Power.* In such instances, the organization at best has exhortatory power. Although the veto power may not prevent a smaller power from stating its case before the organization, the permanent member can be sure that its veto power will prevent any action by the organization. When this happens, those opposing the use of force will have to take counteraction outside the organization. During the Iranian case in 1945, it was not the United Nations that got Soviet troops out of the province of Azerbaijan. What got them out was the willingness of the United States to support the Iranians with military force if their troops met resistance when they entered their northern province.

3. *The United Nations Is Unable to Act against Even an Ally of One of the Permanent Members because the Veto Power of the Ally's Patron Will Bring the Organization to a Halt.* The Security Council was able to respond to the North Korean invasion of South Korea only because the Soviet Union was boycotting the council at that time and, by practice, a nonvote or abstention was not counted as a veto. When the tide of battle turned in favor of the UN forces, the Soviet delegate returned to the presidency of the council, which by rotation was its turn in August 1950, and ended the council's decision making through its veto power. At this point, the Truman administration came up with the Uniting for Peace Resolution, which was adopted by the General Assembly. Under this resolution, issues that become deadlocked by a veto in the Security Council can be transferred to the General Assembly by a procedural and veto-free vote of the council. However, any "action" taken by the assembly on matters so referred are merely recommendations. While the United States was able to gain a mantle of international "legitimacy" for its Cold War policies in this manner, that was about all it got. No nation was obligated to act on the assembly's resolutions, and most did not.

4. *Since Concert Systems Are Oligarchic by Nature, Smaller States Will Have Only Persuasive or "Moral" Power in Affecting Decisions.* As the United Nations Charter makes clear, resolutions adopted by a two-thirds majority in the General Assembly are *recommendations* only, and no state is obligated to abide by them including those who vote for them. The influence of small states within the United Nations depends on their value as counters in the competition among the oligarchs for the imprimatur of General Assembly resolutions.

All these limitations stem from the constitutional foundation of the United Nations itself. In addition to the limitations inherent in the constitutional structure of the United Nations, there are also limitations that stem largely from the nature of state behavior within an anarchic international system.

LIMITATIONS NOT INHERENT IN THE UNITED NATIONS CHARTER
5. *No Nation Is Obligated to Contribute Anything to Enforcement or Peace-keeping Operations.* Even though each of the first four limitations noted stems clearly from the organization's charter, no amount of "reforming" or "strengthening" of the organization's charter will ever really get around this limitation for one simple reason: Practice in both the League and the United Nations has established the norm that each member decides for itself what, if any, contribution it will make to enforcement or peace-keeping operations.

Consider, for example, the frequently heard proposal to abolish the veto power. How would the abolition of the veto have made a difference in the cases just considered? Suppose there had been no veto power during the Korean War. Would the Soviet Union have sent its own men to fight against its ally if a majority of the council passed a resolution authorizing UN forces to resist the North Korean invasion? Clearly not. Most of the states that supported every resolution on Korea—in both the council and the General Assembly—hardly lifted a finger to support the war effort—India's sole contribution, for example, was one ambulance corps. Or consider the Hungarian crisis of 1956. Does any reader believe that the Soviet Union would have allowed Hungary to leave the Soviet bloc if a veto-free majority so voted in the Security Council?

In his *Evolution of the United Nations System*, Professor Amos Yoder notes that the Soviet Union's intervention in Hungary and Czechoslovakia (1968) "demonstrated the basic weakness of the Charter—it is not designed to enforce a decision against one of the great powers." He then goes on to point out the informal limitations to the charter as well, when he adds that, "Theoretically, the General Assembly could have mobilized the world community to oppose the invasion or impose sanctions, but none of the countries was willing to confront the Soviets to that extent or to go to war with the Soviets, who were at that time a nuclear power."[34] This latter *reality*, rather than any constitutional weakness, was the real reason for the United Nations's inaction in the Hungarian case.

6. *Even if the Great Powers Work Together in Good Faith, and with the Best of Will, They May Genuinely Be Unable to Agree on What to Do. In that event the country or countries wanting to do the least will prevail, especially if none of the other Great Powers is willing to act unilaterally.* Such, of course, is what the Clinton administration found out in the Bosnian case until Serbian atrocities made the Europeans' passive policy of safe havens untenable. During his 1992 election campaign and in the early months of his administration, President Clinton talked repeatedly about employing "assertive multilateralism," as an alternative to having America playing the role of a "global cop." Clinton told the World Affairs Council of Los Angeles, "In Bosnia, Somalia, Cambodia, and other war-torn areas of the world, multilateral action holds promise as never before, and the UN deserves full and appropriate contributions from all the major powers."[35]

Once in office, President Clinton quickly learned that members of the Security Council can prefer limited involvement even when one of the Great Powers is willing to lead and take action in the face of risks. Ironically, what finally got the UN Security Council to act in the Bosnian conflict was the administration's threat to act unilaterally if the organization refused to go along. When the administration first proposed its Lift and strike in the spring of 1993, the Europeans quickly vetoed it. Two years later, when the Clinton administration decided to strike the Serbs militarily, with or without either NATO or the United Nations, both organizations followed his lead.

7. *Finally, and Perhaps Most Vexing of All, Even When Small and Relatively Insignificant Powers Fight among Themselves and Commit All Kinds of Atrocities, Powers, Great and Small, Will Usually Do Little to Stop the Atrocities if the Costs and Risks of Doing So Are High, if Their Individual National Interests Are Largely Unaffected by the Conflict, and Their Military Leverage Is Small.* In such cases, the organization will descend into *the production of paper—*pieces of paper containing noble sounding platitudes, reminders about the solemn obligation of the disputants to resolve differences peacefully, calls for an end to the violence, and the creation of study or fact-finding commissions, contact groups, or some combination of these shop-worn techniques. Meanwhile, the party with the most power on the ground will win. However, while the fighting goes on, the members of the organization will agonize in words while doing little in deeds.

Turkish Atrocities against Armenia and Inaction by the League

The inaction of the United Nations in the face of great human tragedies in the post–Cold War era should have surprised no one because the lineage of such inaction can be traced back to one of the very first cases to come before the League of Nations—the genocidal invasion of Armenia by Turkey after World War I.

During the war, Kemal Atatürk's nationalist forces decided to create an ethnic Turkey by purging the country of its alien nationalities. As part of this policy, which today would be called "ethnic cleansing," Turkish forces engaged in atrocious massacres, which led to the deportation of between five hundred thousand and one million people in 1915. Troops would move into Armenian villages, round up all of the young men, and kill them by firing squads. The remaining women, children, and old men would then be taken on forced marches to "agricultural colonies" in the Syrian and Arabian deserts. All possessions were left behind, and along the way food was totally inadequate. The bedraggled, hungry, and weary prisoners were subject to mutilation, beatings, violation, torture, and death through enervation and illness.

About their aims, the Turks were perfectly candid. As one Turkish official told an American diplomat: "One hundred years ago we had a Greek question and a Serbian question and a Wallachian question. The result was Greece, Serbia, and Romania. Fifty years ago we had a Bulgarian question. The Result was Bulgaria. In 1910 we had an Albanian question. The result was Albania. Today we have an Armenian question—but we will have no Armenia. We are going to scatter the Armenians, dismember their cities—and there will be no Armenian nation. Armenia will be part of the Turkish empire."[36]

After Turkey's defeat in World War I, the Allies recognized Armenia as an independent state. Although Turkey accepted the independence of Armenia under the Treaty of Sevres in August 1920, its forces quickly invaded Armenian territory, committing terrible atrocities against the ill-prepared and ill-equipped Armenians. Such was the situation when the first meeting of the assembly convened in fall of 1920. To the vast majority of delegates, the League was facing precisely the kind of situation for which it had been created—a large and predatory country had invaded a smaller neighbor whose territorial integrity and political independence were in jeopardy.

Delegate after delegate gave passionate speeches demanding that the council take steps at once. Typical was the plea of the Greek delegate Seferiades: "A platitudinous resolution on our part would only be the signal for fresh massacres. If you mean to act, act! In the name of humanity, which we represent, I declare from the impartial height of this tribune that if new massacres take place in Armenia, the blood of the victims will be on our heads."[37]

When British and French delegates tried to temper such zeal by pointing out that "action" would mean large and costly military forces without a foreseeable termination date, their remarks were condemned as cowardly, immoral, and unfaithful to the obligations of the charter.

What sobered the assembly was an estimate of what it would actually take to "save" the Armenians. According to the respected Norwegian Fridtjof Nansen, experts calculated that successful action would require raising an international force of 60,000 men and borrowing twenty thousand pounds sterling. On hearing what action "in the name of humanity" would require, the assembly passed resolutions recommending contributions to a program of aid for the Armenians *but requiring no state to contribute anything.* In the end, only Greece and Romania indicated a willingness to contribute forces to aid Armenia, but their beneficence stemmed largely from the fact that both had designs of their own on Turkish territory.

Having decided not to insist on enforcement, the assembly called on the council to create a person or commission to negotiate a settlement. A Committee of Six was appointed with Woodrow Wilson as its head. While the six deliberated, the Armenians turned to the Soviet Union for protection against the Turks. By the time Wilson and his colleagues had drawn new boundaries for the young republic, Armenia had joined the Union of Soviet Socialist Republics. Despite the loss of Armenia's independence, the League Council still took note of the revised boundaries in 1922.

Then and ever since, the League and the United Nations have always responded to such atrocities not by the courses of action prescribed in their charters but on the basis of the costs in terms of lives and treasure that members would incur in seeking to right wrongs that have no impact on their national interests even broadly conceived. We learn this sad but irrefutable lesson from the very first year of the "international community's" experience with peace through "a community of power" rather than a "balance of power." From the very outset, the British historian F. S. Northedge notes, there was a "tendency for events to be decided by armed force while the League could do little but sit and observe. . . . "[38]

The Armenian case was just the first in a series of cases that would follow. A bullying revisionist state would move against an object of prey in an area of little interest to any of the Great Powers. States that might be able to help the victim would be far way, and any assistance that would make a difference would cost far more in treasure and lives than the interests of the helping power would allow. On the other hand, the publicity of the incident, the existence of a formal international institution created precisely to deal with such breaches of the peace, and the very pledges undertaken by the members of those organizations would make inaction appear immoral and cowardly, if not scandalous.

In such situations, a set of predictable stages would unfold. First, there would be calls for a cessation of hostilities and fact finding. Then, or coincidentally, mediators or commissions of conciliation would be appointed. Small states that expected to do nothing, and could in fact do little, would make high-sounding speeches reminding the Great Powers of their responsibilities. The Great Powers would obfuscate and use rhetoric about peace and restraint to hide their inaction. In many cases, the victim would be devoured, and then action would be "too late," as in Vilna, Memel, Ethiopia, Manchuria, Hungary, Tibet, and West Irian. In cases in which bullies overextended themselves, they might, in fact, pull back with face-saving gestures in the interests of "peace" and in deference to the wishes of the international organization, as in the Corfu Channel case of 1923 or the Greek-Bulgarian crisis of 1925. In cases where none of the disputants proved able to prevail, the dispute might become "frozen," as in Cyprus, the Arab-Israeli conflict, or Bosnia after the Dayton Accords. Rare would be those cases in which the League or the United Nations responded to military violations of the organizations' charters with military counterforce. The cases are fewer than the fingers on one's hand—Korea and Kuwait.

No nation—great or small—can have any confidence that members of "the international community" will come to its aid if it is ever attacked by another country—great or small. Interest, not international obligation, will determine whether any members of the "community" will come to the aid of a victim of aggression. Under almost no circumstance will a smaller power send its sons and daughters into battle to save any other community member. If aid is to come, it will come only from a Great Power that has an interest in supporting the status quo. The most that victim nations can expect from the United Nations is talk (which is always cheap), paper, study commissions, mediators, and humanitarian assistance for the victims of aggression who manage to flee the hostilities. Such are the sad lessons based on more than eighty years of experience with international organizations designed to enforce the peace.

The Problem of the United Nations Is Not a Problem of Will

All too frequently, supporters of unrealistic goals for the United Nations seek to explain the organization's "failures" as a problem of will, implying that *if the members, and especially the Great Powers, wanted to make the organization work, they could do so.* But such calls for greater "will" vastly oversimplify the situation. Fundamentally, the problem of "will" is a problem of lives, interests, and money! Having will means spending your money and sending your children off to die whenever and wherever aggression occurs regardless of the consequences. While nations promise to do all kinds of things by signing pieces of paper, they frequently renege on those pledges when the costs and risks of doing so are high and their own interests are not directly involved No cost-free magic wand called "will" can make any of these obstacles to a world of peace and harmony go away.

Even when the Great Powers do possess the will "to do something," they may honestly differ on how to deal with a problem, as in the case of Bosnia. Then again in all too many situations, the members of an international organization may lack usable instruments of force or the use of force might cause untold damage to innocent civilians, a problem that President Clinton faced in seeking to rescue the Kosovars.

Is There Any Point in Keeping the United Nations?

Given all of these inherent limitations and limiting factors, it is easy to see why many people want to throw up their hands. However, perfectionist and impossible expectations can get in the way of recognizing all of the good work that the League and the United Nations have done in getting states to dampen down violence, in allowing disputing parties to disengage through the provision of observers and buffer forces, by insulating conflicts among minor powers from intervention and competition by the Great Powers, and by contributing to the amelioration and resolution of political conflicts. Over the course of almost eighty years the League and the United Nations have frequently contributed to the restoration and maintenance of peace, if not always justice, in conflicts among nations both large and small. To cite just one example, the existence of a United Nations made it much easier for Soviet premier Nikita Khrushchev to retreat during the Cuban missile crisis than would have been possible without the organization.

Almost forty years ago, the British journalist Andrew Boyd suggested that we look at the United Nations as a "do-it-yourself kit with an incomplete set of instructions."[39] Boyd was right on the mark because improvisation has been the hallmark of many successes of the League and the United Nations, a most notable example of which was Canadian prime minister Lester Pearson's proposal to create a United Nations Emergency Force to police the truce between Arab and Israeli forces after the 1956 war. Over the previous eighty years, a great deal of learning has taken place about how international organizations can effectively contribute to maintenance of peace and the resolution of conflict.

Of all people, Americans have, perhaps, the greatest interest in supporting and strengthening the United Nations because, *by their very nature*, international organizations are "friendly" to status quo powers. By standing for the maintenance of peace and the territorial integrity of their members states, international organizations have an inherent bias in favor of the existing distribution of territory, power, and status. Revisionist powers, on the other hand, have the most to lose when the spotlight of international publicity exposes tactics involving stealth and prevarication, as Stalin found out in the Iranian case. While this power of publicity can and does create problems for status quo powers when they are reluctant to act, international organizations can be valuable adjuncts to the diplomacy of status quo powers in maintaining order, promoting the peaceful resolution of disputes, and, perhaps most important of all, providing a mantle of multinational legitimacy when the status quo powers do choose to act. One need only note the differences between Korea and Vietnam to understand the importance of the legitimacy that international organizations can bestow.

Summary of Salient Points

There is no viable alternative to power politics

1. Alternatives to war have been around for centuries, and none has managed to prevent states from resorting to violence whenever they cannot get what they want peacefully. For these alternatives to work, peace must be the highest aim of states, and states must be willing to cede what they possess in the interest of peace.

2. Arbitration, commissions of conciliation, and international courts founder because no state can be forced to use them or comply with them. While tens of thousands of disputes have been resolved through arbitration, such treaties usually contain loopholes that allow states to refrain from arbitrating disputes involving "national honor, independence, vital interests, or the interests of third parties." When states refuse to arbitrate, those states seeking change or the amelioration of grievances have little choice but acquiescence in the status quo, diplomatic negotiation and bargaining, or military force.

3. Efforts to create peace through paper agreements such as the Kellogg-Briand Pact or FDR's Atlantic Charter also founder on the problem of enforcement. As Thomas Hobbes put it, "Covenants without swords are mere words."

4. Efforts to abolish or limit arms also founder on the questions of sovereignty and conflict. No state is obliged to enter into arms control talks or agreements, and when conflict exists among nations, the achievement of weapons reductions becomes almost impossible. On the other hand, when conflict disappears, so does the interest in arms control. Most arms control agreements in the past have done one or more of the following: abolished weapons that states were no longer interested in building, channeled arms spending into other weapons systems, or created ceilings that actually allowed nations to build up their arms.

5. Preserving the peace through international organizations like the League and the United Nations means freezing the map and all of the injustices that map may contain.

6. Plans that place authority for the enforcement of the peace in "the international community" through collective security systems, such as Woodrow Wilson's League of Nations,

assume that peace is the highest aim of states (higher, in fact, than justice), that nations will go to war for principle rather than interest, that potential "law breakers" will be deterred by "the organized community of mankind," and that nations will be willing to give up what they may possess in the interest of peace. Experience with the League of Nations has found all of these assumptions wanting.

7. Plans that place authority for maintaining and enforcing the peace in a condominium or concert of Great Powers are, by their very nature, incapable of dealing with the greatest threat to world peace—Great Power revisionism.

8. The major flaw of efforts to create international peace and security through international organization lies in the fact that no nation will sacrifice lives and treasure to defend another nation for the sake of principle alone. Belief in the deterrent power of "the international community" has proven to be a delusion.

9. Still, of all powers, status quo powers have the greatest interest in supporting and strengthening the United Nations. By their very nature, international organizations are "friendly" to status quo powers. Revisionist powers, on the other hand, have the most to lose when the spotlight of international publicity exposes tactics involving stealth and prevarication, as Stalin found out in the Iranian case. Thus, international organizations can be valuable adjuncts to the diplomacy of status quo powers in maintaining order, promoting the peaceful resolution of disputes, and, perhaps most important of all, providing a mantle of multinational legitimacy when the status quo powers do choose to act.

Notes

1. Frederick L. Schuman, *International Politics* (New York: McGraw Hill, 1933), 214.
2. Nine with European states, eleven with Latin American states, and one with China.
3. Schuman, *International Politics*, 208.
4. These quotations are taken from Robert H. Ferrell, *American Diplomacy: The Twentieth Century* (New York: W. W. Norton, 1988), 93–99.
5. Schuman, *International Politics*, 207–8.
6. Ibid., 664.
7. *FRUS*, 1941 (Washington, DC, 1958), I: 366.
8. Ibid.
9. *FRUS*, 1942 (Washington, DC, 1961), III: 500–1.
10. Ibid., 501–2.
11. Ibid.
12. Where they did conflict with particular interests, as in the case of the British colonies, they were considered "inapplicable" to Britain, of course, but not to FDR. On this point, see Miles Kimball, *The Juggler: Franklin Roosevelt as Wartime Statesman* (Princeton: Princeton University Press, 1991), 67.
13. Arthur Bliss Lane, *I Saw Poland Betrayed: An American Ambassador Reports to the American People* (Boston: Western Islands, 1965, original edition 1948), 44.
14. See his *Cold War Diplomacy* (New York: D. Van Nostrand, 1977), ch. 1.

15. From Ferrell, *Peace in Their Time: The Origins of the Kellogg-Briand Pact* (New Haven: Yale University Press, 1952), 5.
16. Elizabeth Olson, "Breaking a Logjam on Talks to Cut World Nuclear Stockpiles," *The Christian Science Monitor,* September 17, 1998, 7.
17. Taken from R. A. C. Parker, *Europe 1919–45* (New York: Delacorte Press, 1970), 246.
18. Richard C. Hottelet, "Saddam outlasts the UN," *The Christian Science Monitor,* December 12, 1999, 8.
19. Schuman, *International Politics,* 229.
20. Inis Claude, *Swords into Plowshares* (New York: Random House, 1984), 296–300.
21. Frank H. Simonds and Brooks Emeny, *The Great Powers in World Politics* (New York: American Book, 1937), 608.
22. These quotations are taken from F. H. Hinsley's brilliant book on the history of international peace schemes, *Power and the Pursuit of Peace: Theory and Practice in the History of Relations between Nations* (New York: Cambridge University Press, 1963), ch. 2.
23. His *Etrait du Project de Paix Perpetualle de Monsieur l'Abbe de Saint-Pierre,* which is discussed fully in Hinsley, *Power and the Pursuit of Peace,* ch. 3.
24. Ibid.
25. For an extensive discussion of the role of the League in resolving all of the disputes that came before it, see Stanley Michalak, "The UN and the League," in *The United Nations and the International System,* ed. Leon Gordenker (Princeton: Princeton University Press, 1972), 68–69.
26. F. S. Northedge, *The League of Nations: Its Life and Times, 1920–1946* (New York: Holmes and Meier, 1986), 85.
27. Quoted in Schuman, *International Politics,* 706–7.
28. For a brief overview of this case, Schuman, *International Politics,* 772–73.
29. Frederick S. Dunn, *Peaceful Change* (New York: Council on Foreign Relations, 1937), 111.
30. *FRUS, 1942* (Washington, DC, 1961), III: 568–69.
31. Ibid., 569.
32. Adam Ulam, *The Rivals: America and Russia Since World War II* (New York: The Viking Press, 1971), 36.
33. For a brilliant study of the politics of this process see Richard Jackson, *The Non-aligned, the UN, and the Superpowers* (Boulder, CO: Praeger Press, 1983).
34. Amos Yoder, *The Evolution of the UN System* (Washington, DC: Taylor and Francis, 1993), 73.
35. *Foreign Policy Bulletin,* November/December 1992, 16.
36. Quoted in "Turkish Efficiency in Starving Armenia," *Literary Digest,* May 17, 1919, 32.
37. League of Nations, *Official Records,* Assembly, 2nd Session, 297.
38. Northedge, *The League of Nations,* 79.
39. Andrew Boyd, *The United Nations: Piety, Myth, and Truth* (New York: Penguin Books, 1963).

The Prospects for Peace in the Post–Cold War World: Where You Stand on Questions of War and Peace Depends on Where You Sit

The United States as a Revisionist Power

In the final analysis, the question of peace depends on the attitudes of nations toward the existing distribution of power, status, territory, and resources. All the alternatives to power politics call on states to renounce their right to change the territorial or political status quo by force. While this approach might seem "good" and "sensible" to a satisfied nation without a military threat to its security, the same is not true for states seeking change.

The United States could support all the various alternatives to war after the turn of the nineteenth century because it had become a satiated status quo power, secure behind its ocean moats, and an industrial power seeking markets and opportunities for investment abroad. In fact, there is nothing new at all about our current commitment to free trade, the peaceful resolution of conflict, and the rule of international law. Nor is there anything new about our currently fashionable faith that increasing interdependence among peoples will foster tolerance and promote the growth of democracy.

To cite just one trivial illustration, consider the following thesis presented by Columbia University professor James T. Shotwell in his 1927 inaugural address as visiting Carnegie professor of international relations at the Hochschule für Politik in Berlin. In a complex and interrelated modern world, Shotwell argued, war no longer profited a nation: "War, having ceased to be an effective instrument of politics should on that account be renounced by all civilized governments."[1]

Sitting in Shotwell's audience were all the members of the German War Office staff, fully bedecked in uniform and with all of their wartime decorations on display. Surely, the only peace on their minds was a piece of Poland, a piece of Czechoslovakia, all of Austria, all of the Saar, a remilitarization of the Rhineland, and an army big enough to attain these things through the threat of force, if possible, but through another war if necessary. Although the German government signed the Kellogg-Briand Pact, as did Japan and Italy, its signature was merely tactical, a way of disarming its opponents and making it harder for France to concert allies against Germany.

But forget about such notorious revisionist powers. Consider the foreign policy of the United States before it became a great, satiated, and secure industrial power—a power lacking the prospect of a military challenger that might temper its zeal for a world of international law, free trade, ever-increasing prosperity, and peace. Consider the United States before it became strong enough to lecture Europeans about the need for them to forgo their old, irrational, and unprofitable balance-of-power machinations. Look at our own behavior when we had revisionist aims, and measure that behavior against the high standards and high ideals we would later set for—and expect of—other nations.

THE INDIANS. They welcomed us, but there were too few of them and too many of us. The British, in their Grand Proclamation of 1763, tried to reserve all the territory west of the Alleghenies as an exclusive preserve for Indians, but within eight years the proclamation was amended to allow white men to settle along the Ohio River into Kentucky. After the Revolution, the newly independent nation claimed all of the Indians' land as a right of conquest because they sided with the British. Yet, pronouncing a right and enjoying it are quite different things. Indian wars against the advancing settlers were frequent in the aftermath of the Revolution because the British remained in their forts in the Northwest in violation of the Peace of Paris, and their military officers armed the Indians and encouraged attacks against American settlements.

Jay's Treaty got the British out of the Northwest, but the push "to overspread the continent" led to more encroachment and more war. In fact, many in the South and West favored war with Britain in 1812 to solve "the Indian problem." The dominant American viewpoint was that the Indians should assimilate, "become like us," or move west of the Mississippi. When war came, the British again offered to organize and supply Indian tribes, which were divided. The despair that many Indians felt about the possibility of ever getting along with the American white man was well expressed by Shawnee chief Tecumseh, who fought on the side of the British: "Let the white race perish! They seize your land! They corrupt your women. They trample on the bones of your dead! Back whence they came, on a trail of blood, they must be driven! Back—aye, back to the great water whose accursed waves brought them to our shores! Burn their dwellings—destroy their stock—slay their very wives and children that their very breed may perish! War now! War always! War on the living! War on the dead!"[2]

After the war, Presidents Monroe, Jackson, and Van Buren embarked on a series of Indian removal policies that were designed to take the remaining Indian land in the Old South and Old West (present day northern Illinois, southern Michigan, and Wisconsin) to make room for white settlers. Under these policies, the tribes would be relocated to a new Indian territory west of the Mississippi, which would be permanently closed to white settlement. According to Andrew Jackson, "Your white brothers will . . . lay no claim to the land and you can live upon it, you and all your children, as long as the grass grows or the water runs, in peace and plenty. It will be yours forever."[3]

By 1840, Indian removal policies had gained more than 400 million acres in return for 54 million acres of territory west of the Mississippi that were ceded to the Indians. In terms of cost, the land was obtained for about 10¢ an acre, which the federal government then sold to the public for $1.25 an acre. Profits gained from the sale of these Indian lands eliminated the national debt and created such a surplus in the national treasury that the federal government could embark on a national network of roads and canals. But permanent did not mean permanent; within a generation these eastern tribes found themselves confronted with demands to cede their new lands for white settlement.

The various wars between the Americans and the Indians were bloody and filled with atrocities on both sides. But the choice of the Indians was always the same—assimilate or go west—with west always meaning farther west—first the Alleghenies, then the Ohio, then the Mississippi, then the Rockies, until there was no more west; as the Pacific coast and inland areas were settled, the Indians found themselves being pushed toward the center of the country. Ultimately, they were surrounded, outnumbered, defeated, and placed into reservations.

Does anyone believe that Indians would be living on reservations today if we had taken our disputes with them to some arbital tribunal, conciliation commission, or international court? The Indians went into reservations for one simple reason: military power! *War worked for America,* yielding benefits that no people would ever have gained peacefully and amicably, or through a neutral arbitrator, court, or commission of conciliation.

The Cherokee Indians did try to get the United States to adopt the kind of peaceful resolution techniques the America would later preach to other nations. In 1831 and 1832, they took their case against Georgia's appropriation of their lands to the United States Supreme Court, and while they failed in their first attempt, they succeeded in their second. In *Worcester v. State of Georgia,* the Court ruled that Georgia's laws of dispossession violated federal treaties with the Cherokees. However, the

Court's ruling would only be as good as the executive branch's faithful execution of that ruling, which President Jackson refused to carry out. "John Marshall made his decision, now let him enforce it," Old Hickory reputedly proclaimed.[4]

In dealing with the Indians, the federal and state governments stated the terms, and if the Indians refused to go along, they went to war. When the peace treaties ending these wars stood in the way of our desire to expand further, we broke them. When it came to dealing with the Indians, the American view of treaties was very much like that of the Soviet leader Lenin, who once quipped that, "Treaties are like pie crusts, made to be broken." But don't take my word for it. Get a classic text like Samuel Eliot Morison's *Oxford History of the American People* or Paul Johnson's more recent *A History of the American People*, and read all of the pages listed under Indians in the indexes.

MEXICO'S LOSS OF NEW MEXICO AND CALIFORNIA. President James Polk was an expansionist pure and simple. While he did not want a war with Mexico, he did want Mexico's territories of California and New Mexico. Seeking to avoid bloodshed, he instructed his envoy, John Slidell, to offer Mexico five million dollars for New Mexico and twenty-five million dollars for California. On his arrival, the Mexican government thought that Slidell had come to offer compensation to Mexico for its loss of Texas. When officials got wind of what Polk's envoy was really seeking, they refused even to speak to him.

Unable to gain what he wanted peacefully, Polk sent General Zachary Taylor into disputed territory between the Neuces and Rio Grande rivers. When the Mexicans took the bait and a military skirmish occurred, Polk claimed that Mexico "has invaded our territory and shed blood upon the American soil." His pretext for war had come. Through the Treaty of Guadeloupe Hidalgo, Mexico lost about half of its territory and the boundary of Texas was settled at the Rio Grande River. For its loss, the United States paid Mexico $15 million and agreed to assume $3.25 million worth of debts that Mexico owed to American citizens.

In seeking northern Mexico and California, the United States did not have a dispute with Mexico that was justicable. Neither Mexico nor any other country would have freely submitted such an outrageous demand to an arbitration panel. While the Mexican government had defaulted on liabilities to American citizens, the United States had no grievance against Mexico worthy of a war, to say nothing of taking half of its territory.

THE WAR WITH SPAIN. America's war with Spain was not in response to any threat to the nation's security. In fact, the Spanish government sought to resolve American grievances through the kind of peaceful means that the United States would later insist that others employ. When some intemperate private remarks that the Spanish minister made about President McKinley became public knowledge, the Spanish government recalled the minister and offered an apology. It also offered to submit to arbitration the question of claims arising from the sinking of the *Maine*. But the vast majority of the American people, led by the Hearst press, did not want peace; they wanted war. They wanted to liberate Cuba without regard to whether or not Cubans could govern themselves. In the end, the nation wound up with the Philippines, Puerto Rico, Hawaii, and Guam, all of which were spoils of war.

THE PANAMA CANAL. On August 12, 1903, the Colombian Senate refused to cede territory to the United States for the purpose of building a trans-isthmus canal through Panama, *which they had every right to do*. When this occurred, President Theodore Roosevelt was so irate that he drafted a message to Congress, which he decided not to submit, recommending seizure of the proposed canal route by force. Seeking to secure forty million dollars in payment from the United States for relinquishing its rights to build a canal in Panama, agents of the French New Panama Canal Company decided to foment a revolution in the province of Panama, which the canal would traverse.

When the Colombians tried to put down the rebellion, Roosevelt ordered four naval units to the area with orders to prevent the landing of Colombian troops. Since the Colombians could not get their troops to Panama through the jungle, Roosevelt's actions secured the independence of the new republic. As the president, himself, put it, "I took the Canal zone and let Congress debate."[5]

A peaceful resolution of America's dispute with Colombia never crossed Roosevelt's mind. He wanted a canal and he wanted it on our terms; it was as simple as that. The United States had pledged to guarantee Columbia's "right of sovereignty over Panama" in the Colombian Treaty of 1846, but that pledge meant nothing to Roosevelt, who used American military force to do precisely the opposite. In the eyes of the president, the issue was not merely American interests; the basis for his actions, Roosevelt claimed, was a "mandate from civilization!"

The Relativity of Attitudes toward War and Peace

None of these examples was presented to expose America as a hypocritical nation or to bash the United States. Nor is this about "good guys" and "bad guys," "aggressive nations" and "peace-loving nations." Nor is my purpose to get Americans to wring their hands, offer apologies to other nations, or engage in self-flagellation.

My purpose is to illuminate how attitudes toward war and peace differ for satisfied and dissatisfied nations—for nations that have whatever they want and those who do not. What determines a nation's posture toward the desirability of international law, the peaceful resolution of international disputes, and the "irrationality of war" depends on where a nation sits.

Whenever the United States, or any other Great Power, wants something badly enough and cannot get it peacefully, it will resort to military force if it thinks it is powerful enough to do so. If Mexico had been colonized and heavily populated by Prussians, most probably there would never have been a Mexican War, and neither Texas nor the Southwest would be part of America today. The engine of America's transformation from a small strip of land along the Atlantic coast to a vast continental nation was the power of the gun. However, when Japan sought to create a similar empire in Asia, American policymakers trotted out the Open Door notes and the Kellogg-Briand Pact and proclaimed that the United States would not recognize any treaty or agreement that would impair American rights in China or would violate the "sovereignty, independence, or territorial and administrative integrity" of China. As Balzac put it in his *Old Goriot*, "There are no principles, . . . there are only circumstances."[6]

To be sure, there was strong opposition to our wars against the Indians, the Mexicans, and the Spaniards, to say nothing of our frequent interventions in Latin America. Peace groups are as American as apple pie, to use the cliché, the first one having been organized in 1833. Yet, when the great debates and the great decisions took place in the nineteenth century, the peace groups lost.

The tide of battle could turn in favor of the peace lobbyists in the 1920s because America had become a satisfied power, no American interests were at stake, no obligations were involved, no costs would be incurred if others broke their pledge, and no lands or markets were to be risked or forgone. When Sal Levinson, founder of the Committee to Outlaw War, and feminist groups like Carrie Catt's Committee Against War or Jane Adams's League for the Cause and Cure of War embarked on their crusade against war, America's revisionist past had become relegated to the category of ancient history. And the American people? When they thought about the folly, futility, and irrationality of war, they thought not about the benefits gained by America's own past wars but about World War I, its punitive Versailles peace treaty, the wrangles over reparations and debts, France's postwar alliance system, its intervention in the Ruhr, and all the "little" postwar conflicts in Memel, in Vilna, in the Balkans, and in the Corfu Channel.

In signing the Kellogg-Briand Pact and "saying 'no'" to war, the signatories made a pledge akin to W. C. Fields's humorous boast about "saying 'no'" to alcohol: "Don't tell me you can't give up drinking; I've done it thousands of times." When some of the signatories later violated the pact, as America might have done on occasion in the nineteenth century, the nation failed to see the mirror image of its own past.

The Problem of Change in an Anarchical International System

Thus, we return to the central problem of international politics: nothing other than satiation, self-restraint, or fear keeps states from employing force to change things they do not like or to keep things the way they are. None of the alternatives to the use of force has been effective because there are just some things that some states will neither yield nor put up with without a fight.

"The problem" of international politics has never been a problem of "peace" for one simple reason: no state has ever wound up in a war when peace was its highest aim. To have peace, states that do not like things the way they are could just decide to accept the world as it is. Conversely, status quo powers merely have to acquiesce in changes that may not be to their liking.

Peace is always a matter of choice, and "peace" has never been a problem for states that do not want war. The problem of war exists because, in many situations, some things are just more important than peace—things like survival, dignity, honor, justice, and security. No one, in fact, has expressed this sentiment better than Woodrow Wilson in his address to Congress calling for a declaration of war with Germany: "It is a fearful thing to lead this great peaceful nation into war, into the most terrible and disastrous of all wars, civilization itself seeming to be in the balance. *But the right is more precious than the peace, and we shall fight for the things which we have always carried nearest our hearts—for democracy, for the right of those who submit to authority to have a voice in their own government, for the rights and liberties of small nations, for a universal dominion of right by a concert of free peoples as shall bring peace and safety to all nations and make the world itself at last free.*"

Precisely because things are "more precious than peace," nations have forgone arbitration, commissions of conciliation, and the peaceful resolution of conflict. The eminent psychologist Ralph K. White wrote a book entitled *Nobody Wanted War: Misperception in Vietnam and Other Wars* in the midst of the Vietnam War.[7] While it is obvious that neither the United States nor Vietnam "wanted" the war that occurred, preventing that war would have required one of the sides to forgo aims that were "more precious than peace"—securing a communist government in South Vietnam for North Vietnam, maintaining a noncommunist government in South Vietnam for the United States.

When the North Vietnamese could not get what they wanted peacefully, they resorted to force—support for guerrilla warfare in the South at first and, then, conventional war when that effort failed. The North Vietnamese had no more right to rule all of Vietnam than West Germany had to rule East Germany or South Korea had to rule North Korea. That the South Vietnamese government resisted should have surprised no one. Nor should the fact that the United States came to the assistance of the South Vietnamese been surprising to anyone. States forgo "peaceful alternatives" to power politics because they believe that some things are just worth fighting for.

Seeking to buttress peaceful alternatives to war with international organizations designed to maintain the peace through the use of retaliatory force have also faltered, and for one very simple reason: it is not the small powers that cause wars but the Great Powers. When revisionist Great Powers go on the march, international organizations dissolve and are succeeded by balance-of-power systems in which status quo and revisionist powers resort to alliances, armaments, spheres of influence, proxy wars, deterrence, and coercive diplomacy to secure their interests and goals.

Two final alternatives to power politics remain: hegemony by one imperial power, such as Napoleon's empire of the French, or a world government that would replace the anarchic international state system. No one wants the hegemonic alternative for obvious reasons: the experience of Napoleon and the concomitant issue of "who will keep the hegemon responsible?"

We are left, then, with world government, the creation of an institution with a monopoly of force that would stand above states and enforce the decisions of—what? A majority of states? A majority of peoples? A majority of two houses, one representing states and the other peoples? And what body would enforce the laws of these bodies? A secretary general selected by whom? A president of the world?

Schemes for world government are as old as the state system itself. For a quick summary of the classic ones, read F. H. Hinsley's *Power and the Pursuit of Peace*. For a good overview of American schemes since World War II, read Wesley T. Wooley's, *Alternatives to Anarchy: American Supranationalism since World War II*.[8] For an idea of contemporary thinking about world order, read Mel Gurtov's *Global Politics in the Human Interest*.[9]

As interesting as all of these schemes may be, they founder on one point: *the question of how*. How do we get from the world in which we live—the world in which states can use violence to try to get or keep whatever they want—to a world in which states have given over their arms to some structure with a "monopoly on the legitimate use of physical force," to quote again the German sociologist, Max Weber.

Thus, we are back where we started. But if we wait, perhaps in the long term two forces may work to create a community of nations in which states will work cooperatively on matters of concern to all and resolve disputes peacefully—a community in which leaders might not even conceive of using force to resolve disputes with one another. In his *Essay on Perpetual Peace*, which was written in 1795, Immanuel Kant foresaw just such a future based on the spread of commercial trading republics.

Kant's vision has been articulated repeatedly over the previous two hundred years, as we have seen in the examples of Professor Shotwell's inaugural address and more recently in the writings of Princeton University professor Michael Doyle, who argued in 1983 that in the last 150 years democracies have seldom fought against one another. Drawing on the writings of Kant and John Stuart Mill, Doyle argued that a culture of democratic states inculcates tolerance, respect for the rule of law, and the peaceful resolution of disputes.[10] On the basis of "Doyle's law," some have argued that a major goal of American foreign policy should be the promotion of democracy abroad.[11]

The problem with Doyle's law is that our own record in promoting democracy abroad is not a very good one because, frankly, we do not know how to create or foster little Americas or little Swedens. Democracies are developed, not constructed; they require habits of mind that involve tolerance for the views of others and internalized norms of restraint and responsibility. Democracies have never been manufactured by constitutional engineers. It took more than a hundred years for France to go from the dreams of 1789 to the humdrum of a functioning democracy. After almost one hundred years of trying to teach Latin Americans "how to elect good men," there is still not one political system in Latin America, with the possible exception of Costa Rica, that could match Ireland or Norway or Italy as a healthy and functioning democracy. In his efforts to reform the Soviet system, Mikhail Gorbachev might have acted differently had he studied carefully Edmund Burke's *Reflections on the Revolution in France* and Alexis de Tocqueville's *Democracy in America.*

It is easy, if not facile, to assert that a world of economically interdependent, democratic states would be a world without war; however, any such world lies very far in the future given historical experience, and we are almost totally lacking in a road map of how to get there. The fate of China is uncertain and the whole area of the former Soviet Union remains a big question mark, to say nothing about the future of Africa and much of Latin America both economically and politically.

Nor has the final word been said on the relationship between economic interdependence and global peace. Kant believed that increasing interdependence would bring peace just as Professor Shotwell did in 1923 and just as many people so believe today. Still, it remains to be seen whether today's global economy will usher in a period of world of peace and siblinghood or whether it will merely provide another context within which traditional wars will continue to take place. Only time will provide an answer to that question, but for a more sober assessment, consider the closing quotation from Professor Donald Kagan:

> The current condition of the world . . . where war among the major powers is hard to conceive because one of them has overwhelming military superiority and no wish to expand, will not last. A reunified Germany,

223

with its colossal economic resources, will sooner or later acquire compa-
rable military power, and the same is true for Japan. The power of China
is growing with its economic success, and it is unlikely for long to main-
tain a secondary role on the international scene. Nor should Russia's cur-
rent difficulties blind us to its inherent strength, and the certainty that it
will, sooner or later, emerge on the world scene as a great power with
desires and goals of its own, not necessarily compatible with those of other
nations or with the status quo. It would be foolhardy, moreover, to assume
that the return of Germany, Japan, and Russia to full status as great pow-
ers will be the only changes in the world system and that we can foresee
what others may come. In the past such unforeseen changes have threat-
ened peace, and we have no doubt that they will do so again.[12]

Notes

1. Robert Ferrell, *Peace in Their Time* (New Haven: Yale University Press, 1951), 67. The quotation is taken from Shotwell's own account of this lecture, which appears in his *Lessons of the Last World War: A Brochure* (New York, 1942), 12.
2. Paul Johnson, *A History of the American People* (New York: HarperCollins, 1997), 271.
3. Alan Wexler, *Atlas of Westward Expansion* (New York: Facts on File, 1995), 91.
4. Taken from Samuel Eliot Morison, *The Oxford History of the American People* (New York: Oxford University Press, 1965), 451.
5. This and the other quotations in this section are taken from Thomas K. Bailey, *A Diplomatic History of the American People*, 5th Edition (New York: Appleton-Century-Crofts, 1955), ch. xxxii.
6. (Baltimore: Penguin Press, 1972), 134.
7. (Garden City, New York: Doubleday, 1968).
8. (Bloomington: Indiana University Press, 1988).
9. (Boulder, CO: Lynne Rienner Publishers, 1988).
10. See his "Kant, Liberal Legacies, and Foreign Affairs," in *Philosophy and Public Affairs*, 2 Parts, 12, no. 3 (Summer 1983), 203–35 and no. 4 (Fall 1983), 323–53 and "Liberalism and World Politics," *American Political Science Review* 80, no. 4 (1986), 1151–69.
11. See, for example, Joshua Muravchik, *Exporting Democracy: Fulfilling America's Destiny* (Washington, DC: American Enterprise Institute, 1991) or Tony Smith, *America's Mission: The United States and the Worldwide Struggle for Democracy in the Twentieth Century* (Princeton: Princeton University Press, 1995).
12. Donald Kagan, *On the Origins of War and the Preservation of Peace* (New York: Anchor Books, 1995), 568–69.

Index